# Windows Server 2019
# Administration Fundamentals
## *Second Edition*

A beginner's guide to managing and administering Windows
Server environments

**Bekim Dauti**

BIRMINGHAM - MUMBAI

# Windows Server 2019 Administration Fundamentals
## Second Edition

**Commissioning Editor:** Vijin Boricha
**Acquisition Editor:** Rahul Nair
**Content Development Editor:** Carlton Borges
**Senior Editor:** Rahul Dsouza
**Technical Editor:** Komal Karne
**Copy Editor:** Safis Editing
**Project Coordinator:** Vaidehi Sawant
**Proofreader:** Safis Editing
**Indexer:** Tejal Daruwale Soni
**Production Designer:** Nilesh Mohite

First published: December 2017
Second edition: October 2019

Production reference: 1101019

Published by Packt Publishing Ltd.
Livery Place
35 Livery Street
Birmingham
B3 2PB, UK.

ISBN 978-1-83855-091-2

www.packt.com

*With all respect for mankind's achievements in every aspect, especially technological, the stopping and prevention of wars remains the main challenge that mankind has to overcome.*

*– Bekim Dauti*

`Packt.com`

Subscribe to our online digital library for full access to over 7,000 books and videos, as well as industry leading tools to help you plan your personal development and advance your career. For more information, please visit our website.

## Why subscribe?

- Spend less time learning and more time coding with practical eBooks and Videos from over 4,000 industry professionals

- Improve your learning with Skill Plans built especially for you

- Get a free eBook or video every month

- Fully searchable for easy access to vital information

- Copy and paste, print, and bookmark content

Did you know that Packt offers eBook versions of every book published, with PDF and ePub files available? You can upgrade to the eBook version at `www.packt.com` and as a print book customer, you are entitled to a discount on the eBook copy. Get in touch with us at `customercare@packtpub.com` for more details.

At `www.packt.com`, you can also read a collection of free technical articles, sign up for a range of free newsletters, and receive exclusive discounts and offers on Packt books and eBooks.

# Foreword

Windows Server 2019 is the latest and greatest server operating system from Microsoft, which combines hybrid cloud and cloud-connected workloads into one box and provides a huge list of new and improved capabilities, which have been addressed in this book.

While Windows Server 2019 is a solid release from Microsoft that addresses some immediate pain points and provides a firm foundation for future data center developments. There is a lot to learn, but there is no definitive guide besides this book that covers everything you need to know about Windows Administration. The book is not just designed to give you theoretical knowledge; it also covers how to implement this theory in practice, and it gives you tips on how to do so step by step via the exercises.

This is not the first book from Bekim Dauti. He has been blogging for years and has authored different books on Windows. His experience will help you to learn what you need to learn much more quickly.

I hope you will enjoy reading the book as much as I did.

Dr. Erdal Ozkaya

Head of Information and Cyber Security

# Contributors

## About the author

**Bekim Dauti's** profession is the administration of computers and networks, as well as training in Cisco and Microsoft.

He has a bachelor's degree from the University of Tirana and a master's degree from UMUC Europe, both in IT. Additionally, he has more than 15 years' experience as a Cisco Certified Academy Instructor and more than 10 years' experience as a Microsoft Certified Trainer. Bekim holds several certifications from vendors such as ECDL, Certiport, CompTIA, Cisco, Microsoft, and Sun Microsystems. Bekim has contributed to more than 15 books and dozens of articles for PC World Albanian and CIO Albania. He founded Dautti LLC.

These days, he blogs on `Bekim Dauti's Blog`. He works as a system administrator at Kosovo Telecom JSC.

*I thank God for giving me life, health, and the opportunity to contribute through knowledge sharing. May God Almighty reward my family, friends, the folks at Packt Publishing, my teammates at Kosovo Telecom JSC's SysAdmin team, my colleagues both at Dautti Sh.p.k. and QuickStart Inc., and everyone who supported me in writing this book. Last, but not least, peace and blessings to every reader.*

# About the reviewer

**Premnath Sambasivam** is a technical analyst with 7 years of experience in Windows, VMware, and SCCM administration. He is an MCSE Cloud Platform and Infrastructure certified professional. He has also developed and deployed Microsoft System Center Configuration Manager solutions to manage more than 6,000 assets in his clients' environments. Premnath is a Microsoft enthusiast who loves to learn about and explore Azure and PowerShell. He is currently working as a Projects Lead for one of the major retail brands in the USA. He reviewed the book *Mastering Windows Server 2019* earlier this year, which was also published by Packt Publishing.

*I would like to thank my wife and son for encouraging me to spend time learning, since reviewing books also refreshes our memory and enables us to learn about the latest technologies and software improvements. Special thanks to my mom and dad for always being supportive.*

# Packt is searching for authors like you

If you're interested in becoming an author for Packt, please visit authors.packtpub.com and apply today. We have worked with thousands of developers and tech professionals, just like you, to help them share their insight with the global tech community. You can make a general application, apply for a specific hot topic that we are recruiting an author for, or submit your own idea.

# Table of Contents

# Section 2: Setting Up Windows Server 2019

# Section 4: Keeping Windows Server 2019 Up and Running

## Section 5: Getting Ready for the Certification Exam

# Preface

Windows Server 2019 is the latest server operating system developed by Microsoft as part of the Windows NT family of operating systems, based on the Windows 10 platform.

With Windows Server 2019, Microsoft is continuing to build an advanced and secure cloud platform that began with Windows Server 2016. This vision was to bring the cloud to everyone by providing platforms and tools to help build IT solutions that drive success. With Windows Server 2019, Microsoft has consolidated its status in the world of cloud service providers by competing head to head with **Amazon Web Services Cloud** (**AWS Cloud**). For this reason, there has been no better time to become a system administrator.

This book will begin with the computer network essentials and then move into the world of Windows Server 2019. It covers all aspects of the administration-level tasks and activities that are required to become an expert in Microsoft Windows Server 2019. It begins by introducing Windows Server and Windows Server 2019, and then gradually builds up its content with the installation and deployment of Windows Server 2019 in Chapter 3, *Installing Windows Server 2019*. After becoming familiar with Windows Server's 2019 post-installation tasks in Chapter 4, *Post-Installation Tasks in Windows Server 2019*, you will start to functionalize Windows Server 2019 by adding roles to it. By doing so, you will find out what a domain controller is, how to set up a file and print server, configure a web server and host a website, virtualize your IT environment, automate Windows Server 2019 deployment, centrally manage the Windows Server 2019 updates, and many more interesting things. With the help of multiple hands-on exercises, you will gain an immense understanding of Windows Server 2019, which will help you to solve difficult tasks easily. At the end of the book, you will be exposed to maintenance and troubleshooting tasks where, with the help of best practices, you will manage Windows Server 2019 with ease.

At its heart, this book aims to teach you the system administrator's craft. In order to validate your skills and the knowledge gained from this book, each chapter ends with a concept summary and questionnaire to help you take full advantage of the content provided. By the end of this book, you will have enough knowledge to administer and manage Windows Server 2019 with ease, and also be able to pass the MTA: Windows Server Administration Fundamentals: 98-365 exam with no difficulty.

# Who this book is for

If you are a system administrator or an IT professional interested in deploying and configuring Windows Server 2019, then this book is for you. Additionally, this book will also help you to study and pass the MTA 98-365 exam.

# What this book covers

Chapter 1, *Getting Started with Windows Server*, provides you with an introduction to Windows Server. At the beginning of this chapter, there is a recap of the most basic concepts of computer networks. So, this chapter is organized into two parts, where each part attempts to provide a concise, yet complete, description of the basic concepts of computer networks. Definitions of key terms such as hosts, nodes, peer-to-peer, and clients/servers are covered in the *Computer network overview* section.

Chapter 2, *Introducing Windows Server 2019*, introduces you to Windows Server 2019. Windows Server 2019 is developed by Microsoft as part of the Windows NT family of operating systems and concurrently with Windows 10 version 1809. The *Windows Server overview* section uncovers the essentials of Windows Server 2019. In addition, it outlines the various Windows Server 2019 editions and compares Windows Server 2019 to Windows Server 2016 with a focus on what is new in Windows Server 2019.

Chapter 3, *Installing Windows Server 2019*, provides you with detailed instructions for installing Windows Server 2019. The step-by-step instructions, driven by easy-to-understand graphics, show you how to master the installation of Windows Server 2019. You will quickly learn the installation process without hitting any obstacles. This chapter is an excellent collection of how-to tips and provides information on getting the job done efficiently.

Chapter 4, *Post-Installation Tasks in Windows Server 2019*, explains the steps that are required during the post-installation stage of Windows Server, including managing devices and device drivers, checking the registry and status of services, and taking care of the initial server configuration. This chapter is divided into three parts: each topic is accompanied by step-by-step instructions driven by targeted, easy-to-understand graphics.

Chapter 5, *Directory Services in Windows Server 2019*, introduces you to directory services. Now that you have learned how to install Windows Server 2019 and run the initial server configuration, it is time to set up the very first services in your organization's IT infrastructure. With that in mind, this chapter explains directory services. Additionally, you will become familiar with **Organizational Units (OUs)**, default containers, user accounts, and groups so that you can organize the user and computer accounts in your domain.

Chapter 6, *Adding Roles to Windows Server 2019*, provides a broader explanation of what a role is, as well as the importance of roles in determining the server's function when providing network services. You will also get to know all the roles and features that Windows Server 2019 supports. You will learn how to add roles to your server, as well as the requirements after you have added roles so that you can set up your server whenever it is required.

Chapter 7, *Group Policy in Windows Server 2019*, helps you to gain an understanding of **Group Policy** (**GP**) in Windows Server. You will learn about GP processing, become familiar with the GP Management Console, find out about both computer and user policies, and get to know local policies for when your server is not part of a domain. At the same time, you will learn the steps involved in configuring computer and user policies in a domain-based network.

Chapter 8, *Virtualization with Windows Server 2019*, teaches you virtualization concepts, as well as getting you familiar with Hyper-V software, which enables the virtualization of Windows-based servers. You will discover the steps it takes to add the Hyper-V role to your server, get familiar with Hyper-V Manager, and learn the steps it takes to create virtual machines. That way, you will be able to understand what virtualization is, and how you can enable the Hyper-V role and create virtual machines.

Chapter 9, *Storing Data in Windows Server 2019*, explains storage technologies. As well as understanding storage technologies in general, you will learn about a variety of related topics. These include physical interfaces and disk controllers. We will also explore how data is stored in a medium, the types of storage systems used in network environments, and various storage protocols. Additionally, you will get to know the concepts and types of RAID.

Chapter 10, *Tuning and Maintaining Windows Server 2019*, covers the best practices and considerations for server hardware. By understanding the importance of a server's role in a computer network, and learning about each server component, we can be vigilant when selecting server hardware. In addition to this, this chapter teaches you server performance monitoring methodologies and procedures. Performance monitoring will help you to identify the cause of server performance issues early on.

Chapter 11, *Updating and Troubleshooting Windows Server 2019*, outlines the server startup process; advanced boot options and Safe Mode; backup and restore; the disaster recovery plan; and how to update the operating system, hardware, and software. Event Viewer is mentioned too, which will help you to monitor different logs in your system, thus helping you to troubleshoot and solve problems. In this way, you will be able to minimize downtime, which, from a business point of view, is expressed in money loss.

Chapter 12, *Preparing for the MTA 98-365 Exam*, offers an overview of the MTA 98-365 exam, including a look at the skills measured in the exam. Additionally, this chapter contains explanations as to what the MTA 98-365 exam or Windows Server Administration Fundamentals certification is and how to register for the exam. Furthermore, you will find useful resources to help you gather as much information as possible about the exam in general, discover what it takes to pass it, and, by doing so, launch a successful career.

Appendix, *Assessments*, provides you with answers to the chapter questions. Each chapter is accompanied by a considerable number of questions to help you reinforce the concepts and definitions provided. With this appendix, you can check your answers to those questions.

# To get the most out of this book

You must have solid experience of working with the Windows 10 operating system and have solid knowledge of computer networks and network operating systems.

Make sure you have a computer with a processor that supports virtualization technology and has between 8 and 16 GB of RAM.

# Download the color images

We also provide a PDF file that has color images of the screenshots/diagrams used in this book. You can download it here: https://static.packt-cdn.com/downloads/ 9781838550912_ColorImages.pdf.

# Conventions used

There are a number of text conventions used throughout this book.

CodeInText: Indicates code words in text, database table names, folder names, filenames, file extensions, pathnames, dummy URLs, user input, and Twitter handles. Here is an example: "Provide credentials to access the Deployment Share folder."

Any command-line input or output is written as follows:

```
Export-SmigServerSetting -FeatureID DHCP -Path C:\DHCP\Store
-Verbose
```

**Bold**: Indicates a new term, an important word, or words that you see on screen. For example, words in menus or dialog boxes appear in the text like this. Here is an example: "Select **Settings** from the **Start** menu."

 Warnings or important notes appear like this.

 Tips and tricks appear like this.

# Get in touch

Feedback from our readers is always welcome.

**General feedback**: If you have questions about any aspect of this book, mention the book title in the subject of your message and email us at customercare@packtpub.com.

**Errata**: Although we have taken every care to ensure the accuracy of our content, mistakes do happen. If you have found a mistake in this book, we would be grateful if you would report this to us. Please visit www.packtpub.com/support/errata, selecting your book, clicking on the Errata Submission Form link, and entering the details.

**Piracy**: If you come across any illegal copies of our works in any form on the internet, we would be grateful if you would provide us with the location address or website name. Please contact us at copyright@packt.com with a link to the material.

**If you are interested in becoming an author**: If there is a topic that you have expertise in and you are interested in either writing or contributing to a book, please visit authors.packtpub.com.

# Reviews

Please leave a review. Once you have read and used this book, why not leave a review on the site that you purchased it from? Potential readers can then see and use your unbiased opinion to make purchase decisions, we at Packt can understand what you think about our products, and our authors can see your feedback on their book. Thank you!

For more information about Packt, please visit packt.com.

# Section 1: Introducing Windows Server and Installing Windows Server 2019

The first section covers Windows Server, in general, and Windows Server 2019, in particular. It also covers the installation of Windows Server 2019. Upon the completion of this section, you will have enough knowledge about Windows Server in general, and Windows Server 2019 in particular. Additionally, you will be able to clean install, upgrade, and migrate to Windows Server 2019, as well as be able to complete network and unattended installation too.

This section comprises the following chapters:

- Chapter 1, *Getting Started with Windows Server*
- Chapter 2, *Introducing Windows Server 2019*
- Chapter 3, *Installing Windows Server 2019*
- Chapter 4, *Post-Installation Tasks in Windows Server 2019*

# Getting started with Windows Server

1

This chapter is designed to provide you with an introduction to Windows Server in general, and Windows Server 2019 in particular. Windows Server 2019, the newest version of the Microsoft OS for servers, is the follow-up to Windows Server 2016. Besides introducing Windows Server, right at the beginning of this chapter, you will find an overview of the very basic concepts of computer networks. This chapter is organized into two parts; each part provides a concise but complete description of these concepts.

Definitions such as hosts, nodes, peer-to-peer, and clients/servers are covered in the Understanding Computer Network section. Windows Server 2019 is covered in the Understanding Servers Windows Server Overview section. Finally, once you are acquainted with the essentials of Windows Server in general and Windows Server 2019, in particular, through chapter exercise you will have the option to download Windows Server 2019 and create an installation media.

The following topics will be covered in this chapter:

- Understanding computer networks
- Understanding servers
- Understanding Windows Server
- Chapter exercise—downloading Windows Server 2019

## Technical requirements

In order to complete the exercise in this chapter, you will need the following equipment:

- A PC with Windows 10 Pro, at least 16 GB of RAM, 1 TB of HDD, and access to the internet

# Understanding computer networks

It all began many years ago when the need for **sharing resources** became a necessity. As time went by and demands increased, the development and advancement of computer network technologies also took place. With that, more computers were connected to computer networks and geographical distances were diminished in terms of communication. It created a need for well-defined terms and concepts to describe computer networking. Because of that, different types of computer networks, network topologies, architectures, and components have emerged.

Let's begin by understanding what a computer network is.

# What is a computer network?

From my experience, people often confuse what a computer network is with what a computer network does. While the first explains what constitutes a computer network, the latter shows the benefits of a computer network. In *Figure 1.1* we can see that a **computer network** is a group of computers connected to each other in order to share resources. The resources are usually data, network services, and peripheral devices:

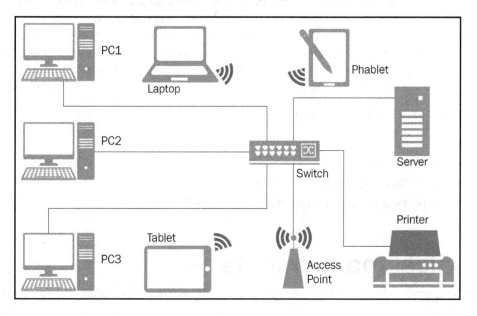

Figure 1.1: A typical computer network

A computer network is divided into different types. Let's take a look at each of them individually.

# Types of computer networks

In general, the categorization of computer networks consists of the **area** they cover and the **purpose** they serve. Some of the most popular types of computer networks nowadays are described in the following subsections.

## Personal Area Network (PAN)

A Personal Area Network (*Figure 1.2*) is a computer network that is used to connect and transmit data among devices located in a private area that is partially or completely protected from external access. Bluetooth and Wi-Fi are the most common communication technologies used to interconnect devices in a PAN. Often, a PAN is also known as a **Home Area Network (HAN):**

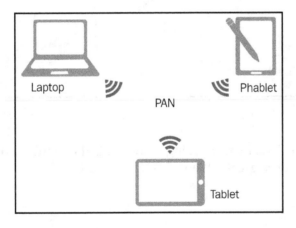

Figure 1.2: A PAN

Another type of network is **local area network (LAN)**. However its coverage is far greater than a PAN. Let's learn more about it next section.

# LAN

A LAN (*Figure 1.3*) is a computer network that connects two or more computers in a local area. Try to understand a local area as one single room, a floor, several floors, a building, or several buildings adjacent to each other at a distance that Ethernet communication technology permits. A LAN usually utilizes a central device that uses twisted pair, coaxial, or fiber optic cables as a networking media to interconnect computers:

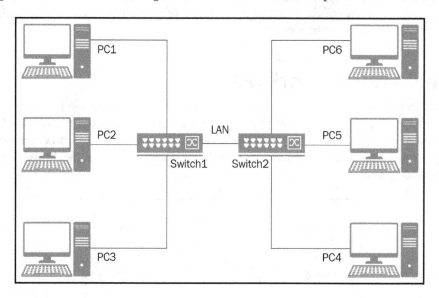

Figure 1.3: A LAN

The next type of network that we are going to look at is the **Metropolitan Area Network (MAN)**. Its coverage is even greater than a LAN.

# MAN

In contrast to a LAN, a MAN (*Figure 1.4*) represents a group of LANs interconnected within the geographical boundary of a town or city. Nowadays, fiber optics and gigabit layer 3 switches are used to interconnect LANs and route the traffic among them, as seen in the following figure:

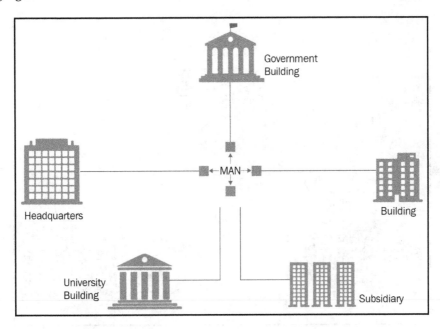

Figure 1.4: A Metropolitan Area Network

Finally, we will understand what is a **wide area network** (**WAN**) which has the greatest coverage.

# WAN

Unlike a MAN, a WAN (as shown in *Figure 1.5*) is a computer network that covers a wide geographic area using dedicated telecommunication lines such as telephone lines, leased lines, or satellites. WANs cover large geographic areas and, as such, they do not have geographic restrictions. The internet is the best example of a WAN:

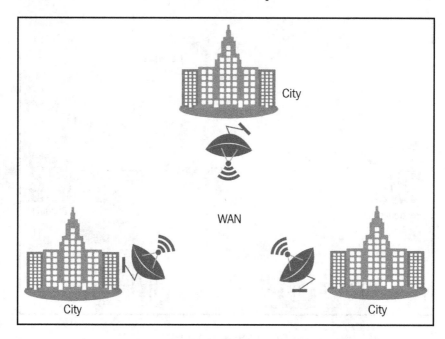

Figure 1.5: A Wide Area Network

Now that we've understood the different types of computer networks, let's take a look at the underlying components that make up these networks.

# Understanding computer network components

Just as PCs have **components**, computer networks have their own components, too. Usually, while PCs and peripheral devices are known to most people, components such as networking devices, networking media, and **network operating systems** (**NOS**) are mostly known by IT professionals.

Let's first understand what clients and servers in a computer network are.

# Understanding clients and servers

Let's assume that the network resource is the point of reference for both clients and servers. Then, in a computer network, **clients** usually request access to resources. On the other hand, **servers** are responsible for providing resources and managing access to those resources. Both clients and servers play an active role in the computer network. In *Figure 1.6*, a server with a directly connected printer provides print resources to PCs in the role of resource requests:

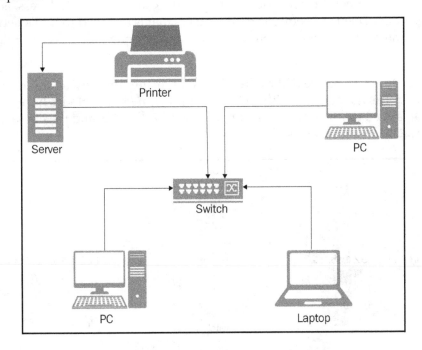

Figure 1.6: Client and server in a computer network

 Interestingly, the origin of the word **servers** comes from the word **serve**. If you search for the word serve in the Merriam-Webster dictionary, among the results, you will find one that says: *to provide services that benefit or help*. From that, we can think of a server in a computer network as the computer that provides services to clients. In conclusion, the server serves the clients.

Although clients and servers are the most important elements of a computer network, it depends upon hosts and nodes. Let's see how it fits into this structure.

# Understanding hosts and nodes

Have you ever heard terms such as hosts and nodes and wondered what they are? Although our first impression might drive us toward thinking that they are the same thing, they are not! While all hosts can be nodes, not every node can act as a host. Hence, a **host** is any device with an IP address assigned to its network interface that requests or provides networking resources on the network. Usually, clients, servers, and routers act as hosts.

 An Internet Protocol address, popularly known as an IP address, is a logical element comprised of numbers that is assigned to host's network interface in order to identify it in a computer network.

However, a **node** is any device that can receive and transmit the networking resources on the network but has no interface with an IP address assigned to it. Nodes have a network interface that is used for their management. In *Figure 1.7*, the PCs and the file server act as hosts, while switches act as nodes:

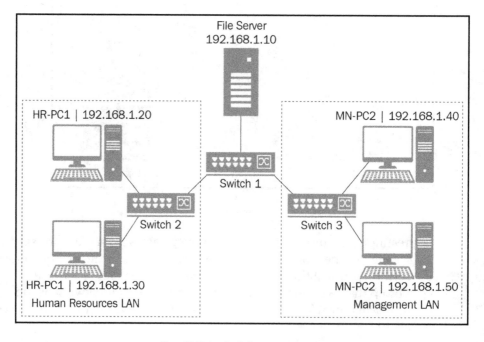

Figure 1.7: Hosts and nodes in a computer network

Now that we have learnt what a network is and its components we are well equipped to understand its architecture.

# Understanding computer network architectures

A computer network architecture represents a computer network design that enables network components to communicate with one another. Computer architecture is actually a framework that incorporates many aspects, such as physical and logical topology, network components, communication protocols, and its operational principles and procedures. Among network architectures, the most popular are **Peer-to-Peer** (**P2P**) and client/server.

Let us first understand the P2P network architecture.

## P2P network architecture

**P2P**, often known as a workgroup, is a computer network (see *Figure 1.8*) in which hosts do not have predefined roles. Instead, they change roles from client to server, and vice versa, based on their actual activities on the network. For example, if **PC1** is requesting resources from **PC2**, then **PC1** acts as the client and **PC2** acts as the server. If **PC2** requests resources from **PC1**, then **PC2** acts as a client and **PC1** acts as the server. Usually, PANs represent the best examples of P2P computer networks:

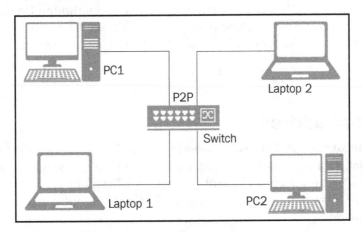

Figure 1.8: A Peer-to-Peer computer network

Peer-to-Peer (P2P) network architecture refers to a network model in which hosts or computers are equal in terms of capabilities and responsibilities. Having said that, depending on the circumstances, each host may be a client or server depending on whether it requests or provides services in that network.

The next type of network architecture is the Client/Server architecture.

# Client/server network architecture

A **client/server**, often known as a domain-based network, is a computer network (see earlier *Figure 1.7*) in which hosts have a predefined role. In such a network, hosts that request resources act as clients, whereas hosts that provide resources act as servers. In general, the client/server network architecture is a network with dedicated servers. Usually, LANs, MANs, and WANs represent the best examples of client/server computer networks.

At this point we have a greater understanding of how a network operates. However for a computer to communicate in a network it requires an IP address. We will learn more about this in the next section.

# Understanding IP addressing and subnetting

For a computer to be able to communicate in a computer network, it must have an **IP address**. As explained earlier, the IP address identifies the computer on that network. In addition, in complex networks, we encounter the term **subnet**, which helps to identify the specific network within the overall network. So far, the world of networks recognizes two IP-addressing technologies: IPv4 and IPv6. Nevertheless, even though IPv6-addressing technology is becoming more and more plausible, it still prefers the role of spectator in the great arena of the internet, in which IPv4-addressing technology continues to be the norm.

Let's first take a look at IPv4 network addresses.

## IPv4 network addresses

An **Internet Protocol version 4 (IPv4)** addressing technology—is often referred to as just an IP address. The label v4 represents the fourth version of IP addressing as specified in IETF publication RCF 791. It is a logical element in a network that consists of 32 bits organized into 4 octets with 8 bits each, divided by a decimal point for simplicity of interpretation (for example, 192.168.1.1).

Additionally, the IETF's RFC 791 document organizes IP addresses into 8-bit, 16-bit, or 24-bit prefixes, which introduces the **classful addressing** that enables IP addresses to be organized into classes of A, B, C, D, and E. With classful addressing, the IP address is split into the bits used for the network portion and bits used for the host portion for a given class.

Now let's take a look at the IPv6 addressing technology which was introduced to overcome the IPv4 address exhaustion of IPv4 network addresses.

# IPv6 network addresses

An **Internet Protocol version 6 (IPv6)** addressing technology - is another logical element that identifies a device on a computer network. The label v6 represents the sixth version of IP addressing, as specified in IETF publication RFC 2460. Unlike IPv4, IPv6 is a 128-bit address size organized into 8 hextets with 16 bits each, divided by a colon for simplicity of interpretation (for example, `2001:0DB8:85A3:0000:0000:8A2E:0370:7334`). The fact that IPv6 uses 128 bits makes it possible to use $2^{128}$ IPv6 addresses which when calculated gives an approximate number of 340 undecillion IPv6 addresses . Undoubtedly, that represents an extremely large number of available IPv6 addresses.

Next, let's take a look at IPv4 subnetting which plays an important role in identifying the network addresses

# IPv4 subnetting

**Subnetting** represents a logical division of one large network into multiple smaller networks. In subnetting, a subnet mask plays an important role in identifying the network and determining the size of the network. Additionally, subnetting enables you to identify the network address, host addresses, and broadcast address of a given network. By definition, a subnet mask is a 32-bit address used in combination with an IPv4 address to indicate a network and its hosts.

The default subnet masks, otherwise known as **classful networks**, for each class of IPv4 addresses are shown:

| IPv4 Class | Default subnet mask |
|------------|---------------------|
| A | 255.0.0.0 |
| B | 255.255.0.0 |
| C | 255.255.255.0 |

 You can learn more on IPv4-addressing technology, address space exhaustion, and classful networks at `https://blogs.igalia.com/dpino/2017/05/25/ipv4-exhaustion/`.

So far we have understood what a computer network is and the various types, components, and architectures. In the next section, we will introduce to Windows Server and its related concepts.

# Understanding servers

Throughout its history, **Windows Server** has evolved from a simple file server to an operating system that is capable of handling network services in complex environments such as corporate networks. Thus, Windows Server can provide network services such as domain controllers, web servers, print servers, and file servers. It often acts as a separate platform in which enterprise applications such as Exchange Server, SQL Server, SharePoint Server, and others are executed. With its robust performance and advanced security, nowadays, Windows Server is shaping **cloud computing**.

# Understanding server hardware and software

As you may recall, computer hardware and software represent the physical and logical components of a server, respectively. Thereof, since the primary role of the server is to provide network services to the clients, a server requires powerful hardware too. This is because software such as Windows Server is designed to process large workloads; therefore, reciprocally, its hardware is required to be durable and made of high-quality materials so it can continually deliver services and support network-based operations. Thus, apart from distinguishing it from the ordinary computer, a server is also specific to the types of services it provides. For example, a database server requires more memory and storage space.

The CPU, memory, disk, and network are known to be the **key system components** that affect the overall performance of your servers. It is recommended that the performance of key system components is continuously monitored in order to maintain the optimal performance of servers for both normal and heavy workloads.

Let's first understand what a CPU is.

# Understanding a  CPU

A **Central Processing Unit** (**CPU**), or processor, is a chip on a server's motherboard. In literature, you often encounter the term **computer's brain**. It is a component that does all the processing and calculations. Intel and AMD are the biggest CPU manufacturers for PCs and servers. Their newest CPUs on the market are based on 64-bit architecture, which differs from 32-bit architecture-based processors. In 64-bit architecture, 64 bits of data are exchanged between the CPU and RAM in each communication session. On the other hand, in 32-bit architecture, only 32 bits of data are exchanged per communication session between RAM and CPU. That is half as less data being communicated via 32-bit architecture as compared to a 64-bit architecture.

In order to give out the performance, the CPU depend on RAM. Let us learn about this next.

# Understanding memory

RAM represents the server's working memory, which is used by Windows Server 2019 and server applications. Thus, the more RAM on the server, the more applications can run simultaneously. You can learn more about RAM in the *Understanding memory* section in `Chapter 10`, *Tuning and Maintaining Windows Server 2019*.

Now let's understand what a disk is in the case of servers.

# Understanding disks

As you know, data is usually stored on a **disk**. In the case of servers, they mostly have more than one disk, which is referred to as the server's disk sub-system. As for disk performance, read/write speed is an element that must be taken into consideration, because the faster the disk's throughput, the higher the performance of your disk sub-system.

Now let's understand what a network interface is.

## Understanding a network interface

A **network interface** enables the server to connect to an organization's LAN and to the internet. Servers usually have more than one network interface. The faster the server's network connection speed is, the more data the server can send and receive to and from the network.

Now that we have understood what a server is, let's take a look at the various server sizes, form factors, and shapes.

# Understanding server sizes, form factors, and shapes

Regarding size and form factors, servers come in three different shapes:

- **Rack-mountable servers** are designed to be installed in a frame called a rack (see *Figure 1.9*). These servers usually populate on-premises server rooms or data centers:

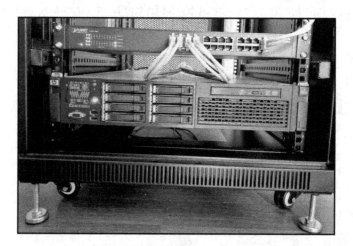

Figure 1.9: An HP server in a rack

- **Blade servers** are small modules known as blades that are installed on a server's chassis to save space and power. These servers usually populate data centers or supercomputer facilities.
- **Tower servers** are single big case servers that stand upright. These servers are usually either used for testing purposes or to provide local services in a SOHO.

 A 64-bit Windows Server installed on a 64-bit hardware server can process double the amount of data compared to a 32-bit Window Server installed on a 32-bit hardware server.

Just like your computer, the server too has its own operating system that enables network services. Let us learn more about it.

# Understanding a Network Operating System

A **Network Operating System** (**NOS**) is software that is capable of managing, maintaining, and providing resources in a network. Additionally, an NOS is capable of sharing files and applications, providing web services, managing access to resources, administering users and computers, providing tools for configuration, maintaining and providing resources, as well as other functions related to network resources. With that in mind, a NOS is an important component when it comes to managing computer network resources.

These days, versions of Windows Server, Linux Server, and macOS Server are all considered to be an NOS because they are all capable of providing network services. Let's understand each one of them individually.

# Windows Server overview

As you know, Windows OS is a Microsoft product. Its server line began with Windows NT 3.5 in the early 90s, which was then followed by other Windows Server versions, starting with Windows Server 2000. At its core, it's a GUI-based OS; however, as of Windows Server 2008, a Server Core edition was introduced, which is a CLI-based OS. From Windows Server 2003 to Windows Server 2008, the architecture was both 32-bit, and 64-bit; however, since Windows Server 2012 it's only 64-bit. The **New Technology File System** (**NTFS**) continues to be its native filesystem; from Windows Server 2012, **Resilient File System** (**ReFS**) was introduced to replace NTFS. However, even on Windows Server 2019 (see *Figure 1.10*), NTFS is a native filesystem. Nowadays, Windows Server powers many organizations' backend systems and is thus able to provide network services for Windows-based hosts as well as to hosts with a non-Windows OS.

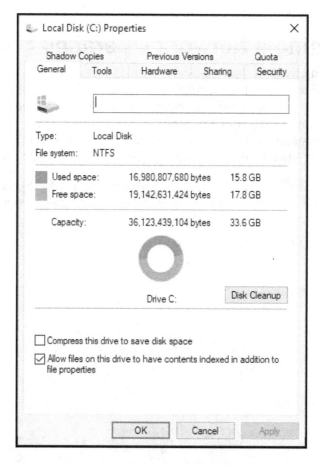

Figure 1.10: The NTFS continues to be used by Windows Server 2019

The ReFS overview can be found at `https://docs.microsoft.com/en-us/`
`windows-server/storage/refs/refs-overview.`

# Linux Server overview

If there is something interesting to talk about in the world of OSes, the Linux operating
system is unequivocal. This is because the world of technology does not recognize any
innovative initiatives as having gathered more volunteers than Linux did. Everything
started as a desire to improve functionality in an existing operating system such as MINIX.
Instead of an improved MINIX, it turned out that, in the early 1990s, Linus Torvalds
developed a new operating system called Linux. So, the GNU GPL project took over the
licensing of Linux, the penguin became a Linux mascot, the first Linux booklet published
was *Linux Installation and Getting Started*, the first Linux virus was *Bliss*, and *Linux
Journal* and *Linux Weekly News* marked the first-release Linux magazines. Just like that,
many other global activities followed that would form the so-called Linux community,
which then turned out to be one of the world's largest volunteer communities, contributing
globally to the further development of Linux. Nowadays, due to its security and open
source nature, Linux Servers (see *Figure 1.11*) power the majority of web servers and
supercomputers.

Figure 1.11: The long-term support version of Ubuntu Server

Find out how to run Linux distros on Windows Server 2019 at `https://`
`docs.microsoft.com/en-us/windows/wsl/install-on-server.`

## macOS Server overview

**macOS Server** may be younger than Windows Server and Linux Server operating systems, but with its reliability, it is slowly gaining the industry's support. At its core, macOS Server is, in fact, a modified Unix OS that already conforms to the familiar Apple GUI for PCs. Much like Windows and Linux, the macOS Server is also offered on 32-bit and 64-bit platforms. However, ever since Apple was designated to use Intel processors for their computers and servers, the macOS Server is only available on 64-bit. Nowadays, although we cannot speak of the exact number of servers powered by the macOS server, Apple continues to provide support for macOS server which has recently offered flexibility in the hardware that supports the macOS Server.

 You can learn more about macOS server at `https://www.apple.com/macos/server/`.

In this section, we have understood what is a server, learned about server hardware such as CPU, memory, disk, network interface, understood server sizes, form factors, and shapes, and what is NOS. In the next section, we will be introduced to Windows Server and its timeline.

# Understanding Windows Server

What would your answer be if someone asked you what Windows Server is? I guess your answer would be more or less like the following: *Windows Server is the server's operating system developed by Microsoft as part of the Windows NT family of operating systems*. In general, whether it is a server based on Windows Server, Linux Server, or macOS Server, it really does not make any difference as long as the version that is being used continues to provide adequate services within an organization's network. However, looking at them from the perspective of deployment, user interface, managing resources, and maintaining a server, many differences are evident.

Let us take a look at the Windows Server timeline to understand how it has evolved over the years.

# Windows Server timeline

So far, in the 23-year history of Windows Server, I think Microsoft has been quite intuitive to adopt new requirements in the server world. Personally, I feel that the Windows Server timeline looks interesting and I want to share it with you. Particularly, notice the transition of the Windows Server technology over time. Simply, it's impressive.

Windows Server timeline is shown in the following table:

| Server for the masses era 1996-2000 | Enterprise era 2000-2008 | Datacenter era 2009 - 2013 | Cloud for the masses era 2016 - present |
|---|---|---|---|
| • Windows NT Server 3.5<br>• Windows NT Server 4.0 | • Windows 2000 Server<br>• Windows Server 2003 | • Windows Server 2008<br>• Windows Server 2012 | • Windows Server 2016<br>• Windows Server 2019 |

In this section, we have learnt about Windows Serve and got acquainted with its timeline. In the following section we will learn the steps for downloading Windows Server 2019.

# Chapter exercise – downloading Windows Server 2019

In this chapter exercise, you will learn how to download Windows Server 2019.

# Downloading Windows Server 2019

To download Windows Server 2019 on your Windows 10 computer, complete the following steps:

1. Press the Windows key + *R* to open **Run**.
2. Enter `microsoft-edge:` and press *Enter*.
3. In Microsoft Edge, click the address bar and enter `https://www.microsoft.com/en-us/evalcenter/`, and then press *Enter*.
4. On the **Evaluation Center** page, click the search icon in the right-upper corner and enter `Windows Server 2019`, then press *Enter*.
5. From the *Search* results, select **Windows Server 2019**.

6. Select your *evaluation file type*, and then click **Continue**.
7. Complete the form as shown in Figure 1.12, and then click **Continue:**

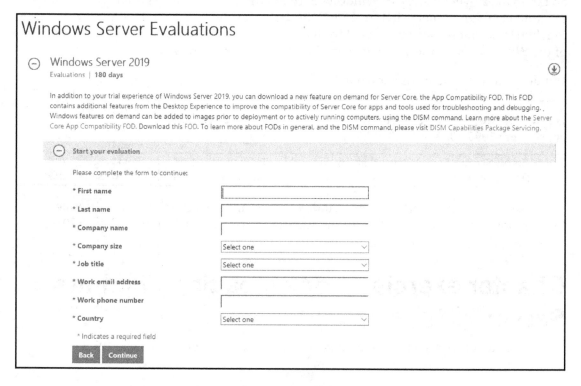

Figure 1.12. Downloading Windows Server 2019 evaluation

8. Select your *language*, and then click **Download**.
9. Shortly after, the **Windows Server 2019** download will begin. If not, you may want to click the **Download** button.

 Once your Windows Server 2019 download completes, you should burn the ISO file to a USB flash drive. If you do not know how, then follow the instructions at `https://www.lifewire.com/how-to-burn-an-iso-file-to-a-usb-drive-2619270`. Once completed, you are all set to move on with the installation of the Windows Server 2019 evaluation version.

# Summary

In this chapter, you learned about computer networks, server's hardware and software, and Windows Server.

Specifically, in the *Understanding Computer Networks* section, you learned what a computer network is, and were introduced to different types of computer networks, computer network components, computer network architectures, and IP addressing and subnetting. Furthermore, in the *Understanding servers* section, you learned about server hardware and software; server sizes, form factors, and shapes; and **Network Operating System** (**NOS**). Finally, in the *Understanding Windows Server* section, you learned about the Windows Server timeline.

To make things interesting, the chapter included a chapter exercise that provided instructions on how to download Windows Server 2019 from the Evaluation Center portal. With the things you have learned in this chapter, you will be able to identify types of computer networks, network architectures, and IP addressing and subnetting. You'll also be able to identify key hardware components, and understand an NOS, and the Windows Server timeline.

In the following chapter, you will learning about Windows Server 2019 specifically.

# Questions

1. A computer network architecture represents the computer network design that enables the network components to communicate with one another. (True | False)
2. _____ usually request access to resources, _____ are responsible for providing resources and managing access to the resources.
3. Which of the following are considered to be computer networks?
   - PAN
   - HAN
   - LAN
   - MAN
   - SAN
   - WAN
   - All of the above

4. Windows Server is the server's operating system developed by Microsoft as part of the Windows NT family of operating systems. (True | False)

5. _____ is able to provide network services such as domain controllers, web servers, print servers, and file servers.

6. The subnet helps to identify a specific network within the overall network. (True | False)

7. Which of the following are considered to be network architectures? (Choose two)
    - Peer-to-Peer (P2P)
    - Client/server
    - Network Operating System (NOS)
    - Network topology

8. The CPU, memory, disk, and network are known to be the key system components that affect the overall performance of your servers. (True | False)

9. The _____ represents its physical component while the _____ represents its logical component of a server.

10. Which of the following are considered to be IP addressing technologies? (Choose two)
    - IPv2
    - IPv4
    - IPv6
    - IPv8

# Further reading

- *An Overview of Networks*: https://intronetworks.cs.luc.edu/current/html/intro.html
- *Get Started with Windows Server 2019*: https://docs.microsoft.com/en-us/windows-server/get-started-19/get-started-19
- *Windows Server vs Linux: The Ultimate Comparison*: https://phoenixnap.com/blog/linux-vs-microsoft-windows-servers

# Introducing Windows Server 2019

This chapter is designed to teach you about Microsoft's new operating system for servers called Windows Server 2019.

In the first part of this chapter, you will learn about the different Windows Server 2019 editions, the differences between Windows Server 2019 and Windows Server 2016, and the minimum recommended system requirements. In the second part of this chapter, you will learn about the new features introduced in Windows Server 2019. System Insights, hybrid cloud, Storage Migration Service, Storage Replica, the improved Windows Defender, and support for Docker containers and Kubernetes are just some of the new features introduced with Windows Server 2019.

This chapter concludes with a chapter exercise on downloading Windows Admin Center.

The following topics will be covered in this chapter:

- Windows Server 2019 overview
- What's new in Windows Server 2019?
- Chapter exercise—downloading Windows Admin Center

## Technical requirements

To complete the lab for this chapter, you will need the following equipment:

- A PC with Windows 10 Pro, at least 8 GB of RAM, 500 GB of HDD, and access to the internet
- **Virtual machine** (**VM**) with Windows Server 2019 Datacenter (Desktop Experience), at least 4 GB of RAM, 100 GB of HDD, and access to the internet

# Windows Server 2019 overview

**Windows Server 2019** (see *Figure 2.1*) is the latest version of the server operating system from Microsoft, as part of the Windows NT family of OSes. Announced in March 2018, it was then released for general availability some time in October 2018. Just like Windows Server 2016, Windows Server 2019 is also based on Windows 10 code.

Consequently, since new feature releases of Windows 10 are delivered via the so-called **Windows as a service** format, Windows Server 2019 interestingly marks the first server build in which Microsoft intentionally skipped the **Release to Manufacturing** (**RTM**) delivery format. Among other new features that have accompanied the appearance of Windows Server 2019 are System Insights, hybrid cloud, Storage Migration Service, Storage Replica, the improved Windows Defender, support for Kubernetes, and more:

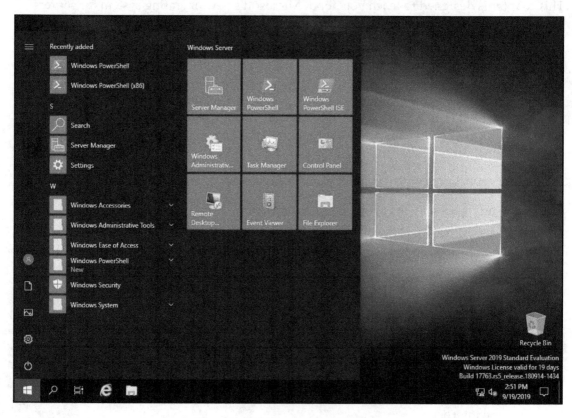

Figure 2.1: Windows Server 2019 Desktop and Start menu

It is also worth mentioning that Microsoft has not forgotten system administrators, for whom it has developed a very nice admin tool known as **Windows Admin Center** (see the *What is Windows Admin Center?* and *Downloading Windows Admin Center* sections later on in this chapter).

 Windows Admin Center is a new server management tool that uses web technology. Its interface is based on Azure's interface, enabling multiple server management features. Once you install Windows Server 2019 and get access to the desktop, the Windows Admin Center dialog box pops up. It is free of cost and can be downloaded from `https://www.microsoft.com/en-us/evalcenter/evaluate-hyper-v-server-2019`.

To begin, let's take a look at the various editions of Windows Server 2019.

# Windows Server 2019 editions

In general, Windows Server 2019 seems to walk in the footsteps of its predecessor Windows Server 2016 in terms of available editions. Hence, if we remove from the list the Windows Server 2016 Storage Server editions, then the editions available in Windows Server 2019 are as follows:

- **Windows Server 2019 Datacenter** is the most comprehensive edition designed for enterprises that own highly virtualized data-centers or act as cloud providers.
- **Windows Server 2019 Standard** is the full-featured edition designed for medium-sized businesses that own servers on-premises.
- **Windows Server 2019 Essentials** is designed for small businesses that own a single server in their IT infrastructure.
- **Microsoft Hyper-V Server 2019** is designed as a free product that delivers enterprise-class virtualization for data-centers and hybrid clouds.

The above points give us a fair idea of the various editions within Windows Server 2019. But how different is it from its previous version? Let us discuss.

# Windows Server 2019 versus Windows Server 2016

Apparently, the first impression is that Windows Server 2019 is an upgraded version of Windows Server 2016. However, once you start digging into the features of Windows Server 2019, you will realize that it is actually more than that. Hence, the following will highlight just a few of the differences between these two OSes:

- **Features related to hybrid capabilities**: Only Windows Server 2019 supports hybrid cloud, Storage Migration Service, and System Insights. However, both OSes support Storage Replica.
- **Features related to better security**: Only Windows Server 2019 supports shielded VMs for Windows Server and Linux, whereas both OSes support Microsoft Defender **Advanced Threat Protection** (**ATP**), Device Guard, and Credential Guard.
- **Features related to optimization of performance**: Only Windows Server 2019 supports Linux containers and the Kubernetes platform, whereas both OSes support Windows Server containers including Docker.
- **Features related to infrastructure management**: Only Windows Server 2019 supports cluster-wide monitoring and deduplication for **Resilient File System** (**ReFS**), whereas both OSes support storage health monitoring and VM Storage Resiliency.

By recognizing the differences of Windows Server 2019 with that of Windows Server 2016, you will be able to easily determine which version you need. Now, let's take a look at the minimum and recommended system requirements.

# Minimum and recommended system requirements

It is customary to familiarize ourselves with the so-called **minimum system requirements** before installing the Windows OS. Hence, it is required that your server meets the following minimum system requirements to install Windows Server 2019:

- **Processor**: 1.4 GHz 64-bit processor
- **RAM**: 512 MB (2 GB for Server with the Desktop Experience installation option)
- **Disk space**: 32 GB
- **Network**: An Ethernet adapter capable of at least one Gigabit throughput
- **Graphics device and monitor**: Capable of Super VGA (1024 x 768) or higher resolution
- **Other hardware**: A DVD drive (if you intend to install the operating system from DVD media), a keyboard, a mouse (or another compatible pointing device), and internet access

However, if you want to enjoy the performance power of Windows Server 2019, then ensure that your server meets the following recommended system requirements:

- **Processor**: 2.0 GHz 64-bit processor or higher
- **RAM**: 32 GB or higher
- **Disk space**: 256 GB SSD and 1 TB HDD
- **Network**: At least 1 Gigabit Ethernet NIC
- **Graphics device and monitor**: Capable of Super VGA (1024 x 768) or higher resolution
- **Other hardware**: A DVD drive, a keyboard, a mouse (or another compatible pointing device), and internet access

In this section, we learned about the Windows Server 2019 operating system and various editions of Windows Server 2019, compared Windows Server 2019 with Windows Server 2016, and found out the minimum and recommended system requirements. In the following section, we will delve deeper into the new features of Windows Server 2019.

# What's new in Windows Server 2019?

There is no doubt that **Windows Server 2019** is built on the strong foundation of Windows Server 2016, which makes them share common features; nonetheless, it brings numerous innovations too. This section will try to explain some of the new features, among many, introduced in Windows Server 2019.

## Understanding the System Insights feature

**System Insights** is a new feature available in Windows Server 2019, which locally analyzes Windows Server system data by providing an insight into the functionality of servers and helping system administrators to keep everything running smoothly. It uses **predictive analytics** to analyze past usage trends and predict future resource consumption. All data is collected, processed, and analyzed directly on the local server, although you can optionally forward events to Azure Log Analytics, giving you a unified view of your environment. System Insights can be installed via Windows PowerShell (see *Figure 2.2*):

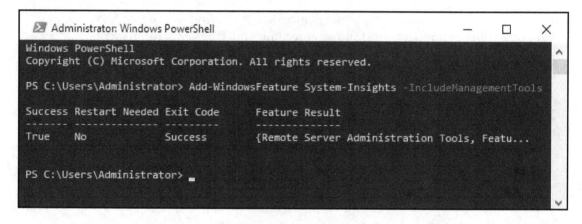

Figure 2.2: Installing System Insights

It can also be installed as a Windows Admin Center extension, as in *Figure 2.3*:

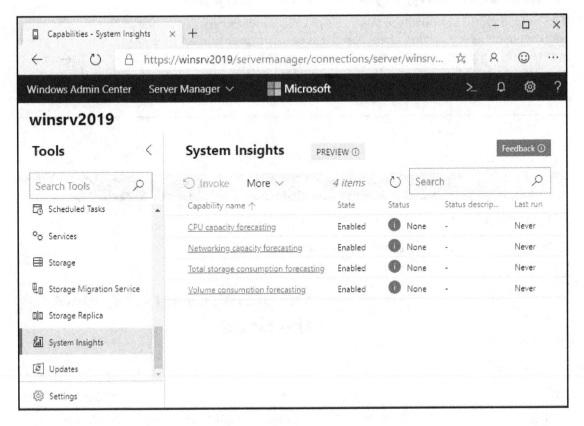

Figure 2.3: System Insights in Windows Admin Center

In addition to System Insights, Windows Server 2019 offers other important features. Now, let's understand hybrid cloud support, another interesting feature of Windows Server 2019.

# Understanding hybrid cloud support

The **hybrid cloud support** (see *Figure 2.4*) in Windows Server 2019 enables the improvement of connections between the servers on-premise, and the cloud services on Azure. Such improvements include better support for Azure Backup, File Sync, disaster recovery, and other Azure services. Additionally, hybrid cloud support enables the apps that are running on the local servers to take advantage of cloud services:

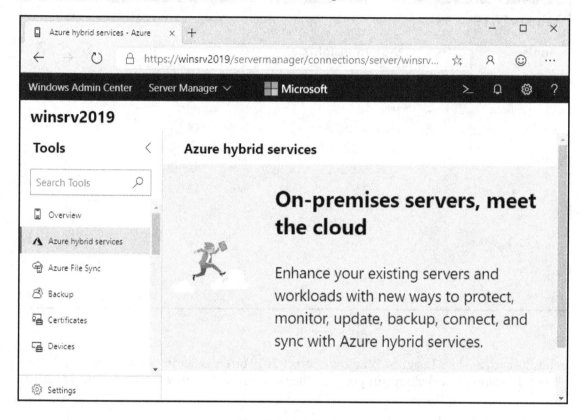

Figure 2.4: Hybrid cloud support

The next brand new feature of Windows Server 2019 that we will look at is Storage Migration Service.

# Understanding Storage Migration Service

**Storage Migration Service** is a brand new feature in Windows Server 2019 that facilitates the process of migrating servers to a newer version of Windows Server. It uses a GUI interface and Windows PowerShell to inventory data on servers and transfer the data and configuration to newer servers. Additionally, it may optionally move the identities of the old servers to the new servers. In that way, the apps and users do not have to change anything. Storage Migration Service can be used as a **Windows Admin Center** extension, as shown in *Figure 2.5*:

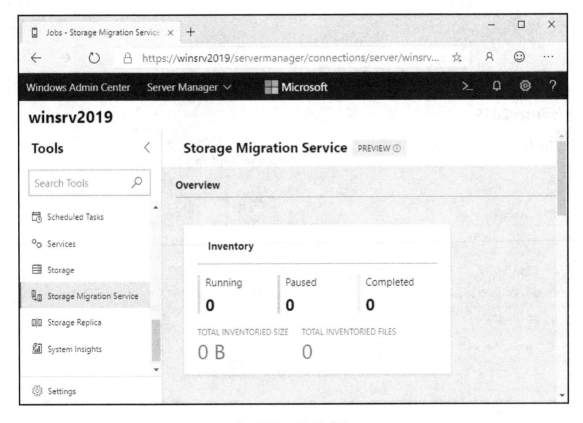

Figure. 2.5: Storage Migration Service

In addition to the new features introduced specifically for Windows Server 2019, there are also those which are introduced in earlier versions but have been improved and enhanced in Windows Server 2019. The next feature that we will learn about is the Storage Replica feature.

# Understanding the Storage Replica feature

**Storage Replica** is a feature that was introduced in Windows Server 2016 but enhanced in Windows Server 2019. It enables the replication of volumes between servers or clusters both synchronously and asynchronously. Usually, such replication is used for disaster recovery purposes. Additionally, Storage Replica allows users to create a stretching failover cluster for high availability with nodes spread over two different sites which maintain the synchronization among storage. It is available in **Windows Admin Center**, as shown in *Figure 2.6*:

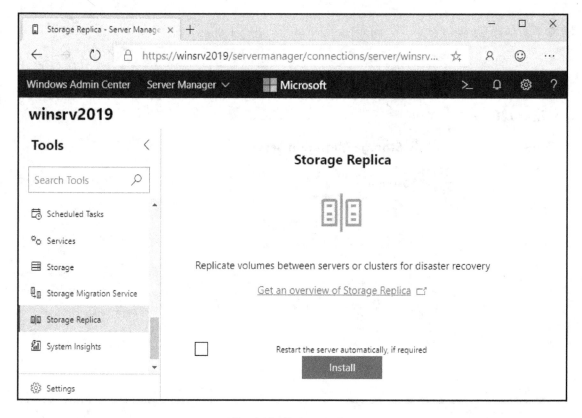

Figure 2.6: Installing Storage Replica

 Stretch cluster represents a method of deploying Storage Replica which allows configuration of computers and storage in a single cluster. In such a deployment method, servers share their storage which is synchronously replicated with the site awareness. Like that, stretching cluster solution in addition to offering high availability, it also enables disaster recovery.

New features introduced with Windows Server 2019 also cover security. Now, let's understand Microsoft Defender ATP, a new security feature.

# Understanding Microsoft Defender ATP

Among the many new features introduced in Windows Server 2019 are those related to security (see *Figure 2.7*) as well. It is worth mentioning here the support for Microsoft Defender ATP. Microsoft Defender ATP is a centralized security platform that is based on a proactive approach for detecting malware. It also deals with post-breach detection, automated investigation, and response. Primarily, it was available for Windows 10 devices. Lately, Microsoft Defender ATP became available for Windows Server 2019 and previous versions of Windows Server:

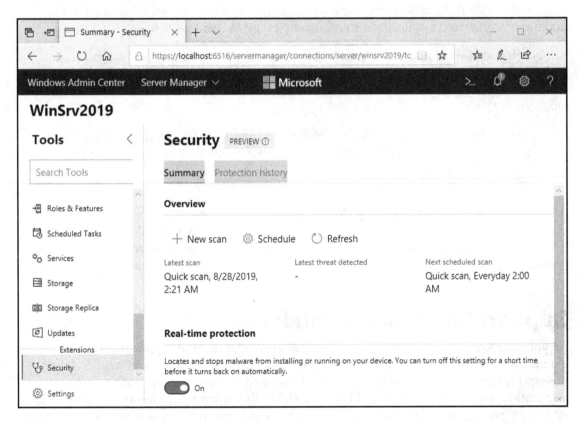

Figure 2.7: Windows Defender via Windows Admin Center

Now, let's learn about support for Kubernetes, which represents a virtualization feature that, in collaboration with Docker, enhances functionality in VMs and increases their security.

# Support for Kubernetes

Originally designed by Google and maintained by the Cloud Native Computing Foundation, Kubernetes is an open source platform that enables the automated deployment, scaling, and operations of application containers in a virtualized environment. Everything began with the introduction of the Docker containerization project, launched in 2013. Docker technology enabled applications to be executed in an environment known as **isolated containers**. However, Docker was not capable of managing large and distributed containerized applications. That is where Kubernetes came in by making containerized applications dramatically easier to manage at scale.

Kubernetes consists of **nodes** and **pods**, where the former can be physical machines or VMs, and the latter represents a single instance of an application. Just like that, Kubernetes has become a key part of the container technology often being used in combination with Docker.

 With the release of Kubernetes v1.14, Windows Server 2019 is the only supported Windows operating system enabling Kubernetes Node on Windows.

If Kubernetes enables automated deployment, scaling, and operations of application containers in a virtualized environment, on the other hand docker enables the application to run its own isolated virtualized environment. So let's learn about support for Docker containers.

# Support for Docker containers

As you may know, Microsoft recommends that every client/server application shall run on a dedicated server. If in the **traditional deployment approach**, this would require a single physical server for each application; in the **virtualized deployment approach**, each application requires its own Virtual Machine (VM). By contrast, the **container deployment approach** (see *Figure 2.8*) implies that the operating system on the host is shared among the applications. In that way, a container enables the application to run in its own isolated environment with no knowledge of any other applications being executed outside its container.

As was the case with Kubernetes (see the *Support for Kubernetes* section), **Docker** has similarly been a game changer in application containerization. Hence, Docker technology has enabled easy-to-build, deploy, and run application images. Docker consists of **Docker Engine**, which powers Docker containers. Originally, it was written for Linux, and, after a lot of development work, it is now supported on Windows and macOS:

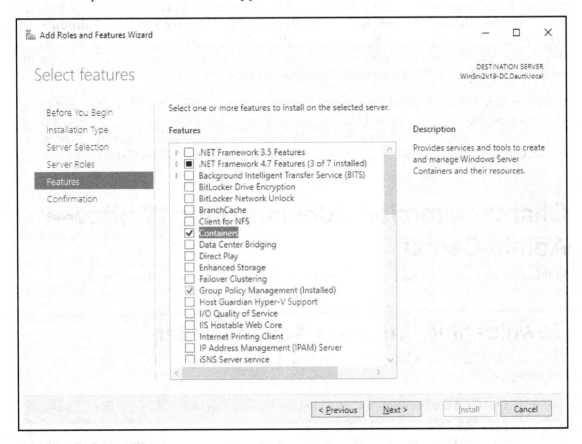

Figure 2.8: Installing the Containers feature

Now, let's understand what Windows Admin Center is and how it makes working with servers much easier. Simply put, instead of logging into your server via Remote Desktop, with Windows Admin Center you bring a very rich server interface to your computer's desktop.

# What is Windows Admin Center?

Formerly known as Project Honolulu, **Windows Admin Center** is a new server management app introduced with Windows Server 2019. It enables system administrators to work with both servers on-premises and in the cloud. Windows Admin Center uses a browser-based interface to manage Windows Server. In that way, Windows Admin Center comes as a substitution platform for older tools such as **Server Manager** and **Computer Management**. You can download Windows Admin Center from Microsoft's website (see this chapter's exercises) and then install it on Windows Server 2019, as well as Windows 10 and earlier versions of Windows and Windows Server.

In this section, we understood the System Insights feature, hybrid cloud support, Storage Migration Service, the Storage Replica feature, and Microsoft Defender ATP. Also, we learned about support for Kubernetes, Docker containers, and Windows Admin Center. In the following section, we will learn how to download Windows Admin Center.

# Chapter exercise – downloading Windows Admin Center

In this chapter exercise, you will learn how to download Windows Admin Center.

## Downloading Windows Admin Center

To download Windows Admin Center for your Windows 10 computer, complete the following steps:

1. Open up the browser and go to `https://www.microsoft.com/en-us/cloud-platform/windows-admin-center`.
2. On the Windows Admin Center download site, click the **Download now** button, as shown in *Figure 2.9*:

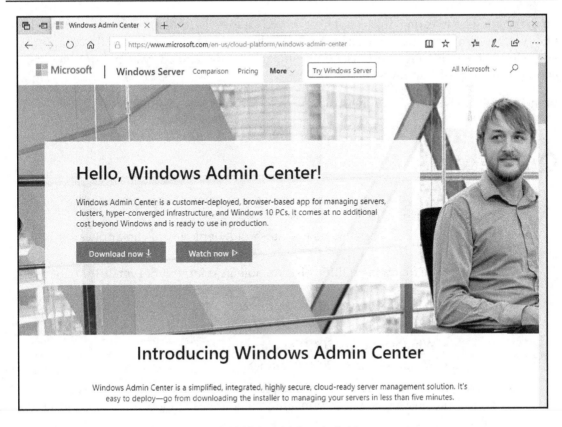

Figure 2.9: Windows Admin Center download site

3. The Windows Admin Center will start downloading.

# Summary

In general, in this chapter, you learned about Windows Server 2019 as the latest version of the Server operating system by Microsoft, which is part of the Windows NT family of OSes.

Specifically, in the *Windows Server 2019 overview* section, you learned about the Windows Server 2019 OS, various editions of Windows Server 2019, the differences between Windows Server 2019 versus Windows Server 2016, and the minimum and recommended system requirements. Furthermore, in the *What's new in Windows Server 2019?* section, you learned about the System Insights feature, hybrid cloud support, Storage Migration Service, the Storage Replica feature, and Microsoft Defender ATP. Additionally, you learned about support for Kubernetes and Docker containers and what Windows Admin Center is.

To make things interesting, this chapter provided an exercise that provided the instructions to download Windows Admin Center. With the things you have learned in this chapter, you will be able to identify editions, minimum, and recommended system requirements, and new features of Windows Server 2019.

In the following chapter, you will learn how to install Windows Server 2019.

# Questions

1. Windows Admin Center is a new server management app introduced with Windows Server 2019. (True | False)
2. _____ technology has enabled easy-to-build, deploy, and run application images.
3. Which of the following editions is available in Windows Server 2019? (Choose two.)
   - Windows Server 2019 Datacenter
   - Windows Server 2019 Enterprise
   - Windows Server 2019 Standard
   - Windows Server 2019 Beginner
4. Microsoft Defender ATP is a unified platform that enables preventative protection, post-breach detection, automated investigation, and response. (True | False)
5. _____ is a new feature available in Windows Server 2019, which locally analyzes Windows Server system data by providing an insight into the functionality of servers and helping system administrators to keep everything running smoothly.
6. Which of the following is the CPU minimum system requirements for installing Windows Server 2019?
   - 1.4 GHz 64-bit processor
   - 1.4 GHz 32-bit processor
   - 2.4 GHz 64-bit processor
   - 2.4 GHz 64-bit processor
7. The hybrid cloud support in Windows Server 2019 enables the improvement of the connections between the on-premises servers and the cloud services on Amazon Web Services. (True | False)

8. _____ is a brand new feature in Windows Server 2019 that facilitates the process of migrating servers to a newer version of Windows Server.

9. Which of the following features is new in Windows Server 2019?
    - Microsoft Defender ATP
    - Storage Migration Service
    - Kubernetes platform
    - All of the above

10. Windows Server 2019 is the penultimate version of the Server operating system by Microsoft, as part of the Windows NT family of OSes. (True | False)

11. _____ consists of nodes and pods where the former can be physical machines or VMs, and the latter represents a single instance of an application.

12. What is the new server management app introduced with Windows Server 2019?
    - Windows Administrative Tools
    - Windows PowerShell
    - Windows Admin Center
    - Active Directory Administrative Center

# Further reading

- *What's new in Windows Server 2019*: https://docs.microsoft.com/en-us/windows-server/get-started-19/whats-new-19
- *Hello, Windows Admin Center!*: https://docs.microsoft.com/en-us/windows-server/manage/windows-admin-center/understand/windows-admin-center
- *Storage Migration Service overview*: https://docs.microsoft.com/en-us/windows-server/storage/storage-migration-service/overview
- *Docker for Windows Desktop... Now With Kubernetes!*: https://blog.docker.com/2018/01/docker-windows-desktop-now-kubernetes/
- Getting started with Docker and Kubernetes on Windows 10: https://learnk8s.io/blog/installing-docker-and-kubernetes-on-windows/

# Installing Windows Server 2019 3

This chapter is designed to provide you with detailed instructions for installing Windows Server 2019. The step-by-step instructions, illustrated with easy-to-understand graphics, explain and show you how to master the installation of Windows Server 2019. With the guidance provided by this easy-to-follow chapter, you will quickly learn the installation process without any obstacles. It is an excellent resource with useful tips on how to get the job done easily and efficiently.

With that in mind, this chapter covers the following installation types: clean installation, installation over a network using the **Windows Deployment Service (WDS)**, unattended installation using **Windows Assessment and Deployment Kit (Windows ADK)** and **Microsoft Deployment Toolkit (MDT)**, in-place upgrade, and migration. It concludes with an exercise about how to set up WDS.

The following topics will be covered in this chapter:

- Understanding the installation of Windows Server 2019
- Performing various Windows Server 2019 installation methods
- Chapter exercise—setting up WDS

## Technical requirements

In order to complete the lab for this chapter, you will need the following equipment:

- PC with Windows 10 Pro, at least 16 GB of RAM, 1 TB of HDD, and access to the internet
- Virtual machine with Windows Server 2008 R2 Standard, at least 2 GB of RAM, 100 GB of HDD, and access to the internet

- Virtual machine with Windows Server 2016 Standard, at least 4 GB of RAM, 100 GB of HDD, and access to the internet
- Virtual machine with Windows Server 2019 Standard, at least 4 GB of RAM, 100 GB of HDD, and access to the internet

# Understanding the installation of Windows Server 2019

One of the daily tasks performed by a system administrator is installing a new operating system. It is more than an installation, as it includes steps such as preparing for the installation, installing the OS, verifying the installation, and initial server configuration. Simply put, it's the starting point for everything! Although there might be rare situations when servers come with preloaded operating systems, in most cases, it is a system administrator's responsibility to get the job done.

Let's begin by understanding what partition schemes are as this will help us to manage the partitions on the disks.

# Understanding partition schemes

The disk partition is a disk's logical division so that an operating system can manage data. Whereas, the partition scheme represents the technology that is used to manage the partitions on the disks. In general, there are two partition schemes:

- **Master Boot Record (MBR)**: This is an old partition scheme known today as a legacy boot option. It operates on a 512-byte disk sector with a maximum of four primary partitions, or three primary partitions and one extended partition. An extended partition can have up to 26 logical partitions. The MBR uses **Logical Block Addressing (LBA)** to support disks up to 2 TB. The MBR has always proven to be a very useful partition scheme for multiboot platforms.

- **GUID Partition Table (GPT)**: This coexists with the MBR and is a new partition scheme that overcomes the limitations of the MBR. The **global unique identifier (GUID)** in a GPT is a 128-bit number that Microsoft uses to identify resources. In a GPT, block sizes from 512 bytes and up are supported, where the most common default these days is 4,000 or 4,096 bytes, and the size of the partition entry is 128 bytes. The GPT is part of the **Unified Extensible Firmware Interface (UEFI)** standard that replaces the old **basic input/output system (BIOS)** to support modern hardware. By its nature, the GPT is fault tolerant and supports up to 18 EB disk storage, and up to 128 partitions on each disk.

Moving forward, let's look at the boot options that will further help us with the installation process.

# Understanding boot options

Depending on the manufacturer, different keys on a keyboard can be used to access the BIOS. The most frequently used keys are *Delete* and *F2*. Upon entering the BIOS, there are several boot options available:

- **Installation media**: In most cases, there may be a DVD disk. Prior to accessing the BIOS, make sure that you insert the bootable DVD disk into the DVD drive. Specify the DVD as a first boot option, then save the changes, and exit the BIOS.
- **USB flash drive**: The capacity of a USB flash drive must be a minimum of 8 GB. Plug in your *bootable* USB flash drive before you access the BIOS. Specify the USB flash drive as a first boot option, then save the changes, and exit the BIOS.
- **Network boot**: This occurs when installing Windows Server 2019 over the network. First things first, enable booting from the **local area network (LAN)** and then specify booting from the network as a first boot option. Save the changes and exit the BIOS.

Regardless of which option you are using, soon your computer will restart and attempt to boot from the specified boot option. *Figure 3.1* shows the boot from a DVD disk:

Figure 3.1: Booting from a DVD disk

 To make a bootable USB flash drive, you can use the Windows 7 USB/DVD download tool. This can be downloaded from `https://www.` `microsoft.com/en-us/download/windows-usb-dvd-download-tool`.

Next, let's look at the advanced startup options, which will be very helpful once the installation is complete.

# Accessing the advanced startup options

In Windows Server 2019, there is no *F8* option. Instead, you can use the **Advanced startup** options to recover the server OS. That said, to access the **Advanced startup** options, complete the following steps:

1. Click the Start button.
2. Select **Settings** from the Start menu.
3. In **Windows | Settings**, select **Update & Security**.
4. Select **Recovery** from the navigation menu on the left side of the screen.
5. Click the **Restart now** button (as shown in *Figure 3.2*) and then click on **Continue**:

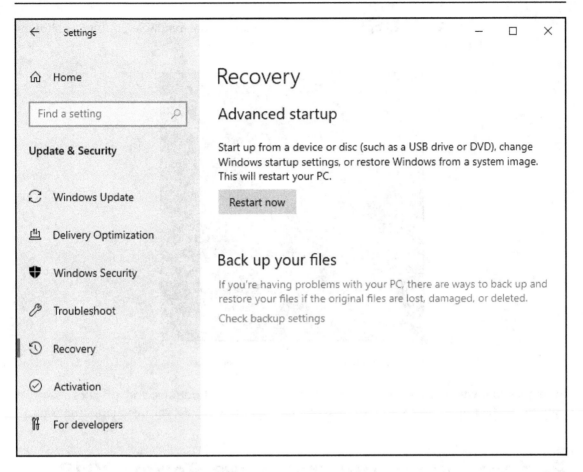

Figure 3.2: Accessing advanced startup options in Windows Server 2019

6. After a short time, options such as **Continue**, **Troubleshoot**, and **Turn off your PC** will be displayed.
7. Click **Troubleshoot** to access the advanced options.

8. From the **Advanced options** screen, select any of the available options, as shown in *Figure 3.3*:

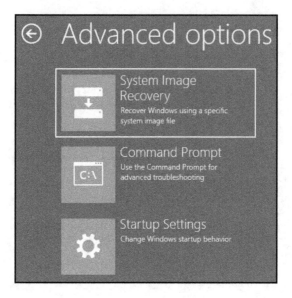

Figure 3.3: Advanced startup options in Windows Server 2019

In this section, we have looked at the partition schemes, boot options, and advanced startup options. In the following section, we will delve deeper into the server installation options.

# Performing various Windows Server 2019 installation methods

When it comes to installing Windows Server 2019, there are many methods. So, depending on the environment in which you will deploy Windows Server 2019, you can choose from the following:

- Clean installation
- Installation over a network using WDS
- Unattended installation
- In-place upgrade
- Migration

Now, let's learn about the installation options.

# Choosing Desktop Experience, Server Core, or Nano Server installation

Windows Server 2019 offers three installation options. However, the selected installation option affects the availability of roles and features, and therefore you should consider the options before choosing your desired installation option:

- **Desktop Experience**: This is an installation option that contains everything from Windows Server 2019, so choosing **Desktop Experience** means that you have installed everything on Windows Server 2019. However, your hardware needs to exceed the minimum requirements specification in order to benefit from the full-featured **Graphical User Interface (GUI)**.
- **Server Core**: This is an installation option recommended by Microsoft due to its minimal hardware resource consumption and higher security. The roles and features can be installed locally through Windows PowerShell or remotely through Server Manager.
- **Nano Server**: This is a replacement for Server Core that takes up far fewer hardware resources, has fewer updates, and supports only 64-bit applications. It is administered remotely since it has no local login capabilities. Simply put, this installation option is best understood as *set it and forget it*.

Now that we are aware of the installation options, let's learn how to perform a clean installation.

# Performing a clean installation

Whether you are installing Windows Server 2019 on a new hard disk or on an existing disk, the clean installation overwrites the existing operating system on a hard disk. Be aware, the clean option requires user interactivity, although that might be more limited than the upgrade option.

To perform the clean installation of Windows Server 2019, complete the following steps:

1. Turn on your computer, depending on the selected boot option, and wait for the boot prompt on the screen. The message on the screen requires user confirmation to boot the system from a DVD, USB flash drive, or network boot.

2. The installation files are loaded in RAM, as shown in *Figure 3.4*:

Figure 3.4: Loading installation files into RAM

3. Enter your language and other preferences, as shown in *Figure 3.5*. Click **Next** to continue:

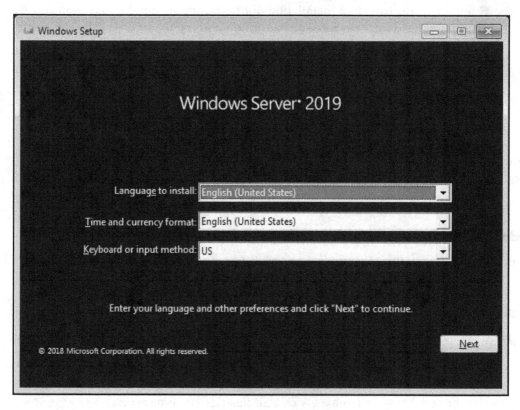

Figure 3.5: Windows Server 2016 setup

4. Click **Install now** to start installing Windows Server 2019, as shown in *Figure 3.6*:

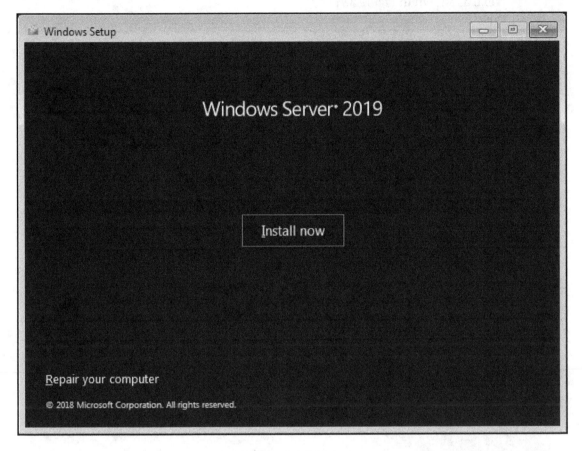

Figure 3.6: Windows Server 2019 is about to start

5. Select **Windows Server 2019 Datacenter (Desktop Experience)** and then click **Next**, as shown in *Figure 3.7*:

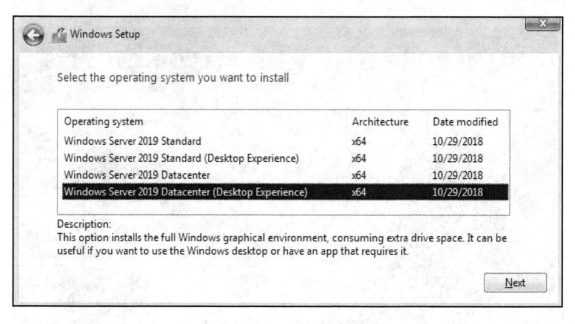

Figure 3.7: The available Windows Server 2019 OSs for the installation

6. Take your time to read the license terms. When done, check **I accept the license terms** and then click **Next**, as shown in *Figure 3.8*:

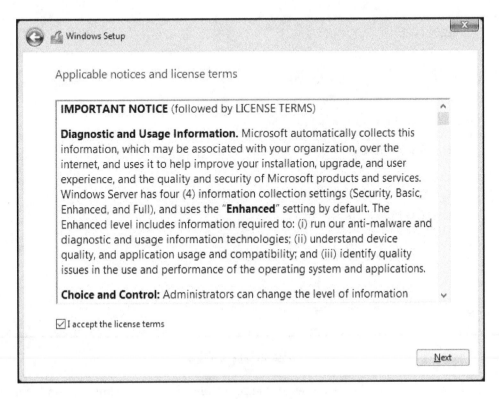

Figure 3.8: The Microsoft Software License Terms

7. Select **Custom: Install Windows only (advanced)**, as shown in *Figure 3.9*, to run the clean installation:

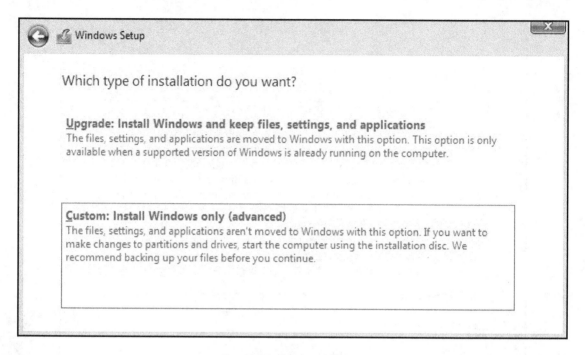

Figure 3.9: The available types of installation

8. After preparing the drive, select the partition where you want to install Windows Server 2019. Click **Next**, as shown in *Figure 3.10*:

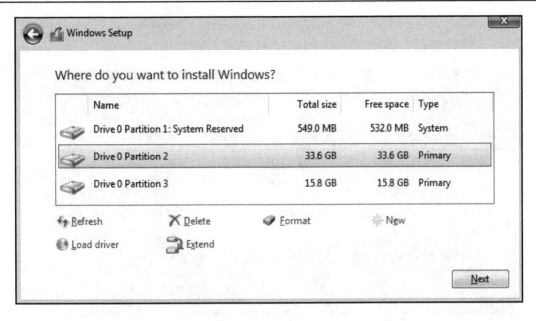

Figure 3.10: Selecting the partition for installing the operating system on a disk

9. **Windows Setup** is installing Windows Server 2019, as shown in *Figure 3.11*. Sit back and relax:

Figure 3.11: Several steps must be completed from the checklist before Windows Server 2019 gets installed

10. After getting the devices ready and performing a few restarts, set up the administrator password and click **Finish**, as shown in *Figure 3.12*:

Figure 3.12: An administrator account is recommended to have a password

11. Congratulations! You have successfully installed Windows Server 2019. Press *Ctrl + Alt + Delete,* as shown in *Figure 3.13*, to unlock the system. Provide the administrator password to make the first login to Windows Server 2019:

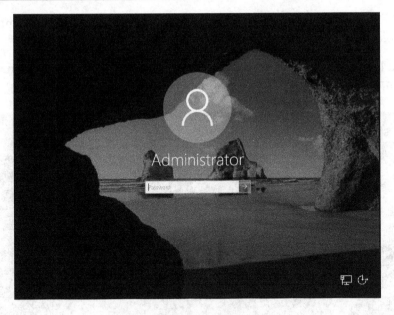

Figure 3.13: The famous key combination Ctrl + Alt + Delete

 If the competition has a single reason to compliment Microsoft, then, without a doubt, it would be for Windows Installer. Windows Installer is an **application programming interface** (**API**) used by Windows for software installation, maintenance, and uninstalls.

Now that we have learned how to perform a clean installation, we are well equipped to apply the various installation methods. Let's begin by performing an installation over a network.

# Performing an installation over a network

Often, organizations deploy hundreds of servers in their IT infrastructures, and they use WDS to enable *installation over the network*. Setting up WDS is fairly easy (see *Chapter exercise – setting up WDS* section later in this chapter): it requires installing and setting up the WDS role to the server and then adding both the install and boot images. As it is the case with the *clean install*, the *installation over network* also requires user interaction. Thus, to install Windows Server 2019 with just a little or no user interaction at all, an unattended installation is used that requires an answer file in order to automate the deployment of an OS. The unattended installation is explained in the next section.

To perform the network installation of Windows Server 2019 using WDS, complete the following steps:

1. The **Preboot Execution Environment** (**PXE**) is created and establishes a communication with the WDS server, as shown in *Figure 3.14*:

```
Hyper-V
PXE Network Boot 09.14.2011
(C) Copyright 2011 Microsoft Corporation, All Rights Reserved.


CLIENT MAC ADDR: 00 15 5D 00 75 0A  GUID: 42DA9F36-9EEB-405B-A79B-73148BA4AE88
CLIENT IP: 172.16.0.150  MASK: 255.255.0.0  DHCP IP: 172.16.0.10
GATEWAY IP: 172.16.0.1

Downloaded WDSNBP from 172.16.0.10 WinSrv2019.Dautti.local

Press F12 for network service boot
Architecture: x64
Contacting Server: 172.16.0.10.
TFTP Download: boot\x64\pxeboot.n12
_
```

Figure 3.14: PXE

2. Load the Windows Server 2019 installation files from the WDS server into the server RAM, as shown in *Figure 3.15*:

Figure 3.15: Installation files are loaded from WDS into the RAM

3. Choose the appropriate settings for the **Locale** and **Keyboard** or **input method** and click **Next**, as shown in *Figure 3.16*:

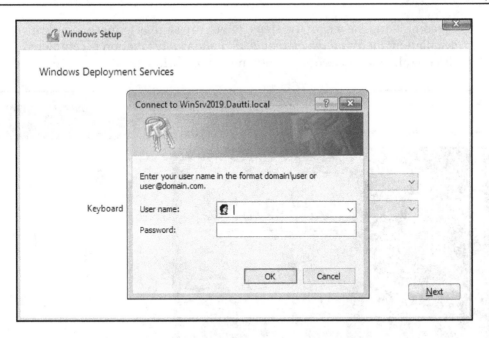

Figure 3.16: During this step, authentication with the WDS server is required

4. After you provide the authenticated user credentials, select the operating system you want to install and click **Next**, as shown in *Figure 3.17*:

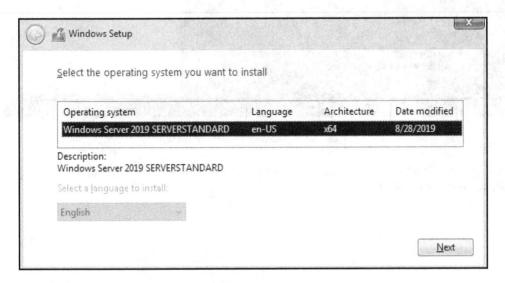

Figure 3.17: Installation over a network (the WDS server)

5. On completing the rest of the steps, which are similar to those in a clean installation, the Windows Server 2019 Standard installation is completed successfully via a network, as shown in *Figure 3.18*:

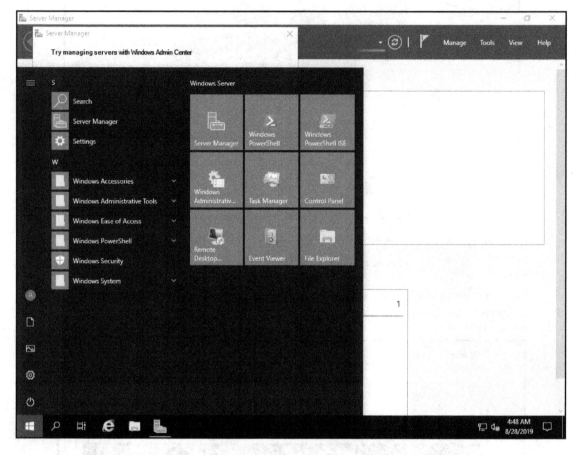

Figure 3.18: Windows Server 2019 Standard user interface

Now, let's move on to the second method to perform an unattended installation using Windows ADK and MDT.

# Performing an unattended installation using Windows ADK and MDT

In contrast to a clean installation, an unattended installation involves little or no interactivity during the installation. In conjunction with WDS, it is known as an **automated installation** and is used to deploy a large number of servers in enterprises. Part of the unattended installation is the *answer file*. This is an XML file that stores the answers for an installation prompt. You can use Notepad to create an answer file from scratch, or you can download sample answer files from the internet. Additionally, Microsoft provides several tools for automating the installation. Apart from WDS, explained in *Performing an installation over a network* section, tools such as Windows ADK and MDT provide a unique platform for automating desktop and server deployments. Both tools are available for download.

To perform an unattended installation of Windows Server 2019, complete the following steps:

1. Download and install the Windows ADK in a Windows 10 computer, as shown in *Figure 3.19*:

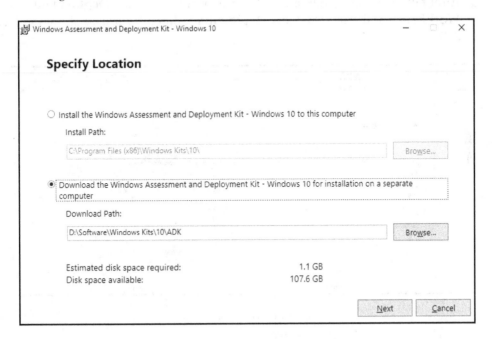

Figure 3.19: Installing Windows ADK

2. Install the MDT, as shown in *Figure 3.20*:

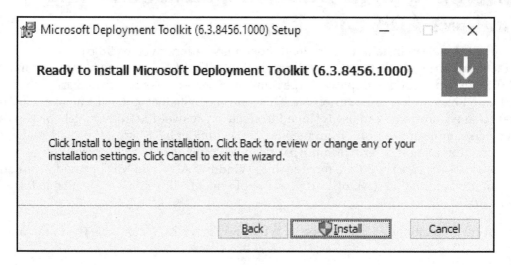

Figure 3.20: Installing the MDT

3. After both Windows ADK and MDT are installed, run the **Deployment Workbench** and select the **New Deployment Share Wizard**, as shown in *Figure 3.21*:

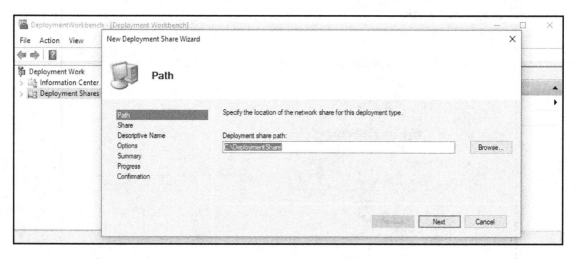

Figure 3.21: The New Deployment Share Wizard

4. After creating the deployment share, run the **Import Operating System Wizard** to import the Windows Server 2019 files.

5. Afterward, run the **New Task Sequence Wizard** to create the answer file for an unattended installation.

6. Then, update deployment share to create bootable PE image.

7. Boot the new server with the `LiteTouchPE_x64` image, located in the `Boot` subfolder of the `DeploymentShare` folder. After the successful boot, select **Run the Deployment Wizard to install a new Operating System**, as shown in *Figure 3.22*:

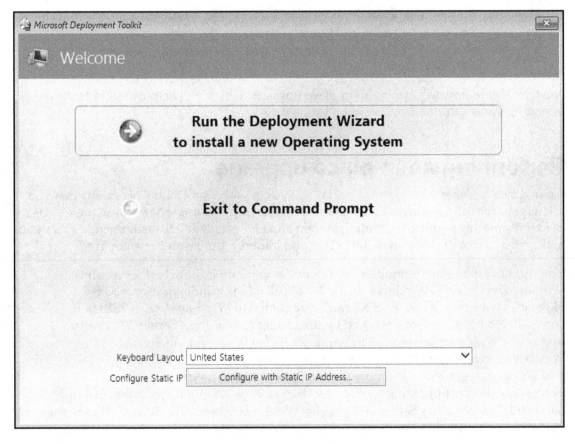

Figure 3.22: Deploying Windows Server 2019 over the MDT

8. Provide credentials to access the `DeploymentShare` folder. Ensure that the provided user has full control of the `DeploymentShare` folder.

9. Select `Task Sequence` (that is, the answer file) created earlier with **Deployment Workbench**, and click **Next**.

10. After providing the **Computer Details**, **Locale**, and **Time**, specifying whether to capture the image and specifying the BitLocker configuration, you are ready to begin deploying Windows Server 2019.

11. Windows Server 2019 is then deployed through the MDT.

12. After the installation progress step completes, the installation takes care of getting the devices ready and Windows Server 2019 Standard is deployed successfully.

 You can download the Windows ADK at `https://developer.microsoft.com/en-us/windows/hardware/windows-assessment-deployment-kit,` and the MDT at `https://www.microsoft.com/en-us/download/details.aspx?id=54259.`

Next, let's learn how to perform an in-place upgrade, which will help us upgrade the old operating system to a new one without losing data.

# Performing an in-place upgrade

An upgrade replaces your existing operating system with a new one. This means that you retain your files and settings. This is often called an **in-place upgrade** because it happens in place on a machine with an operating system already installed. It is recommended that you make a backup of the Windows state, files, and folders before running an upgrade.

You can run an in-place upgrade to Windows Server 2019 if the actual server runs Windows Server 2016, Windows Server 2012/2012 R2, or Windows Server 2008 R2. However, Windows Server 2008 R2 can be upgraded to Windows Server 2019 in three consecutive upgrade processes—first by upgrading to Windows Server 2012, then upgrading Windows Server 2012 to Windows Server 2016, and, finally, upgrading from Windows Server 2016 to Windows Server 2019. The same applies to Windows Server 2012, which can be upgraded to Windows Server 2019 in two consecutive upgrade processes—first by upgrading to Windows Server 2016, and then upgrading Windows Server 2016 to Windows Server 2019. While, Windows Server 2012 R2 and Windows Server 2016 can be upgraded to Windows Server 2019 in a single upgrade process.

To perform an in-place upgrade from Windows Server 2016 to Windows Server 2019, complete the following steps:

1.  Insert the Windows Server 2019 DVD disk, or plug in the USB flash drive, and run the `setup` file, as shown in *Figure 3.23*:

Figure 3.23: Running the Windows Server 2019 setup

2. After a short time, the **Get updates, drivers and optional features** window will display. With the **Download updates, drivers and optional features (recommended)** option selected, click **Next** to continue, as shown in *Figure 3.24*:

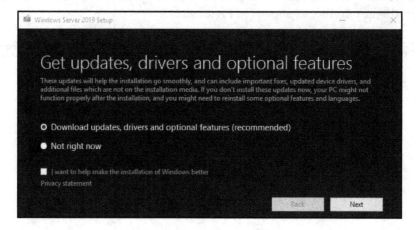

Figure 3.24: Getting important updates to help ease the upgrade

3. Type in the product key and click **Next**.
4. Select the edition that you want to install and click **Next**.
5. Click the **Accept** button to accept the license terms.
6. Choose what to keep, and then click **Next** to continue.
7. Once the updates are downloaded and the **Windows Server 2019 Setup** window ensures that there is enough disk space on the server, you are ready to install. Click the **Install** button to continue with the upgrade, as shown in *Figure 3.25*:

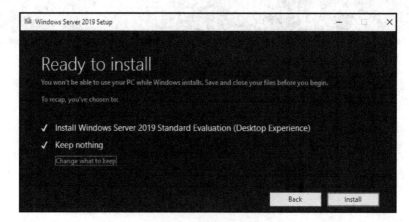

Figure 3.25: Ready to run the in-place upgrade

8. Either sit back and relax or do some other work until the upgrade completes (see *Figure 3.26*):

Figure 3.26: Upgrading from Windows Server 2012 R2 to Windows Server 2019

9. After the first restart, the screen, as shown in *Figure 3.27*, will show up:

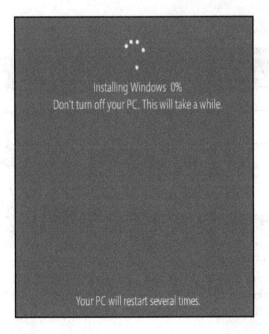

Figure 3.27: During upgrade, the server will restart several times

10. After several restarts, the upgrade from Windows Server 2016 to Windows Server 2019 is completed successfully, as shown in *Figure 3.28*:

Figure 3.28: The system properties confirm the in-place upgrade

Now, let's learn how to perform migration using the **Windows Server Migration Tool** (**WSMT**), which will help us migrate the services from an old server to a new one.

# Performing migration using WSMT

The migration takes place when you bring in a new machine (physical or virtual) and you want to move the roles, features, apps, and settings into it. To do so, first, you want to install the operating system on a new server, and then proceed with the migration. Prior to running a migration, make sure to check whether Windows Server 2019 supports your existing apps. The migration requires the WSMT feature to be installed on a new server (see *Figure 3.29*).

To perform the migration of roles from an old server (Windows Server 2008 R2) to a new server (Windows Server 2019), complete the following steps:

1. In a new server, install the WSMT feature through the **Server Manager**, as shown in *Figure 3.29*:

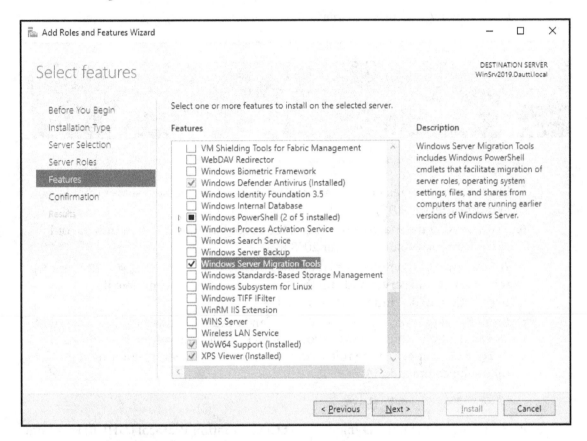

Figure 3.29: Adding the WSMT feature in Windows Server 2019

2. After the installation is complete, close the **Add Roles and Feature Wizard**. The `ServerMigrationTools` folder is created at `C:\Windows\System32\ServerMigrationTools`.

3. Open Windows PowerShell with elevated admin rights, and locate the Server Migration Tools, entering the following command (see *Figure 3.30*):

```
cd ServerMigrationTools
```

4.  From the same Windows PowerShell session, create the `MigrationTools` folder, entering the following command (see *Figure 3.30*):

    ```
    .\SmigDeploy.exe /package /architecture amd64 /OS WS12R2 /path
    C:\MigrationTools
    ```

The following screenshot displays the output of the preceding command:

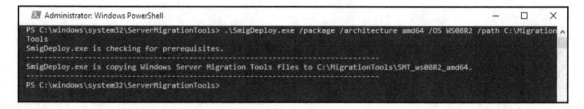

Figure 3.30: Creating the MigrationTools folder with Windows PowerShell

5.  Share the newly created `MigrationTools` folder on the new server (that is, Windows Server 2019).
6.  Try accessing the shared `MigrationTools` folder, and copy that into the old server (that is, Windows Server 2008 R2).
7.  After copying is complete, open up the `MigrationTools\SMT_ws12R2_amd64` folder on the old server and run the `SmigDeploy` app to complete the registration. Exit Windows PowerShell.
8.  From the old server, try to open WSMT (an additional PowerShell console) with elevated admin rights. WSMT (PowerShell console) was added by running the `SmigDeploy` app. List the roles installed on the old server by entering the following command:

    ```
    Get-SmigServerFeature
    ```

9.  Prior to migrating, the **Dynamic Host Configuration Protocol** (**DHCP**) role from an old server to a new one the DHCP service must be stopped. After stopping the DHCP service on the old server, export it by entering the following command:

    ```
    Export-SmigServerSetting –FeatureID DHCP –Path C:\DHCP\Store
    –Verbose
    ```

10. Provide the administrator password to complete the export, as shown in *Figure 3.31*:

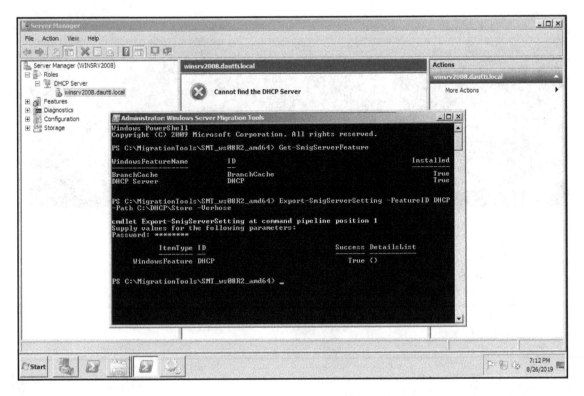

Figure 3.31: Exporting DHCP from the old server

11. On the new server, add the DHCP role using the Server Manager.

12. On the old server, share the DHCP\Store folder.

13. From the new server, try accessing the shared DHCP\Store folder and copy that into the MigrationTools folder. Then, open the WSMT (PowerShell console), and enter the following command to import DHCP:

```
Import-SmigServerSetting -FeatureID DHCP -Path
C:\MigrationTools\DHCP\Store -Force
```

14. Provide the administrator password to complete the import, as shown in *Figure 3.32*:

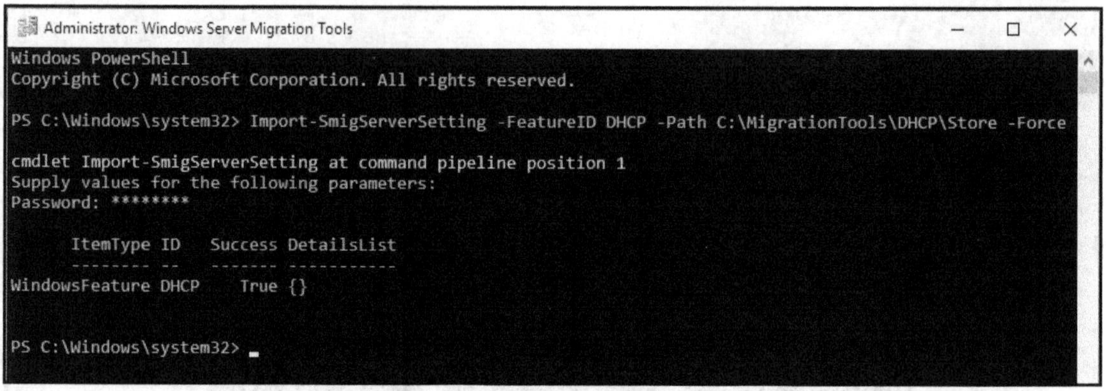

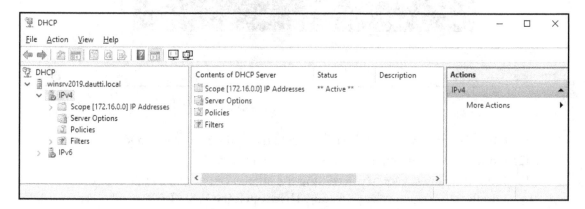

Figure 3.32: Importing the DHCP role into the new server

15. The DHCP role, as shown in *Figure 3.33*, is migrated successfully to the new server through WSMT:

Figure 3.33: The successful migration of the DHCP role in the new server

In this section, we have learned about the various methods of installation such as clean install, installation over a network, unattended installation, in-place upgrade, and migration of installing and deploying Windows Server 2019. In the following section, we will delve deeper into setting up WDS.

# Chapter exercise – setting up WDS

In this exercise, you will learn how to do the following:

- Installing WDS
- Setting up WDS

# Installing WDS

To install WDS in Windows Server 2019, complete the following steps:

1. Click the Start button, and then, in the Start menu, click the **Server Manager** tile.
2. In the **Server Manager** window, in the **WELCOME TO SERVER MANAGER** section, click **Add roles and features**.
3. With the **Add Roles and Features Wizard** open, click **Next**.
4. Select the **Role-based or feature-based installation** option and click **Next**.
5. With the **Select a server from the server pool** option checked, click **Next**.

6. Select the Windows Deployment Services role, as shown in Figure 3.34, and then click Next:

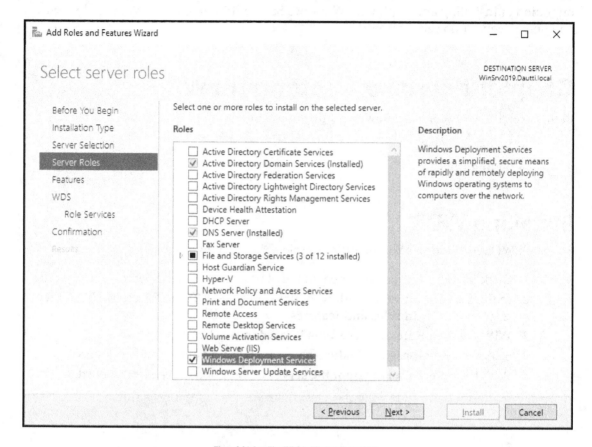

Figure 3.34: Installing WDS in Windows Server 2019

7. Accept the default settings in the **Select features** step, and then click **Next**.
8. Take your time to read the WDS description and the things to note regarding the WDS installation. Then, click **Next**.

9.  Select **Role Services** and then click **Next**, as shown in *Figure 3.35*:

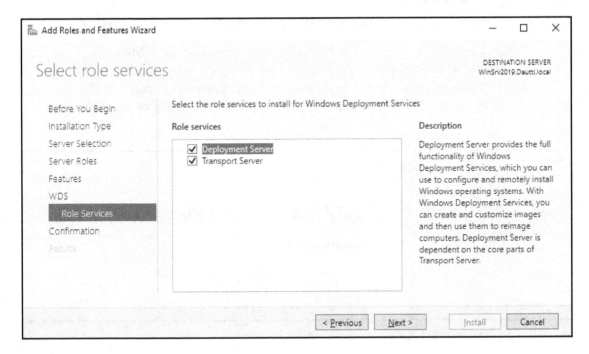

Figure 3.35: Installing Role Services

10. Confirm the installation selections for the WDS role, and click the **Install** button.
11. Either hit **Close** or wait until the installation progress reaches its end.
12. Click **Close** to close the **Add Roles and Features Wizard**.

We have successfully installed WDS. Now it is time to set it up.

# Setting up WDS

To set up WDS in your Windows Server 2019 server, complete the following steps:

1. Click the Start button, and then on the Start menu, click **Windows Administrative Tools**.

2. From the list, double-click the **Windows Deployment Services**. Shortly afterward, the **Windows Deployment Services** console will open, as shown in *Figure 3.36*:

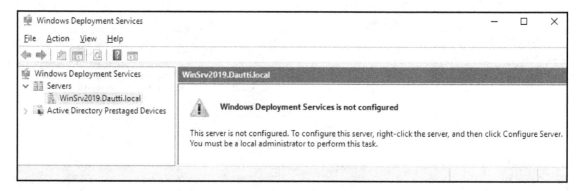

Figure 3.36: Setting up WDS

3. In the WDS window, right-click the server, and then from the context menu, select **Configure Server**.

4. In the **Windows Deployment Services Configuration Wizard**, read the **Before you begin** message and then click **Next**.

5. In the **Install Options** step, select the **Integrated with Active Directory** option and then click **Next**.

6. In the **Remote Installation Folder Location** step, enter the path to the remote installation folder and then click **Next**.

7. In the **Proxy DHCP Server** step, select the options regarding the **DHCP on your network infrastructure** and then click **Next**.

8. In the **PXE Server Initial Settings** step, select the options to define which client computers this server will respond to and then click **Next**.

9. In the **Task Progress** step, wait for the task to be completed and then click **Finish** (see *Figure 3.37*):

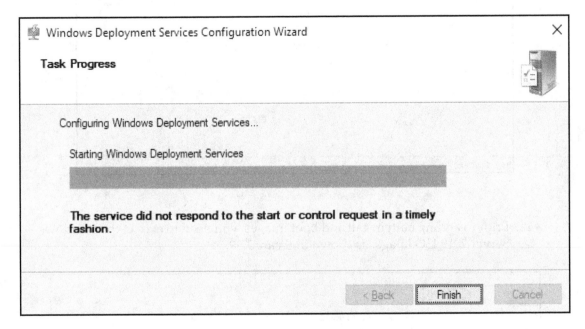

Figure 3.37: Completing the WDS setup

10. In the **Windows Deployment Services** window, right-click the server, and then from the context menu, select **All Tasks** | **Start**, as shown in *Figure 3.38*:

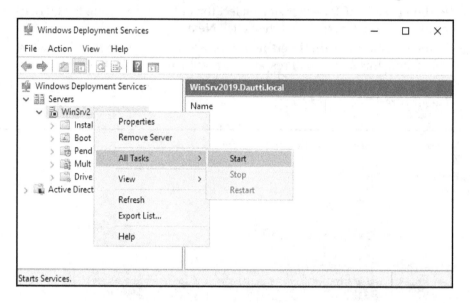

Figure 3.38: Starting the WDS service

11. Prior to adding both install and boot images, you need to extract the Windows Server 2019 ISO image, as shown in *Figure 3.39*:

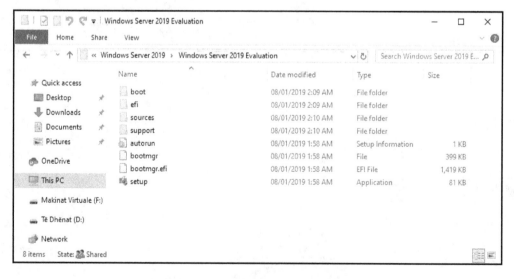

Figure 3.39: Extracting the Windows Server 2019 ISO file

12. In the **Windows Deployment Services** window, right-click the `Install Images` folder and select **Add Install Images...** from the context menu. The following window will open (see *Figure 3.40*):

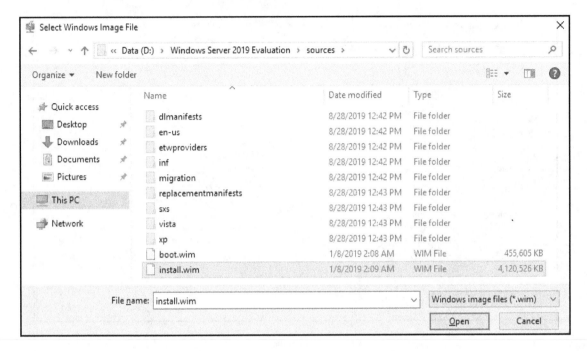

Figure 3.40: Selecting Adding Install Images...

13. In the **Windows Deployment Services** window, right-click the `Boot Images` folder and select **Add Boot Images...** from the context menu. The following window will open (see *Figure 3.41*):

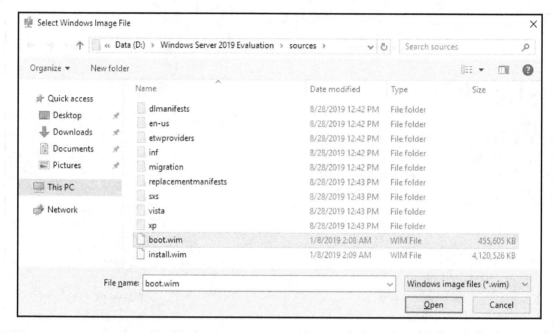

Figure 3.41: Selecting Adding Boot Images...

14. Once the install and boot images are added (see *Figure 3.42*), you can then boot the servers via the network in order to deploy Windows Server 2019:

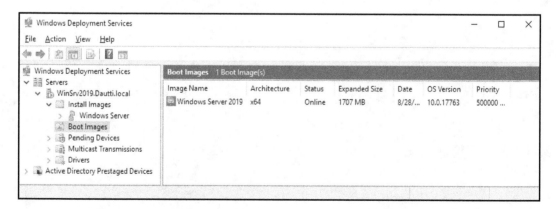

Figure 3.42: Completing adding both install and boot images

The WDS configuration completes this chapter exercise, which helps us to understand the installation of Windows Server 2019 over the network.

# Summary

In this chapter, you learned about various methods of installing and deploying Windows Server 2019.

In the *Understanding the Windows Server 2019 installation* section, we looked at partition schemes, boot options, and advanced startup options. While, in the *Performing various Windows Server 2019 installation methods* section, we learned about various installation methods such as clean install, installation over network, unattended installation, in-place upgrade, and migration of installing and deploying Windows Server 2019. These methods will help you to install Windows Server 2019 in a new server, upgrade a previous version of Windows Server in an old server to Windows Server 2019, perform an installation over a network, automate the deployment of Windows Server 2019, and migrate services from an old version of Windows Server to Windows Server 2019. The chapter concluded with an exercise that provided instructions on how to set up WDS.

In the next chapter, you will learn about studying and post installation tasks in Windows Server 2019.

# Questions

1. _____ is a new partition scheme that overcomes the limitations of the MBR partition scheme.
2. A clean installation enables automated installation over a network. (True | False)
3. _____, a replacement for Server Core, takes up far fewer hardware resources than the two other installation options, has fewer updates, and supports only 64-bit applications.
4. Which of the following tools are provided by Microsoft to automate the Windows Server 2019 installation? Choose two of the following:
   - Windows ADK
   - MDT
   - SharePoint Server 2019
   - SQL Server 2019

5. An unattended installation requires interactivity during the installation of an operating system. (True | False)

6. _____ takes place when you bring in a new machine (physical or virtual) and you want to move the roles, features, apps, and settings into it.

7. Which of these are installation options in Windows Server 2019? Choose three of the following:
    - Desktop Experience
    - Server Core
    - Nano Server
    - KDE and GNOME
    - Windows PowerShell

8. Discuss the pros and cons of the three boot options: installation media (DVD), USB flash drive, and network boot.

9. Discuss the installation types: clean installation, network installation, unattended (automated) installation, in-place upgrade, and migration.

# Further reading

- *Boot to UEFI Mode or legacy BIOS mode*: https://docs.microsoft.com/en-us/windows-hardware/manufacture/desktop/boot-to-uefi-mode-or-legacy-bios-mode
- *Install, upgrade, or migrate to Windows Server*: https://docs.microsoft.com/en-us/windows-server/get-started-19/install-upgrade-migrate-19
- *Windows Deployment Services Overview*: https://docs.microsoft.com/en-us/previous-versions/windows/it-pro/windows-server-2012-r2-and-2012/hh831764(v%3Dws.11)

# 4
# Post-Installation Tasks in Windows Server 2019

In this chapter, we will learn about Windows Server 2019 post-installation tasks.

To make it more understandable, the content of this chapter is organized into three parts. The first part explains the importance of device drivers after every installation of the Windows Server OS. Tasks such as installation, removal, disabling, updating/upgrading, rollback, and other related tasks concerning device drivers are included in this section. The second part covers the registry of the Windows Server OS, which is in fact a hierarchical database, and programs that run in the background. The third part explains the importance of the Windows Server initial configuration that needs to be considered once Windows Server 2019 is installed.

Each topic is accompanied by step-by-step instructions illustrated with targeted, easy-to-understand graphics. This chapter also includes an exercise on performing an initial Windows Server configuration.

The following topics will be covered in this chapter:

- Understanding devices and device drivers
- Understanding the registry and services
- Understanding Windows Server initial configuration
- Chapter exercise—performing an initial Windows Server configuration

# Technical requirements

In order to complete the exercises in this chapter, you will need the following equipment:

- A PC with Windows 10 Pro, at least 16 GB of RAM, 1 TB of HDD, and access to the internet
- A virtual machine with Windows Server 2019 Standard (Desktop Experience), at least 4 GB of RAM, 100 GB of HDD, and access to the internet
- A virtual machine with Windows Server 2019 Standard (Server Core), at least 4 GB of RAM, 50 GB of HDD, and access to the internet

# Understanding devices and device drivers

As you know, computer hardware is nothing more than a collection of physical components and the operating system is just a collection of programmed instructions. Therefore, it is very interesting to learn about the interaction between hardware and software. So, the question arises: how does the OS recognize the physical components?

# Getting to know computer devices and device drivers

Today's PCs in their elementary composition include components such as the computer case, monitor, keyboard, and mouse. However, among today's computer, we also find computers such as the all-in-one, in which the computer case is integrated with the monitor (see *Figure 4.1*). All the visible differences between physical parts of PCs, the general physical components are organized as follows:

- An *internal device* is any device that is located in the computer case. Examples of a computer's internal devices are the power supply, motherboard, and accompanying components, hard drives, extension cards, and other internal hardware components that constitute the core computer architecture (any physical component located inside a computer case).
- An *external device* is any device that is attached or connected to a computer case, and as such becomes part of the whole computer system. Examples of a computer's external devices are the keyboard, monitor, mouse, speakers, earphones, webcam, microphone, and other external hardware components.

- A *peripheral device* is considered to be any device that is physically located near the computer, and as such is not an essential part of the computer system as a whole. Examples of peripheral devices are printers, scanners, projectors, plotters, and other peripheral devices.
- A *network device* is actually a peripheral device connected to a computer over a network cable. Examples of network devices are network printers, network scanners, network backup libraries, **network-attached storage (NAS)**, **storage area network (SAN)**, and other network devices.

Figure 4.1: The all-in-one computer

Another category of computer devices is *input* and *output* devices. These devices either create input or output for the computer core architecture. Lately, with advancements in technology, there are devices that act as an input and output device at the same time. Touch-enabled devices are an example of input/output devices.

Note that, in today's literature, often, external devices are referred to as peripheral devices too because these devices are connected to a computer case to add functionality. This means that almost any device that resides outside of the core computer architecture is considered to be a peripheral device.

A *device driver* is a program that acts as a translator between computer hardware and an operating system. Thus, an OS manages and operates the computer hardware via device drivers. Usually, device drivers come with installation media (in most cases, a DVD) that accompanies the device, or it can be downloaded from the manufacturer's website as well. However, do not be surprised if you recently purchased a hardware device and it did not include any installation media with a device driver. This is mostly because the present OSes are **Plug and Play** (**PnP**) enabled. PnP is explained in the *Getting to know PnP, IRQ, DMA, and driver signing* section later in this chapter.

# Working with devices and device drivers

Usually, devices in Windows Settings are used to manage devices, while Device Manager is used to manage device drivers. That being said, in Device Manager, depending upon the status of the device driver, note that, other than the proper representation of device drivers, there are also the following representations (see *Figure 4.2*):

- **Generic**: This indicates that a generic (that is, an alternative) device driver is installed. As such, the generic driver does not present the proper device driver.
- **A black exclamation point on a yellow triangle**: This indicates that either the device driver is missing, or the installed device driver is not the proper one. As such, you need to install the proper device driver.
- **A downward black arrow**: This indicates a disabled device. As such, the device has a device driver installed but it is currently not enabled. To enable it, simply right-click on a device driver and select **Enable** from the context menu.

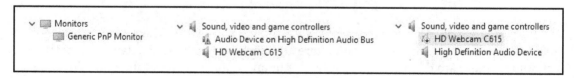

Figure 4.2: Device drivers representation in Device Manager

Now that we have understood what devices and device drivers are, let's learn how to access them.

# Accessing Devices and Device Manager

To access **Devices** from Windows Settings, take the following steps:

1. Click the Start button to open the Start menu.
2. On the Start menu, click the Settings icon.
3. In **Windows Settings**, click **Devices**.

To access **Device Manager** from the *secret* Start menu, take the following steps:

1. Right-click the Start button to open the *secret* Start menu.
2. In the *secret* Start menu, select **Device Manager**.
3. Shortly after, the **Device Manager** window will open, as in *Figure 4.3*:

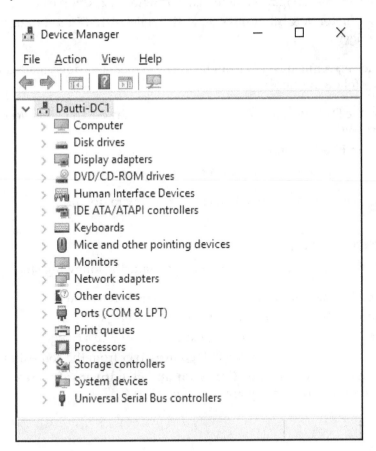

Figure 4.3: The Device Manager

Other than right-clicking the Start button to open the *secret* Start menu, you can use the Windows key + *X* combination. Similarly, you can use the Windows key + *I* combination to open **Windows Settings**. At the same time, to open **Device Manager**, enter `devmgmt.msc` in the **Run** dialog box.

## Adding devices and installing device drivers

To add a device using Windows Settings, take the following steps:

1. Click the Start button to open the Start menu.
2. On the Start menu, click the Settings icon.
3. In **Windows Settings**, click **Devices**.
4. In the **Devices** navigation menu, click **Bluetooth & other devices**.
5. In the **Bluetooth & other devices** section, click **Add Bluetooth or other device** to add a device.

To install a device driver using a file from installation media or downloaded from the internet, take the following steps:

1. Insert the DVD disk in a DVD drive or locate the downloaded *device driver file* on your server.
2. Through **File Explorer**, run the `setup` or `install` file.
3. Follow the instructions in **Setup or Install Wizard**.

Now that the device drivers are installed, let's learn how to update them.

## Updating device drivers

To update the device driver using Device Manager, take the following steps:

1. Right-click the Start button to open the *secret* Start menu.
2. In the *secret* Start menu, select **Device Manager**.
3. In the **Device Manager** window, expand the device's category.
4. Right-click the device and select **Update driver** from the context menu.
5. Select either **Search automatically for updated driver software** or **Browse my computer for driver software** (see *Figure 4.4*):

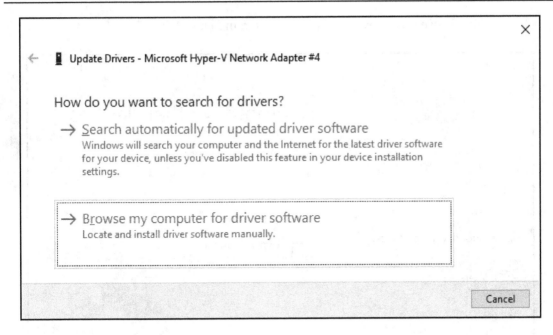

Figure 4.4: Installing a device driver

If you lack a device driver, then let the update driver wizard do the work for you by clicking on **Search automatically for updated driver software**.

 Whether you install or update a driver through **Device Manager**, you will always end up using the **Update driver** option from the context menu.

Now let's learn how to remove and uninstall device drivers.

## Removing devices and uninstalling device drivers

To remove a device using Windows Settings, take the following steps:

1. Click the Start button to open the Start menu.
2. On the Start menu, click the Settings icon.
3. In the **Windows Settings**, click **Devices.**
4. In the **Devices** navigation menu, click **Bluetooth & other devices** and select the device that you want to remove.

5. Click the **Remove device** button as shown in *Figure 4.5*:

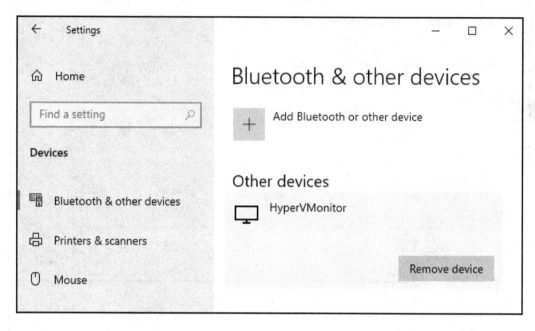

Figure 4.5: Removing a device

To uninstall a device driver using Device Manager, take the following steps:

1. Right-click the Start button to open the *secret* Start menu.
2. In the *secret* Start menu, select **Device Manager**.
3. In the **Device Manager** window, expand the device's category.
4. Right-click the device and select **Uninstall device** from the context menu.
5. Click the **Uninstall** button.

Moving forward, let's learn how to manage and disable device drivers.

## Managing devices and disabling device drivers

To manage a device using Windows Settings, take the following steps:

1. Click the Start button to open the Start menu.
2. On the Start menu, click the Settings icon.
3. In **Windows Settings**, click **Devices**.

4. In the **Devices** navigation menu, click **Printers & scanners** and select the device that you want to manage.
5. Click the **Manage** button.

To disable a device driver using Device Manager, take the following steps:

1. Right-click the Start button to open the *secret* Start menu.
2. In the *secret* Start menu, select **Device Manager**.
3. In the **Device Manager** window, expand the device's category.
4. Right-click the device and select **Disable device** from the context menu.
5. Click the **Yes** button, as shown in *Figure 4.6*:

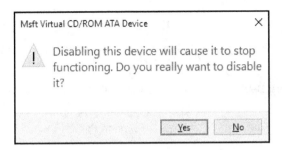

Figure 4.6: Disabling the device driver

Next, let's learn how to roll back device drivers.

## Rolling back device drivers

To roll back a device driver using Device Manager, take the following steps:

1. Right-click the Start button to open the *secret* Start menu.
2. In the *secret* Start menu, select **Device Manager**.
3. In the **Device Manager** window, expand the device's category.
4. Right-click the device and select **Properties**.

5. Select the **Driver** tab and then click the **Roll Back Driver** button, as shown in *Figure 4.7*:

Figure 4.7: Rolling back a device driver

 You will want to roll back a driver if you have installed multiple device drivers or have updated the existing device driver with a newer one and the device is not performing as expected.

Now let's take a look at solutions for technical problems with device drivers.

# Troubleshooting a device driver

If you encounter technical problems with device drivers, then there are several options you can choose (see *Figure 4.8*) to overcome them:

- **Update driver**: This enables you to update the driver automatically or browse your server for driver software.
- **Roll-back driver**: This enables you to roll back the driver if your current driver is causing problems.
- **Disable driver**: This enables you to disable the driver if the current driver is causing major issues, such as server instability.
- **Uninstall driver**: This enables you to uninstall the current driver if you have found the appropriate driver from the device manufacturer.

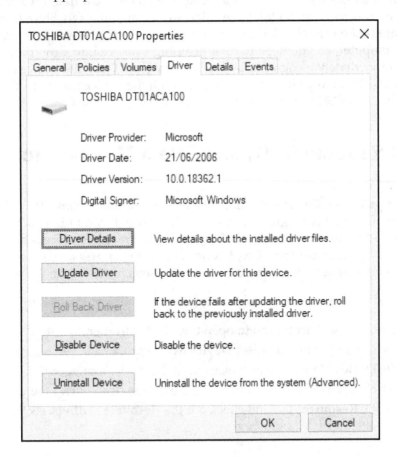

Figure 4.8: Troubleshooting options for device driver

We have now learned various ways of handling devices. Moving on, let's gain an understanding of various system resources, such as PnP, IRQ, DMA, and driver signing.

# Getting to know PnP, IRQ, DMA, and driver signing

In computer hardware, devices use system resources to communicate with one another.

## Understanding PnP

If you like Windows OS just because *it is all about PnP*, then know that it really is! It all started as a joint project between Intel and Microsoft a long time ago. Since then, PnP has massively simplified work with devices and device drivers. As the name suggests, with a PnP-enabled computer, all you need to do is just plug a device into a computer, and then that device is immediately recognized by the Windows OS. Once the device is identified by the Windows OS, it then uses its Driver Store to install the device driver. In Windows Server 2019, the Driver Store is located at `C:\Windows\System32\DriverStore`.

## Interrupt Request (IRQ) and Direct Memory Access (DMA)

In modern computers, an IRQ is identified by a decimal number from 0 to 31. From a technical point of view, it is a signal sent by a device through communication channels in order to get the attention of a processor when that device requires processing. In contrast, DMA, identified by a number from 0 to 8, represents a system resource used by a device to bypass the processor whenever such a device needs direct access to the RAM.

To view IRQ and DMA resource settings using Device Manager, take the following steps:

1. Right-click the Start button to open the *secret* Start menu.
2. In the *secret* Start menu, select **Device Manager**.
3. In the Device Manager window, expand the device's category.
4. Right-click the device and select **Properties** from the context menu.
5. Click the **Resources** tab and check out the **Resource settings:** section, as shown in *Figure 4.9*:

Figure 4.9: Driver's Resource settings

Now let's have a look at a driver's signature and how we can view it.

# Understanding driver signing

*Driver signing* is a driver's digital signature to identify the publisher of the driver package. Technically, a driver's digital signature proves that Microsoft has tested and approved the driver package, ensuring that its installation will not cause any reliability or security issues. To view a driver's digital signing information in Windows Server 2019, take the following steps:

1. Right-click the Start button to open the *secret* Start menu.
2. In the *secret* Start menu, select **Device Manager**.
3. In the **Device Manager** window, expand the device's category.

4. Right-click the device and select **Properties** from the context menu.
5. Click the **Driver** tab and then click the **Driver Details** button to view the **Driver File Details** window, as shown in *Figure 4.10*:

Figure 4.10: Driver's digital signing information

In this section, we have learned what computer devices and drivers are and about the various ways of handling them. We have also seen various system resources that devices use to communicate with each other. In the next section, we will learn about the Windows Server registry and services and ways of managing and working with them.

# Understanding the registry and services

In many IT books, the Windows Registry is often portrayed as the heart of the Windows OS, and services are referred to *as the background programs* of the Windows OS. Regardless of the language used to describe them, the Windows Registry and Windows services really make up the Windows OS core architecture.

# Understanding the Windows Server registry

Whatever hardware or software change is made to the server is stored on the registry. That said, the *Windows Registry* is a hierarchical database that stores the hardware/software configuration and system security information. Once you access the Windows Registry, you will notice that its console tree (left-hand side) consists of five registry keys known as hives (that is, HKEYs). Note that, the syntax of the registry keys and sub-keys follows the standard of the Windows file path separated by a backslash. In Windows Server 2019, there are five HKEYs:

- HKEY_CLASSES_ROOT: It stores information on installed applications and their extensions.
- HKEY_CURRENT_USER: It stores information on the user that is currently logged in.
- HKEY_LOCAL_MACHINE: It stores information specific to the local computer.
- HKEY_USERS: This contains information on logged user profiles.
- HKEY_CURRENT_CONFIG: This contains information gathered during the boot process.

# Understanding Windows Server services

Whether you are running an application or a network service, working behind the scenes are services that support their execution. These background programs can be started, stopped, restarted, and paused through Services Control Manager.

# Getting to know service startup types

When accessing services through Services Control Manager, you will notice (see *Figure 4.11*) that each service has the following startup types:

- **Automatic**: This service starts automatically when the OS starts.
- **Automatic (Delayed start)**: This service starts approximately 2 minutes after all marked automatic services have started.
- **Manual**: This service must be started either by a user or dependent services.

- **Disabled**: This service cannot be started by the OS, user, or dependent services.

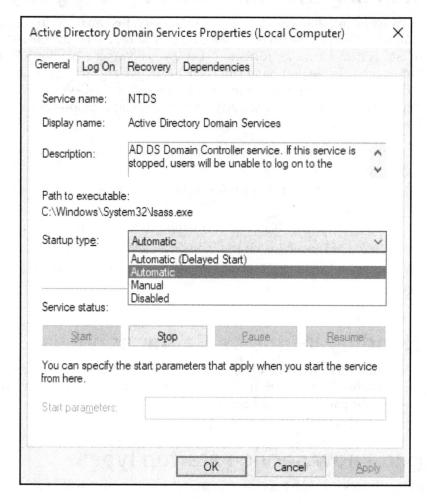

Figure 4.11: Windows Server service startup types

Now that we have looked at services and the registry, let's learn how to access and manage them.

# Working with the registry and services

While Windows Registry is accessed and managed by the Registry Editor, Windows services are accessed and managed via Control Manager. First let's learn how to access the Windows Registry.

## Accessing and managing Windows Registry keys and values

To access the Windows Registry using Registry Editor, take the following steps:

1. Click the search box in the taskbar and enter `regedit` and then press *Enter*.
2. After a short time, **Registry Editor** will open as in *Figure 4.12*:

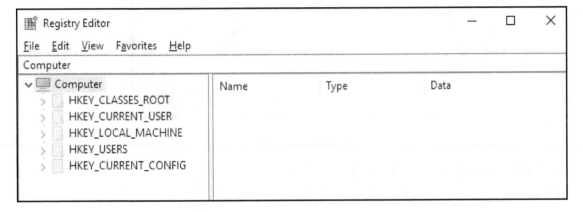

Figure 4.12: Windows Server Registry Editor

Now let's learn how to modify registry values.

## Modifying a registry value

To modify a registry value using Registry Editor, take the following steps:

1. Click the search box in the taskbar and enter `regedit` and then press *Enter*.
2. On the left-hand side of **Registry Editor**, locate the registry key and its sub-key(s).
3. On the right-hand side of **Registry Editor**, right-click the registry value that you want to change and select **Modify...**, as shown in *Figure 4.13*:

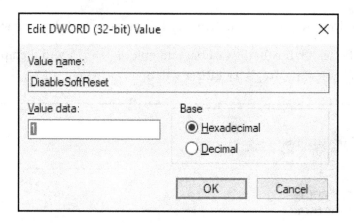

Figure 4.13: Modifying a registry value

Now let's learn how to rename a registry value.

# Renaming a registry value

To rename a registry value using Registry Editor, take the following steps:

1. Click the search box in the taskbar and enter `regedit` and then press *Enter*.
2. On the left-hand side of **Registry Editor**, locate the registry key and its sub-key(s).
3. On the right-hand side of **Registry Editor**, right-click the registry value that you want to rename and select **Rename**, as shown in *Figure 4.14*:

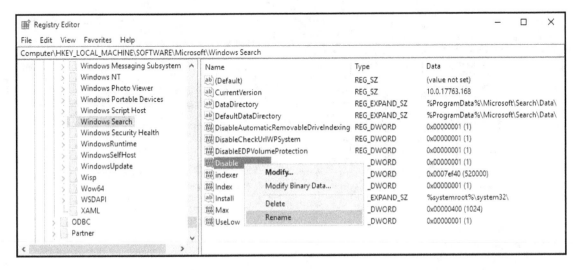

Figure 4.14: Renaming a registry value

Now let's learn how to delete a registry value.

## Deleting a registry value

To delete a registry value using Registry Editor, take the following steps:

1. Click the search box in the taskbar and enter `regedit` and then press *Enter*.
2. On the left-hand side of **Registry Editor**, locate the registry key and its sub-key(s).
3. On the right-hand side of **Registry Editor**, right-click the registry value that you want to delete and select **Delete**, as shown in *Figure 4.15*:

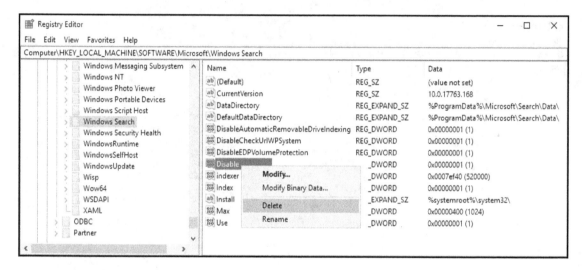

Figure 4.15: Deleting a registry value

 Working with registry keys happens to be the same as working with registry values. Deleting, renaming, and exporting are some of the operations that you can accomplish with registry keys as well.

# Accessing and managing Windows services

To access Windows services, take the following steps:

1. Click the Start button.
2. In the Start menu, select the **Windows Administrative Tools** option.
3. Scroll down and select **Services**.
4. Shortly after, the Windows Services Control Manager is displayed, as in *Figure 4.16*:

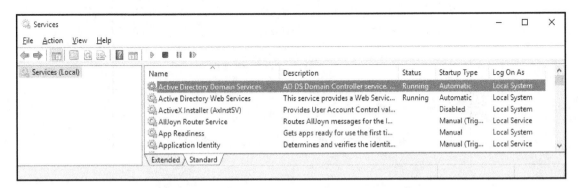

Figure 4.16: Windows Server Control Manager

Now let's learn how to set up service recovery options using Control Manager.

## Setting up service recovery options

To set up service recovery options using Control Manager, take the following steps:

1. Click the Start button.
2. In the Start menu, select the **Windows Administrative Tools** option.
3. Scroll down and select **Services**.
4. On the right-hand side of the **Services** window, right-click the service that you want to set up recovery options for.
5. In the context menu, select **Properties**.
6. From the opened window, click the **Recovery** tab.

7. Select the computer's response if the service fails by specifying the **First Failure**, **Second Failure**, and **Subsequent failures** actions, as in *Figure 4.17*:

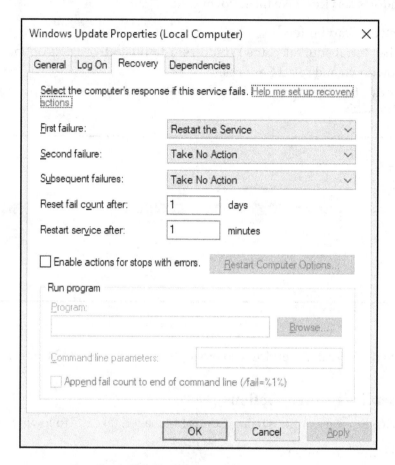

Figure 4.17: Setting up service recovery options in Windows Server 2019

8. Click **OK** to close the dialog box.

Now let's learn how to delay the start of a service.

## Delaying the start of a service

To delay the start of a service using Control Manager, take the following steps:

1. Click the Start button.
2. In the Start menu, select the **Windows Administrative Tools**.

3. Scroll down and select **Services**.
4. On the right-hand side of the **Services** window, right-click the service that you want to delay.
5. In the context menu, select **Properties**.
6. From the **General** tab, click the **Startup type** drop-down list.
7. Select **Automatic (Delayed Start)**, as shown in *Figure 4.18*:

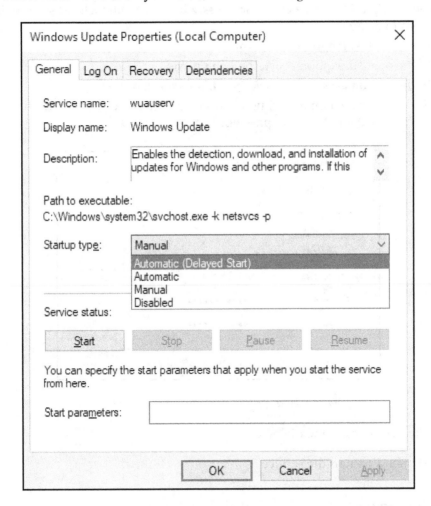

Figure 4.18: Setting up the delayed startup of a service in Windows Server 2019

8. Click **OK** to close the dialog box.

Let's learn how to set up the log on settings for a service.

## Run as settings for a service

To set up the log on settings for a service using Control Manager, take the following steps:

1. Click the Start button.
2. In the Start menu, select the **Windows Administrative Tools.**
3. Scroll down and select **Services**.
4. On the right-hand side of the **Services** window, right-click the service that you want to delay.
5. In the context menu, select **Properties.**
6. In the opened window, click the **Log On** tab.
7. In the **Log on as:** section, click the **This account:** option.
8. Enter a user account including the domain with a backslash, and fill in **Password** and **Confirm password** as in *Figure 4.19*:

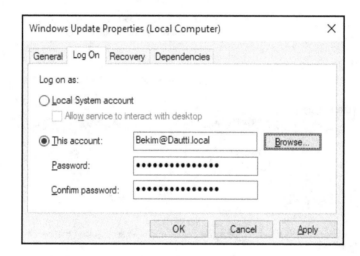

Figure 4.19: Setting up log on settings for a service in Windows Server 2019

9. Click **OK** to close the dialog box.

Now let's learn how to start the service.

## Starting the service

To start the service using Control Manager, take the following steps:

1. Click the Start button.
2. In the Start menu, select the **Windows Administrative Tools.**

3. Scroll down and select **Services**.

4. On the right-hand side of the **Services** window, right-click the service that you want to start.

5. In the context menu, select **Start** as shown in *Figure 4.20*:

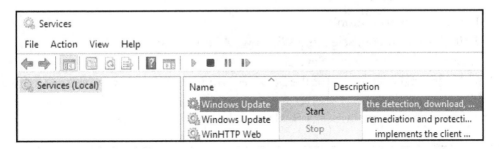

Figure 4.20: Starting the service

Now that we have learnt to start a service, the next section will teach us how to stop the service.

## Stopping a service

To stop a service using Control Manager, take the following steps:

1. Click the Start button.

2. In the Start menu, select **Windows Administrative Tools**.

3. Scroll down and select **Services**.

4. On the right-hand side of the **Services** window, right-click the service that you want to stop.

5. In the context menu, select **Stop** as shown in *Figure 4.21*:

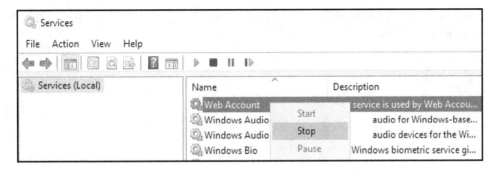

Figure 4.21: Stopping the service

## Restarting the service

To restart the service using Control Manager, complete the following steps:

1. Click the Start button.
2. In the Start menu, select the **Windows Administrative Tools**.
3. Scroll down and select **Services**.
4. On the right-hand side of the **Services** window, right-click the service that you want to restart.
5. In the context menu, select **Restart** as shown in *Figure 4.22*:

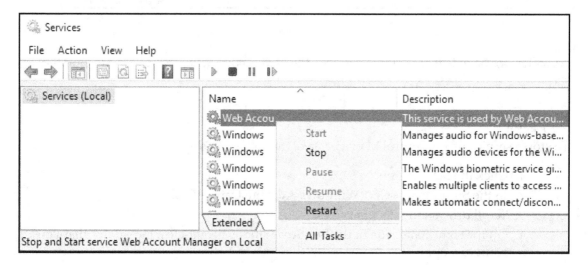

Figure 4.22: Restarting the service

We will now look at registry entries, service accounts, and dependencies, and at the steps to be followed to add them.

# Explaining registry entries, service accounts, and dependencies

In most cases, you will end up adding a new registry key or a registry value while fixing an issue or adding a new feature to your Windows Server. No matter how you do it, you should always be careful when working with the Windows Registry. In regard to services, the service account is the Windows Server native account or an account created by you to manage running services. From a security standpoint, the service account enables services to access both local and network resources. In regard to native accounts that services are running, the following service accounts (see *Figure 4.23*) are available in Windows Server 2019:

- **Local System**: This is a built-in account with the most privileges in a Windows OS. It is also known as a **superuser**, and this account is more powerful than an admin account.
- **NT Authority\LocalService**: This is a built-in account with the same privileges as members of the users group.
- **NT Authority\NetworkService**: This is a built-in account that has more privileges than members of the users group.

As far as service dependency is concerned, it happens that applications use more than one service. That being said, if you try to stop a dependent service, then you need to stop a few others too. Conversely, if you try to start a dependent service, then a few others will need to be started too.

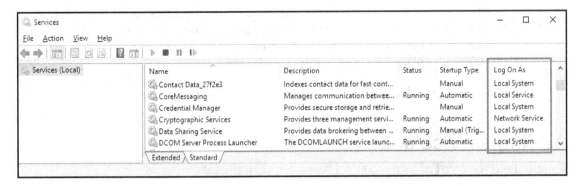

Figure 4.23: Native service accounts in Windows Server 2019

Now let's learn how to add a new registry key.

# Adding a new registry key

To add a new registry key using Registry Editor, take the following steps:

1. Click the search box in the taskbar and enter `regedit` and then press *Enter*.
2. On the left-hand side of **Registry Editor**, right-click the registry key or its sub-key(s).
3. In the context menu, select **New | Key** as shown in *Figure 4.24*:

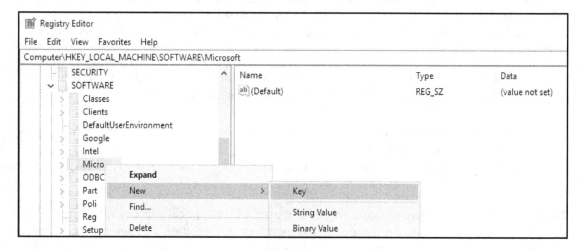

Figure 4.24: Adding a registry entry

 To add a new registry value, right-click the empty space on the right-hand side of **Registry Editor** once you have located the registry key or its sub-key(s). In the context menu, select **New,** and then enter the value that you want to add.

Now let's learn how to add a service account.

# Adding service accounts

To add a service account using Control Manager, take the following steps:

1. Click the Start button.
2. In the Start menu, select the **Windows Administrative Tools**.
3. Scroll down and select **Services**.
4. On the right-hand side of the **Services** window, right-click the service that you want to add a service account too.

5. In the context menu, select **Properties**.
6. In the **Properties** window, click the **Log On** tab, as shown in *Figure 4.25*.
7. In the **Log on as** section, select the **This account** option and click the **Browse** button.
8. Specify the service account in your organization's Active Directory.
9. Enter the service account password and confirm the password.
10. Click **OK** to close the **Properties** window.

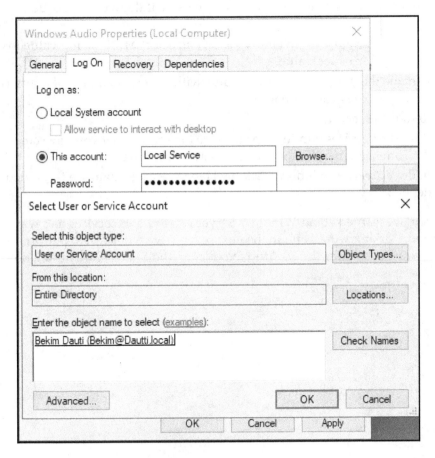

Figure 4.25: Adding a service account

Now let's learn how to add a service dependency.

# Adding a service dependency

To add a service dependency using Registry Editor, take the following steps:

1. Click the search box in the taskbar and enter `regedit` and then press *Enter*.
2. On the left-hand side of **Registry Editor**, locate the service (`HKEY_LOCAL_MACHINE\SYSTEM\CurrentControlSet\Services\`) that you want to add a dependency to.
3. On the right-hand side of it, modify the value if there is a `DependOnService` value.
4. If not, then right-click in empty space, and select **Multi-string value** to create a `DependOnService` value.
5. Rename the `DependOnService` value with the exact name of the service that you want to create a dependency for.
6. Restart the server.
7. With the **Services** window open, locate the service that you have created a dependency for and right-click it to select **Properties**.
8. In the **Properties** window, click the **Dependencies** tab to see the added dependency.

In this section, we learned about Windows Server registry and services and ways of managing and working with them. In the next section, we will learn to perform the servers initial configuration both for the Desktop Experience and Server Core installation options.

# Understanding Windows Server initial configuration

After setting up the device drivers and ensuring that the OS services are up and running, *initial server configuration* is a must. It is an activity that involves changing the server name, joining a domain (this depends on the role of the server), enabling Remote Desktop, setting up a static IP address, changing the time zone, activating Windows Server 2019, turning off **Internet Explorer** (**IE**) enhanced security, and checking for updates. This ensures that the server is ready to take a new role in an organization's IT infrastructure.

# Getting to know the Windows Server initial configuration

The server's initial configuration is a very important task as it determines the functional status of the server just before taking on the task of adding roles. Thus, from my experience, first, you will want to set up the IP address, change the time zone, activate your Windows Server 2019, and then proceed with checking for updates, changing the default server name, joining the domain, enabling Remote Desktop, and finally turning off IE enhanced security. With that in mind, let's perform the server's initial configuration both for Desktop Experience and Server Core installation options.

## Using Server Manager in Desktop Experience

In Desktop Experience, the initial server configuration can be accomplished using Server Manager, as shown in *Figure 4.26*. After first logging into Windows Server 2019, Server Manager starts automatically. It will always start automatically unless you change it.

To run the server's initial configuration using Server Manager in Desktop Experience, click **Configure this local server** on the **WELCOME TO SERVER MANAGER** section (see *Figure 4.26*):

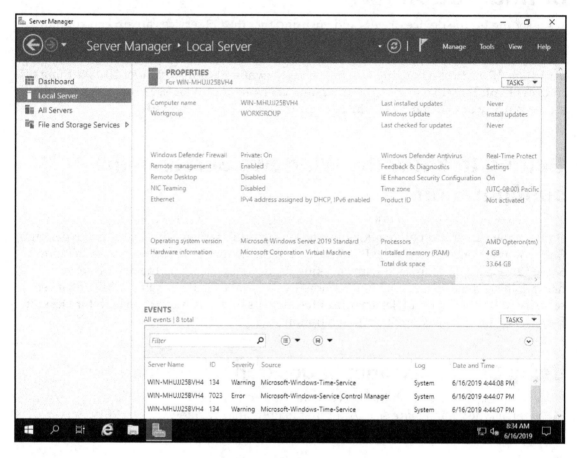

Figure 4.26: Server Manager in Windows Server 2019

Now let's take a look at the Server Configuration tool.

# Using server configuration in Server Core

In Server Core, the initial server configuration can be accomplished through the Server Configuration tool, as shown in *Figure 4.27*. In contrast to Server Manager, the Server Configuration tool is accessed by entering SConfig.cmd at Command Prompt:

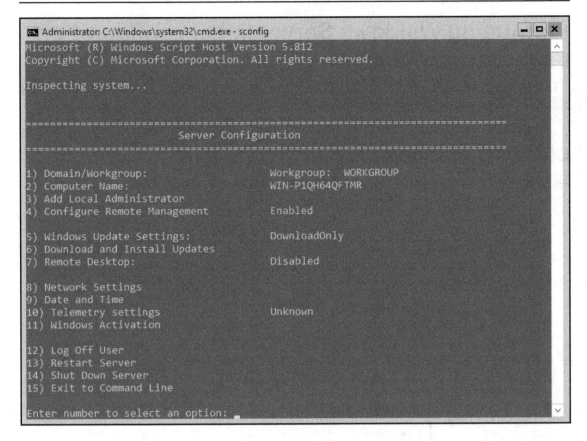

Figure 4.27: Server Configuration in Windows Server 2019

At this point, you are well equipped for the chapter exercise, where we will be performing an initial Windows Server configuration. So let's get straight into it.

# Chapter exercise – performing an initial Windows Server configuration

In this chapter exercise, you will learn how to do the following:

- Perform Windows Server initial configuration using Server Manager
- Perform Windows Server initial configuration using Server Configuration

# Performing Windows Server initial configuration using Server Manager

The following section provides explanations regarding the initial configuration of Windows Server 2019 Standard (Desktop Experience) by using Server Manager.

## Changing the server name

To change the server name as in *Figure 4.28*, take the following steps:

1. In the **Properties** section, click the highlighted default computer name.
2. In the **System Properties** window, click the **Change** button.
3. In the **Computer Name/Domain Changes** window, delete the existing computer name and provide the name for your server, and then click **OK**:

Figure 4.28: Changing the server's name

4. Click **OK** to confirm that you will restart your server to apply these changes.

5. In the **System Properties** window, click the **Close** button.
6. In the Microsoft Windows dialog box, click **Restart Now**.

Now let's learn how to join the server to a domain.

# Joining a domain

Before joining the server to a domain, evaluate the role of your server. If your server is going to be a **Domain Controller** (**DC**), then there is no need for it to join a domain, as adding the AD DS role will automatically make your server a domain controller. Otherwise, if your server is going to have a role other than AD DS, then, as a domain member, it must join the domain as in *Figure 4.29*. To do so, take the following steps:

1. In the **Properties** section, click the highlighted workgroup.
2. In the **System Properties** window, click the **Change** button.
3. In the **Computer Name/Domain Changes** window, select the **Domain:** option and click the textbox to provide your organization's domain, and then click **OK**:

Figure 4.29: Joining a server to a domain

4. In the **Windows Security** window, enter the name and password of an account with a permission to join the domain, and then click **OK**.

5. The **Computer Name/Domain Changes** dialog box welcomes your server to your organization's domain. Click **OK** to close it.

6. Click **OK** to confirm that you will restart your server to apply these changes.

7. In the **System Properties** window, click the **Close** button.

8. In the **Microsoft Windows** dialog box, click **Restart Now**.

Now let's learn how to enable Remote Desktop.

# Enabling Remote Desktop

To enable Remote Desktop, as in *Figure 4.30*, take the following steps:

1. In the **Properties** section, click the highlighted Remote Desktop setting.

2. In the **System Properties** window, select the **Allow remote connections to this computer** option.

3. The **Remote Desktop Connection** dialog box informs you that the Remote Desktop firewall exception will be enabled. Click **OK** to close it:

Figure 4.30: Enabling Remote Desktop

4. To add Remote Desktop users, click the **Select Users...** button.

5. In the **Remote Desktop Users** window, click the **Add** button to add users. Select users or groups from your AD DS. When you have finished adding Remote Desktop users, click **OK** to close the **Remote Desktop Users** window.

6. Again, click **OK** to close the **System Properties** window.

Now let's learn how to set up the IP address.

## Setting up the IP address

To set up the IP address, as in *Figure 4.31*, take the following steps:

1.  In the **Properties** section, click the highlighted Ethernet setting:

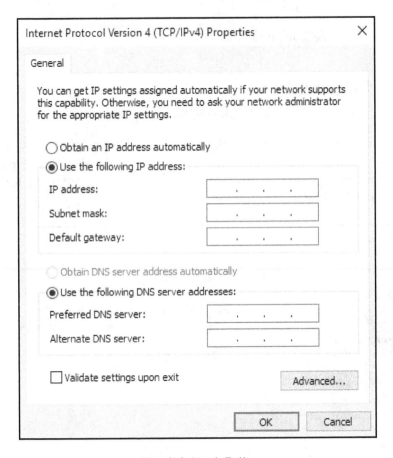

Figure 4.31: Setting up the IP address

2.  In the **Network Connections** window, right-click your server's Ethernet and select **Properties**.
3.  In the **Ethernet Properties** window, select **Internet Protocol Version 4 (TCP/IPv4),** and click the **Properties** button.

4. In the **Internet Protocol Version 4 (TCP/IPv4) Properties** window, select the **Use the following IP address:** option and enter the **IP address**, **Subnet mask**, and **Default gateway** fields. Additionally, select the **Use the following DNS server addresses:** option and fill in the **Preferred DNS server** and **Alternate DNS server** fields. Click **OK** to close.

5. Click the **Close** button to close the **Ethernet Properties** window.

6. In the upper-right corner, click the Close button (the red X) to close the **Network Connections** window.

Now let's learn how to check for updates.

# Checking for updates

To check for updates, as in *Figure 4.32*, take the following steps:

1. In the **Properties** section, click the highlighted **Last checked for updates** setting.

2. In the **Settings** window on the right-hand side of the **Windows Update** section, the available updates are listed (if any). If any updates are ready for installation, then click the **Install now** button:

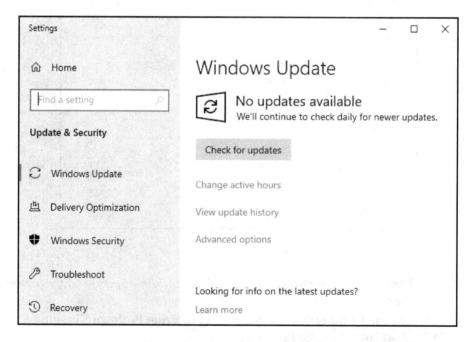

Figure 4.32: Checking for updates

3. Installing updates might take some time! When the installation is done, often, you will be asked to restart the server for the updates to take place.

Now let's learn how to turn off the IE enhanced security settings.

## Turning off IE enhanced security

To turn off the IE enhanced security settings, as in *Figure 4.33*, take the following steps:

1. In the **Properties** section, click the highlighted IE enhanced security configuration setting.
2. In the **Internet Explorer Enhanced Security Configuration** window within the **Administrators:** section, select the **Off** option.
3. Click **OK** to close the **Internet Explorer Enhanced Security Configuration** window:

Figure 4.33: Turning off IE enhanced security

Now let's learn how to change the time zone.

## Changing the time zone

To change the time zone, as in *Figure 4.34*, take the following steps:

1. In the **Properties** section, click the highlighted time zone setting.
2. In the **Date and Time** window, click the **Change time zone...** button.
3. In the **Time Zone Settings** window, click the drop-down list to select your time zone.
4. Click **OK** to close the **Time Zone Settings** window.
5. Again, click **OK** to close the **Date and Time** window:

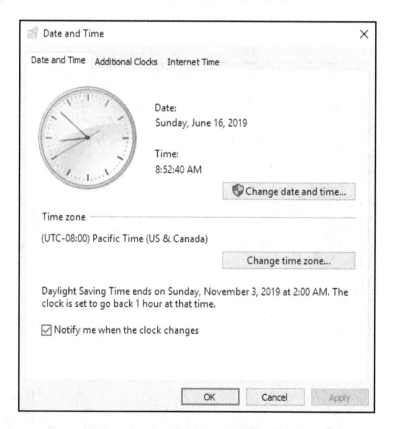

Figure 4.34: Changing the time zone

Now let's learn how to activate Windows Server.

## Activating Windows Server

To activate your Windows Server 2019 (Desktop Experience), as in *Figure 4.35*, take the following steps:

1. In the **Properties** section, click the highlighted **Not activated** setting of the product ID:

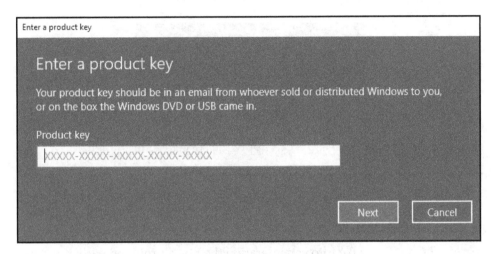

Figure 4.35: Activating Windows Server 2019

2. In the **Enter a product key** window, enter your Windows Server 2019 product key and press *Enter*.
3. Microsoft's Activation Server checks the product key you entered. If it is valid, click **Next** in the **Activate Windows** window.
4. When activation finishes, click **Close** to close the **Thank you for activating** window.

We have learned how to perform Windows Server initial configuration using Server Manager. Let's now learn how to perform this configuration using Server Configuration.

# Performing Windows Server initial configuration using Server Configuration

The following section explains the initial configuration of Windows Server 2019 Standard (Server Core) using Server Configuration.

# Changing the server name

To change the server name, as in *Figure 4.36*, take the following steps:

1. Enter 2 as a selected option and press *Enter*.
2. Enter the new server name and press *Enter*.
3. In the **Restart** dialog box, click **Yes** to restart the server:

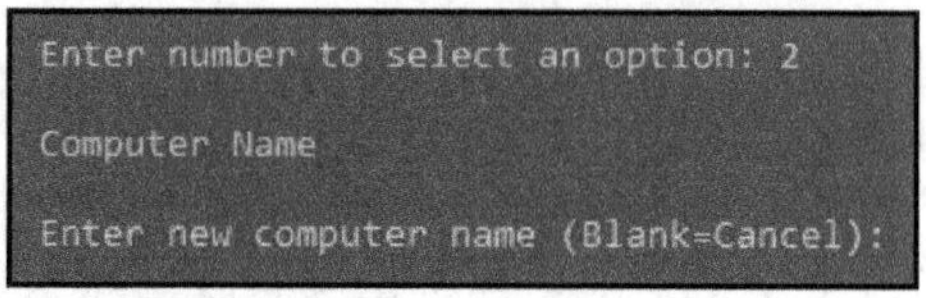

```
Enter number to select an option: 2

Computer Name

Enter new computer name (Blank=Cancel):
```

Figure 4.36: Changing the server name

4. Your server will restart so it can apply the server name change.

Now let's learn how to join the server to a domain.

# Joining the domain

Before joining the domain, take into consideration the notes provided earlier, when we were performing configuration using Server Manager. To join the domain, as in *Figure 4.37*, take the following steps:

1. Enter 1 as a selected option and press *Enter*.
2. To join your server to your organization domain, enter D and press *Enter*.
3. Enter your organization domain and press *Enter*.
4. Enter the authorized domain user and press *Enter*.
5. Enter the password and press *Enter*.
6. In the **Change Computer Name** dialog box, click **No** when asked to change the name of your server:

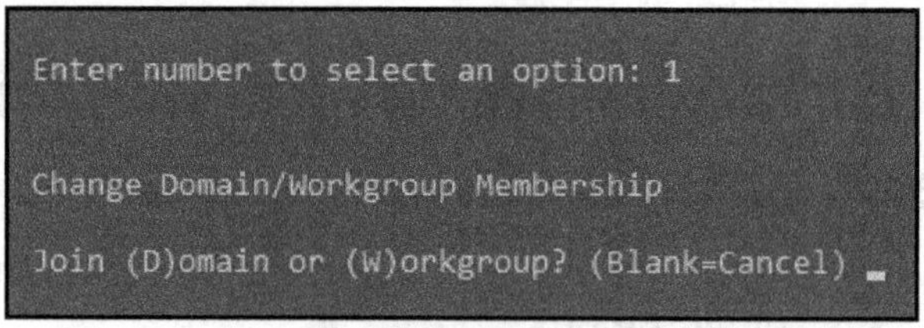

```
Enter number to select an option: 1

Change Domain/Workgroup Membership

Join (D)omain or (W)orkgroup? (Blank=Cancel) _
```

Figure 4.37: Joining the domain

Now let's learn how to enable Remote Desktop.

# Enabling Remote Desktop

To enable Remote Desktop, as in *Figure 4.38*, take the following steps:

1. Enter 7 as a selected option and press *Enter*.
2. To enable Remote Desktop, enter E and press *Enter*.
3. Enter 1 and press *Enter* for more secure access.
4. In the **Remote Desktop** dialog box, click **OK** to confirm Remote Desktop enabling:

```
Enter number to select an option: 7

(E)nable or (D)isable Remote Desktop? (Blank=Cancel)
```

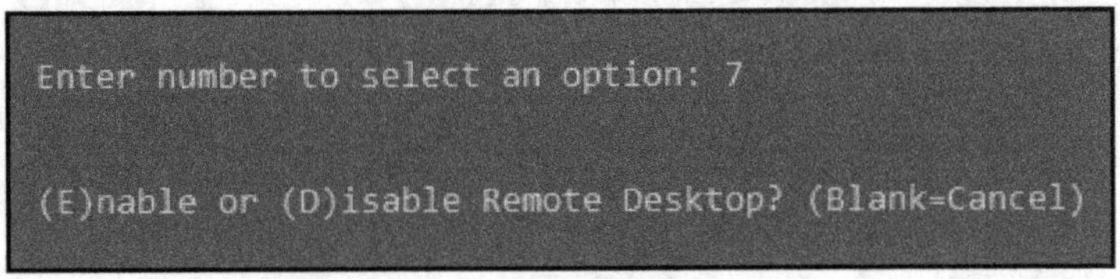

Figure 4.38: Enabling Remote Desktop

Now let's learn how to set up the IP address.

# Setting up the IP address

To set up the IP address, as in *Figure 4.39*, take the following steps:

1. Enter 8 as a selected option and press *Enter*.
2. Enter the number of the network adapter that you want to set up the IP address for and press *Enter*.
3. Enter 1 in the sub-menu to set the network adapter address and press *Enter*.
4. Enter S for the static IP address and press *Enter*.
5. Enter the static IP address and press *Enter*.
6. Enter the subnet mask and press *Enter*.
7. Enter the default gateway and press *Enter*.
8. Enter 2 in the sub-menu to set the DNS servers and press *Enter*.

9. Enter the new preferred DNS server and press *Enter*.
10. In the **Network Settings** dialog box, click **OK** to close it.
11. Enter the alternate DNS server and press *Enter*.
12. Enter 4 in the sub-menu to exit and **Return to Main Menu**:

```
Enter number to select an option: 8


---------------------------------
    Network settings
---------------------------------


Available Network Adapters

Index#  IP address      Description

  1     192.168.1.23    Microsoft Hyper-V Network Adapter

Select Network Adapter Index# (Blank=Cancel):  1


---------------------------------
    Network Adapter Settings
---------------------------------


NIC Index               1
Description             Microsoft Hyper-V Network Adapter
IP Address              192.168.1.23    fe80::a4c4:77e9:2f12:d8eb
Subnet Mask             255.255.255.0
DHCP enabled            True
Default Gateway         192.168.1.1
Preferred DNS Server    192.168.1.1
Alternate DNS Server

1) Set Network Adapter Address
2) Set DNS Servers
3) Clear DNS Server Settings
4) Return to Main Menu


Select option:  _
```

Figure 4.39: Setting up the IP address

Now let's learn how to check for updates.

# Checking for updates

To check for updates, as in *Figure 4.40*, take the following steps:

1. Enter 6 as a selected option and press *Enter*.
2. In a new window, enter A for all or R for recommended updates and press *Enter*.
3. After a short time, Windows Update starts searching for updates.
4. If applicable updates are found, then enter A for all, N for no updates, or S for single update, and press *Enter*.
5. When the updates are downloaded, the installation takes place. Click **Yes** to restart your server:

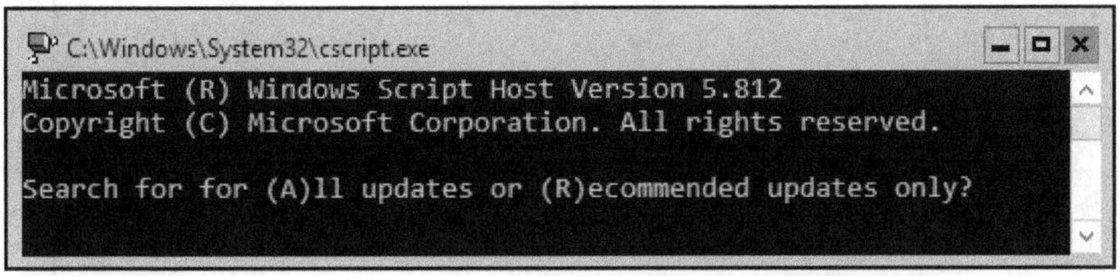

Figure 4.40: Checking for updates

Now let's learn how to change the time zone.

# Changing the time zone

To change the time zone, as in *Figure 4.41*, take the following steps:

1. Enter 9 as a selected option and press *Enter*.
2. In the **Date and Time** window, click the **Change time zone...** button.
3. In the **Time Zone Settings** window, click the drop-down list to select your time zone.
4. Click **OK** to close the **Time Zone Settings** window.

5. Again, click **OK** to close the **Date and Time** window:

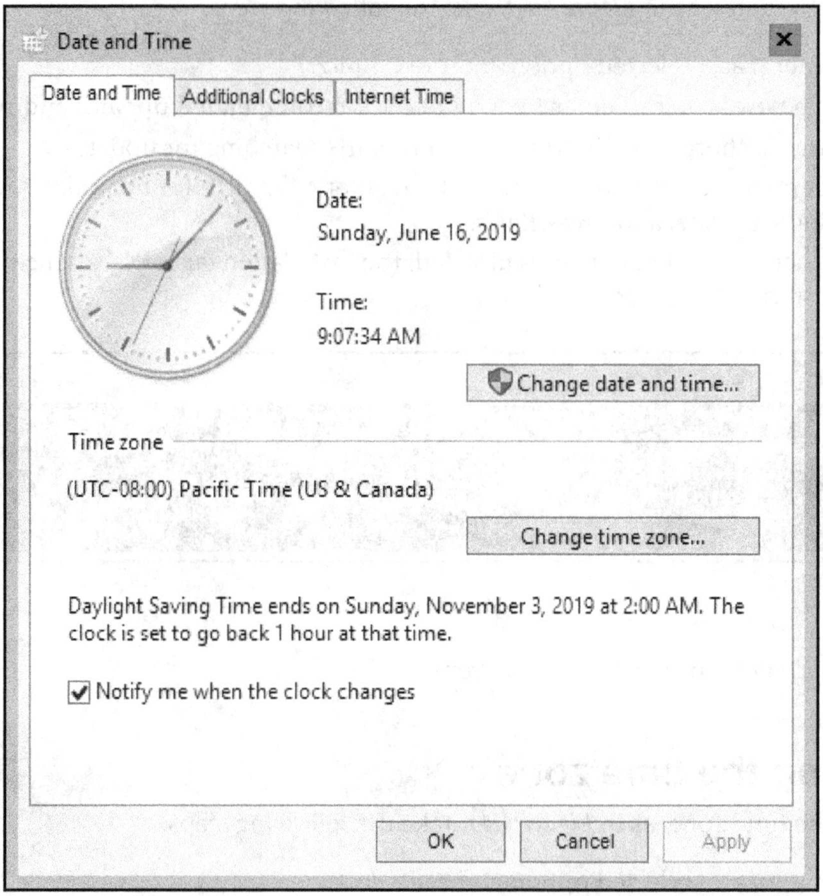

Figure 4.41: Changing time zone

Now let's learn how to activate Windows Server.

# Activating Windows Server

To activate Windows Server 2019 Server Core, as in *Figure 4.42*, take the following steps:

1. Enter 11 as a selected option and press *Enter*.
2. Enter 3 in the sub-menu to install the product key and press *Enter*.

3. In the **Enter Product Key** window, enter the Windows Server 2016 product key and click **OK**.
4. Enter 2 from the sub-menu to activate Windows and press *Enter*.
5. After a short time, your Windows Server 2019 will be activated. Enter `Exit` to close the activation window.
6. Enter 4 from the sub-menu to exit and return to the main menu:

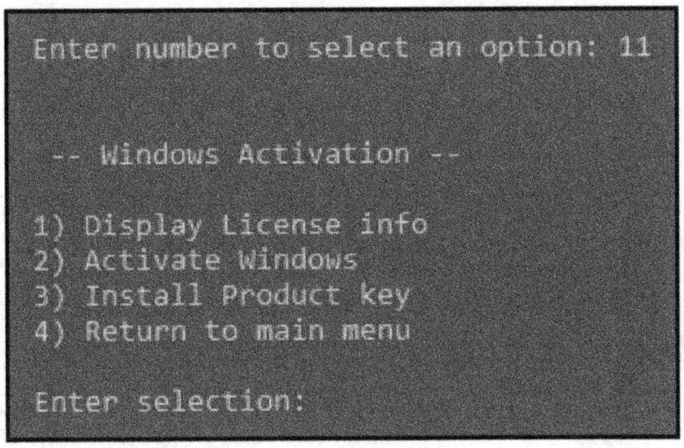

```
Enter number to select an option: 11


-- Windows Activation --

1) Display License info
2) Activate Windows
3) Install Product key
4) Return to main menu

Enter selection:
```

Figure 4.42: Activating Windows Server 2019

The activation of Windows Server 2019 concludes this chapter exercise, which will help us learn how to complete the initial configuration using both Server Manager and Server Configuration.

# Summary

In this chapter, you learned about various post installation tasks in Windows Server 2019. You were introduced to device drivers, registries, and services.

In the first part of this chapter, you became familiar with the way devices are organized in a computer system. You also learned what a device driver is. In addition to hands-on instructions about working with device drivers, you also learned about system resources and the way that devices use system resources to communicate with one another.

Then, in the second part of this chapter, we looked at the Windows Server registry and services. Here, you got a better understanding of registry keys and service startup types. Additionally, using the hands-on instructions, you learned how to work with the Windows Server registry and services.

In the third part of the chapter, you learned about the concept of Windows Server initial configuration, and finally, you were able to run Windows Server 2019 post-installation tasks in the chapter exercise. All that you have learned in this chapter will help you complete post-installation tasks for Windows Server 2019, as well as to complete the initial configuration.

In the following chapter, you will learn about Directory Services in Windows Server 2019.

# Questions

1. A device driver is a program that acts as the translator between computer hardware and an operating system. (True | False)
2. _____ works on the principle that when a device is plugged into a computer, the device is immediately recognized by the operating system.
3. Which two of the following are known as a computer's system resources?
   - IRQ
   - DMA
   - SAN
   - NAS
4. A driver's digital signature identifies its publisher. (True | False)
5. ____ is a hierarchical database that stores hardware and software configurations, and system security information.
6. Which two of the following Windows Server tools are used to operate devices and device drivers?
   - Devices
   - Device Manager
   - Registry Editor
   - Control Manager
7. Which two of the following Windows Server tools are used to operate the registry and services?
   - Services Control Manager
   - Registry Editor
   - Device Manager
   - Devices

8. The _____ is the Windows Server native account or an account created by you to manage running services.
9. Discuss Windows Registry keys.
10. Discuss Windows service startup types.

# Further reading

- *How to Use the Windows Device Manager for Troubleshooting*: `https://www.howtogeek.com/167094/how-to-use-the-windows-device-manager-for-troubleshooting/`
- *Structure of the Registry*: `https://docs.microsoft.com/en-us/windows/desktop/sysinfo/structure-of-the-registry`
- *Understanding and Managing Windows Services*: `https://www.howtogeek.com/school/using-windows-admin-tools-like-a-pro/lesson8/`

# Section 2: Setting Up Windows Server 2019

**2**

The second section covers the roles in Windows Server 2019. Upon completion of this section, you will be able to set up a domain and build up network services on Windows Server 2019 such as DNS, DHCP, print server, web server, WDS server, and WSUS server.

This section comprises the following chapters:

- Chapter 5, *Directory Services in Windows Server 2019*
- Chapter 6, *Adding Roles to Windows Server 2019*

# 5
# Directory Services in Windows Server 2019

Now that you have learned how to install Windows Server 2019 and run the initial server configuration, it is time to set up the very first services in your organization's IT infrastructure.

With that in mind, this chapter explains the domain service as the most important service in networks based on Windows Server. Specifically, this chapter covers Microsoft's **Active Directory (AD)** and **Domain Name System (DNS)** roles in Windows Server 2019. That way, you will be acquainted with topics such as the domain, forest, tree domain, child domain, domain controller, functional level, trust relationship, forward and reverse lookup zones, DNS record, and many others.

At the same time, this chapter provides you with instructions on how to install both AD DS and DNS roles. Also, you will get to know the **Organizational Units (OUs)**, default containers, user accounts, and group scopes and types so that you can organize the user and computer accounts in a Windows Server domain-based network. This chapter also includes an exercise—installing the AD DS and DNS roles and promoting the server to a **Domain Controller (DC)**.

The following topics will be covered in this chapter:

- Understanding the AD infrastructure
- Understanding DNS
- Understanding OUs and containers
- Understanding accounts and groups
- Chapter exercise—installing the AD DS and DNS roles and promoting the server to a DC

# Technical requirements

To complete the exercises for this chapter, you will need the following equipment:

- PC with Windows 10 Pro, at least 16 GB of RAM, 1 TB of HDD, and access to the internet
- Virtual machine 1 (*tree domain*: `Dautti.local`) with Windows Server 2019 Standard (Desktop Experience), at least 4 GB of RAM, 100 GB of HDD, and access to the internet
- Virtual machine 2 (*tree domain*: `ITTrainings.local`) with Windows Server 2019 Standard (Desktop Experience), at least 4 GB of RAM, 100 GB of HDD, and access to the internet
- Virtual machine 3 (*child domain*: `Programming.Dautti.local`) with Windows Server 2019 Standard (Desktop Experience), at least 4 GB of RAM, 100 GB of HDD, and access to the internet

# Understanding the AD infrastructure

**Active Directory** is Microsoft's technology that represents a distributed database that stores objects in a hierarchical, structured, and secure format. AD's objects typically represent users, computers, peripheral devices, and network services. Each object is uniquely identified by its name and attributes. The domain, the forest, and the tree represent logical divisions of an AD infrastructure. An AD uses the following protocols and services:

- **Lightweight Directory Access Protocol** (**LDAP**) is used to access the directory services data.
- Kerberos securely authenticates and proves the identity between users and servers on the network.
- DNS is used to translate domain names into IP addresses.

An AD is managed through the following snap-ins in **Microsoft Management Console** (**MMC**) (`mmc.exe`):

- **Active Directory Administrative Center** (`dsac.exe`), as shown in *Figure 5.1*, is the one-stop place that is used to manage Windows Server's directory services.
- **Active Directory Users and Computers** (`dsa.msc`) is used to manage users, computers, and relevant information.
- **Active Directory Domains and Trusts** (`domain.msc`) is used to manage domains, trusts, and relevant information.

- **Active Directory Sites and Services** (`dssite.msc`) is used to manage the replication and services between sites.
- **Active Directory Module for Windows PowerShell** is used to manage the Windows Server's directory services via `cmdlets`:

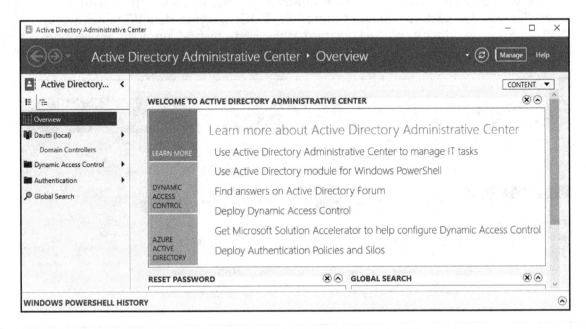

Figure 5.1: The Active Directory Administrative Center in Windows Server 2019

 You can access Microsoft's Script Center at `https://technet.microsoft.com/en-us/scriptcenter/bb410849.aspx` and PowerShell Gallery at `https://www.powershellgallery.com/`. Both are well-known repositories of free and public domain PowerShell scripts. Additionally, substantial collections of AD- and DNS-related entries are included.

To set up domain services in your organization's IT infrastructure, you are required to install the AD DS role to a server. While you can find more information about server roles in `Chapter 6`, *Adding Roles to Windows Server 2019*, AD DS is a role in Windows Server 2019 that lets system administrators manage and store a network's information resources. See *Chapter exercise – installing the AD DS and DNS roles and promoting the server to DC* section later in this chapter to learn how to install AD DS on a server.

We will now learn about various elements of an AD infrastructure. Let's begin with the DC.

# Understanding the DC

A DC (see *Figure 5.2*) is a server that is responsible for securely authenticating users to access resources in an organization's network. In Windows NT, there was one DC per domain configured as a **Primary Domain Controller** (**PDC**), and all other domain controllers acted as **Backup Domain Controllers** (**BDC**). In contrast, in Windows Server 2019, there are no primary and backup approaches used—instead, numbers are used next to DCs to identify priorities (for example, DC1 and DC2):

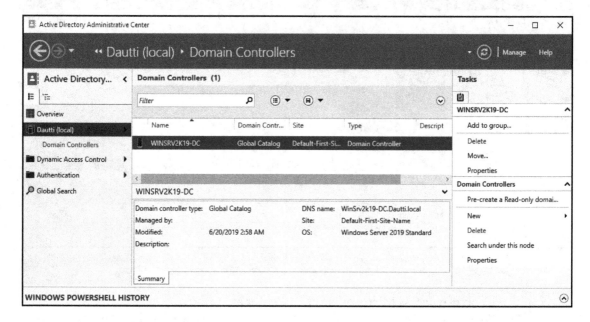

Figure 5.2: Accessing DCs through the Active Directory Administrative Center

 A server that has joined a domain in an organization's network is considered a member server.

The DC is responsible for granting access to domains. Let's understand this next.

# Understanding the domain

A domain is a logical grouping of users, computers, peripheral devices, and network services. From the perspective of network architecture, usually, domains are centralized network environments where authentication is governed by a DC. In Windows Server-based networks, the domain is powered by the AD DS role. *Figure 5.3* presents the step in the **Active Directory Domain Services Configuration Wizard** in which the domain is being set:

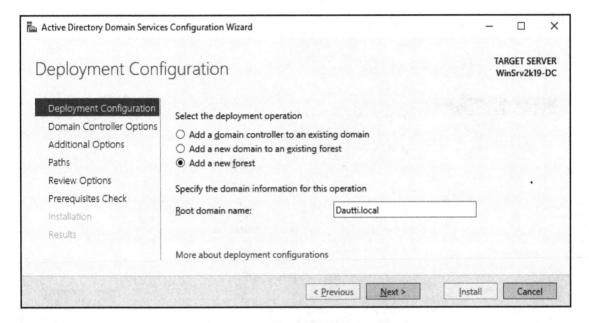

Figure 5.3: Setting up a root domain in Windows Server 2019

 You must understand that there is a profound difference in the meaning of *domain* in the context of a directory domain or a domain server and in the context of a *domain name*. The former means a database of users, servers, devices, and resources within a specific collection of such things. The latter means the logical naming system that governs the internet, including web servers and websites.

Several domains come together to make up a tree domain, as we'll explain in the upcoming section.

# Understanding the tree domain

In an AD structure, a tree domain is in fact comprised of one or more domains. Domains in a tree are linked through transitive trust. With transitive trust, if A trusts B, and B trusts C, then A trusts C. That said, in a tree domain, when a new domain joins an existing tree, then the new domain automatically trusts all existing domains in the tree. Similar to adding a domain, the tree domain is configured during the **Promote this server to a domain controller** process.

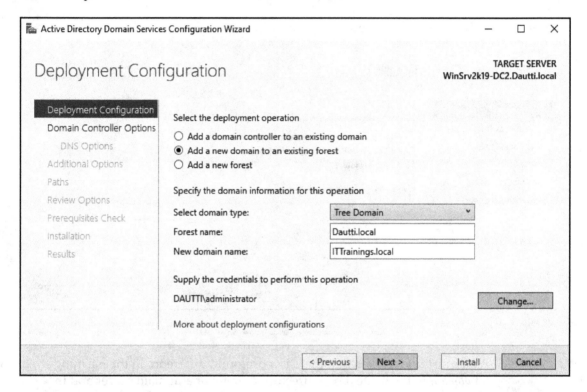

Figure 5.4: Setting up a tree domain in Windows Server 2019

When several tree domains come together, we have a forest, as we'll explain in the next section.

# Understanding the forest

As you know, in real life, a forest consists of trees. Likewise, in AD, a **forest** consists of one tree domain or a collection of tree domains. From that, it can be concluded that the tree domain actually represents a domain, which, if it is a root domain, represents the forest. Just like that, a forest is a domain too. Isn't that a closed circle?

To set up a forest in Windows Server 2019, as was the case with tree domains, use the **Active Directory Domain Services Configuration Wizard** as shown in *Figure 5.5*:

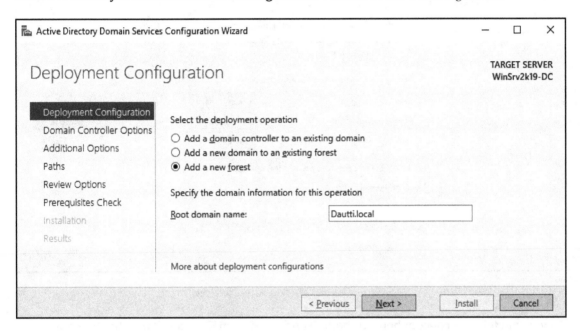

Figure 5.5: Setting up the forest in Windows Server 2019

A level below the tree domain represents the child domains, as we'll explain in the next section.

# Understanding the child domain

To understand the child domain, let's illustrate it with the example from *Figure 5.7*. `Dautti.local` and `ITTrainings.local` are both tree domains; however, `Dautti.local` represents a forest since that is the root domain. From that, `Programming.Dautti.local` represents a child domain of the `Dautti.local` tree domain.

To set up a child domain in Windows Server 2019, you can use the **Active Directory Domain Services Configuration Wizard** (see *Figure 5.6*):

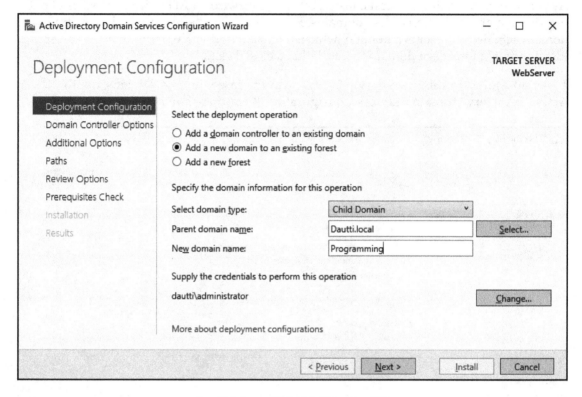

Figure 5.6: Setting up a child domain in Windows Server 2019

As you can tell, the concept behind the tree and child domain is similar to the tree data structure. Now, let's understand the operations master role.

# Understanding operations master roles

By its very nature, an AD DS is complex! However, once you begin deploying it, then everything becomes clearer. Let's look at the operations master role this way. Earlier in the *Understanding the domain* section (see *Figure 5.3*), we created the root domain, Dautti.local, which actually represents a forest. In fact, in this example, the machine that hosts the Dautti.local forest is actually a DC for that particular network.

From what was said, when the AD DS role is being installed and the server gets promoted to a domain controller, the AD DS automatically assigns five master operations roles. The first two, *master schema* and *domain naming master*, are forest-wide operations master roles, whereas, the remaining three, such as the **Relative Identifier** (**RID**), **Primary Domain Controller** (**PDC**) emulator, and infrastructure master, are tree domain-wide operations master roles. While the schema master and domain naming master manages the AD's schema, the read-write copy takes care that only one unique domain is in the forest. On the other hand, RID takes care of assigning **Security Identifiers** (**SIDs**) to DCs, the PDC emulator deals with password updates, and the infrastructure master keeps track of the changes made to other domain objects.

To relate that to our example (see *Figure 5.7*), the root domain such as Dautti.local is actually the master schema and the domain naming master in the whole forest (that is, Dautti). Dautti.local and ITTrainings.local are both tree domains in a forest and, as such, they have their own RID masters, PDC emulators, and infrastructure masters:

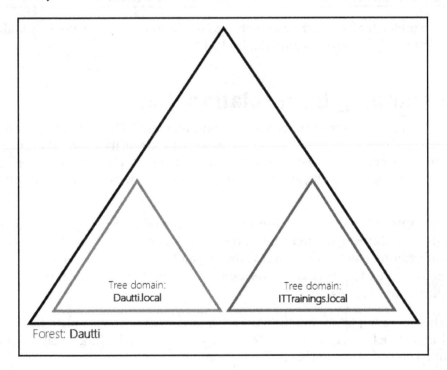

Figure 5.7: AD DS structure

The roles explained previously, always, according to Microsoft, represent the five roles of ADs operations called **Flexible Single Master Operation** (**FSMO**). Now, let's understand the difference between a domain and a workgroup.

# Understanding domain versus workgroup

To better illustrate the difference between domain and workgroup, let's consider network architectures such as **Peer-to-Peer** (**P2P**) networking and the client/server. The following table shows the comparison between domain and workgroup:

| Domain | Workgroup |
|---|---|
| Here, a dedicated server is used to provide services. | Here, computers equally share resources among themselves without the need for a dedicated server. |
| For example, a client/server network. | For example, a P2P network. |

Now that we understood the difference between workgroup and domain, let's understand the trust relationship between a computer and a DC.

# Understanding trust relationship

In AD, there is a **trust relationship** between a computer and a DC and between domains, too. That being said, once a computer joins a domain, the **Security Account Manager** (**SAM**) in the local computer trusts the AD's authentication mechanism, which is a Kerberos in a DC. Hence, the user is being authenticated by a DC in a network and not from the local SAM.

Similarly, the authentication mechanism of each tree domain is trusting every other authentication mechanism of other trusted tree domains within a forest. From *Figure 5.7*, if a user is authenticated by Dautti.local, then its authentication is accepted by ITTrainings.local too, since these tree domains are part of the same forest (that is, the root domain), Dautti.local.

To understand it better, try to link the trust relationship with the administration and communication link between domains. Now, let's understand the functional levels of domain and forest and how to check it.

# Understanding functional levels

There are two types of functional levels, the **Forest Functional Level** (**FFL**) and the **Domain Functional Level** (**DFL**). The FFL controls which versions of Windows Server can run in DCs of the forest, and, at the same time, it enables the available capabilities across all domains in a forest. In contrast, DFL controls which versions of Windows Server can run in DCs of that domain, and, at the same time, it enables the available capabilities in that domain only. In Windows Server 2019, the DFL and FFL should be raised to at least Windows Server 2008 because Windows Server 2003 is no longer supported.

To check the domain and forest functional levels in Windows Server 2019, complete the following steps:

1. Click the **Start** button, and then, on the **Start** menu, click on the **Server Manager** tile.
2. In the **Server Manager** window, click **Tools** from the menu bar and then select **Active Directory Domains and Trusts**.
3. In the **Active Directory Domains and Trusts** window, right-click the root domain and then select **Properties** from the context menu.
4. In the **Properties** dialog box, you will find the **Domain functional level:** and **Forest functional level:** under the **General** tab, as shown in *Figure 5.8*:

Figure 5.8: Checking the DFL and FFL in Windows Server 2019

Be aware that there is no functional level for Windows Server 2019. Instead, the highest functional level offered is **Windows Server 2016**.

Now that we have understood the roles of FFL and DFL, let's understand what a contiguous namespace is.

# Understanding namespaces

In *Figure 5.9*, Dautti.local actually represents a forest and a root domain at the same time, whereas Dautti.local and ITTrainings.local are actually tree domains in the aforementioned forest. Furthermore, the Dautti.local tree domain contains a child domain such as Programming.Dautti.local. From that, it is obvious that the child domain and the tree domain share a common namespace within a forest (that is, Programming.Dautti.local). This is known as a **contiguous namespace**:

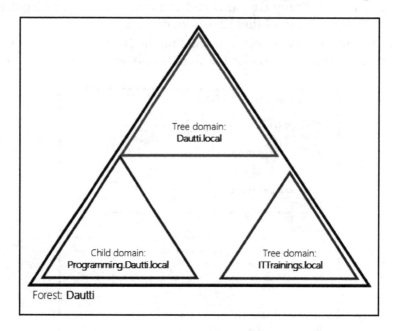

Figure 5.9: The namespace concept in AD DS

To better understand namespaces, try associating it with an URL. Now, let's understand what a site is.

# Understanding sites

As is the case with computer networks, even in ADs there are physical and logical topologies too. Hence, a **domain** represents the logical topology, whereas the **site** represents the physical topology in an AD infrastructure. From that, the site actually represents the physical location of the computer network.

Now, let's understand the process of replication.

# Understanding replication

In an AD infrastructure, replication is a process that synchronizes the common directory partition among all DCs in a forest. Additionally, replication topology is a set of communication paths through which the DC's replication data travels.

Now, let's understand what a schema is.

# Understanding schema

Generally in AD, there are elements such as objects, classes, and attributes that define a schema object. While the **class** represents the object type, the **attribute** represents the characteristics of the object. Thus, the AD stores the objects that are identified by their classes and attributes. Then, the **schema** represents the model that contains the rules of the types of objects that can be stored in AD. Then, it is the *replication* that synchronizes the *schema* among all DCs in a forest.

# Understanding Microsoft Passport

In today's technological trends, in which a user needs to log in to different environments to access applications, websites, and other services, the traditional format of authentication (such as username and password) is neither viable nor secure. The same applies to Microsoft's OSes and services. Therefore, Microsoft has introduced Microsoft Passport, which enables users to authenticate without a password. Microsoft Passport is based on the **Fast ID Online** (**FIDO**) Alliance standards and consists of two components: a single sign-in service and a wallet service. From that, we can deduce that Microsoft Passport is a two-factor authentication mechanism with which users will be able to prove who they are by providing something that they uniquely possess.

In the preceding sections, we understood the various elements related to the AD infrastructure. In the following section, we will delve deeper into the concept of DNS and its various elements.

# Understanding DNS

The DNS concept dates from the 1960s, also known as the ARPANET era. At that time, scientists engaged in the ARPANET project were trying to find a way of memorizing names instead of IP addresses. At the beginning of the 1980s, in the form of **Requests for Comments (RFC)** documents, the first specification documents were published about the DNS.

The nature of a DNS is that it has a tree structure (hierarchical), where each branch represents the root zone and each leaf has zero or more resource records. Each zone can represent a root domain or multiple domains and sub-domains. A domain name consists of one or more parts, known as labels, and are separated by a period (for example, packtpub.com). DNS is maintained by a database that uses distributed clients/server architecture where network hosts represent the servers' names. The following steps illustrate how the DNS works:

1. If you enter www.packtpub.com in the browser's address bar and press *Enter*, your computer's browser will make a request on the internet to access the www.packtpub.com website.
2. The very first server that the browser runs into is the recursive resolver, which, in most cases, may be provided by your **Internet Service Provider (ISP)**.
3. The *recursive resolver* will then contact the root servers that are scattered all over the globe and that contain information about top-level domains; in our example, it is .com.
4. The top-level domains will provide the DNS information to the recursive resolver.
5. Once the recursive resolver receives the information from top-level domains, it will then contact the domain name server, packtpub.com. Using the domain name server's local DNS, it will try to figure out the IP address.
6. Once it learns the web server's IP address, then the recursive resolver provides that IP to your computer's browser in order to access the web server content via its newly accustomed IP address.

Now that we know how the DNS works, we are well-equipped to install the DNS role.

# Installing the DNS role

Similar to the AD DS role, the DNS in Windows Server 2019 is a role too that is installed using Server Manager, as shown in *Figure 5.10*:

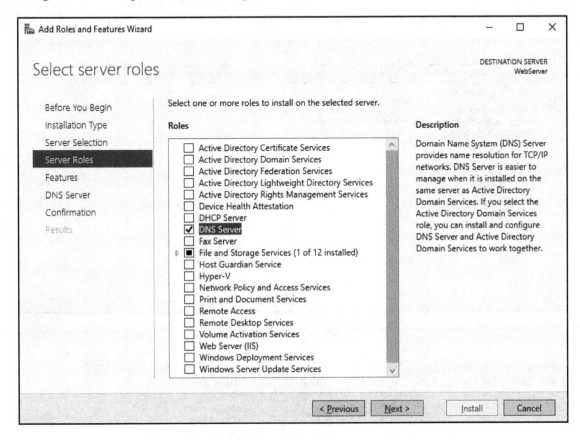

Figure 5.10: Adding the DNS role in Windows Server 2019

Note that, when installing the DNS role, it can be installed either as a separate role (see *Figure 5.10*) or alongside AD DS, as shown in *Figure 5.11*:

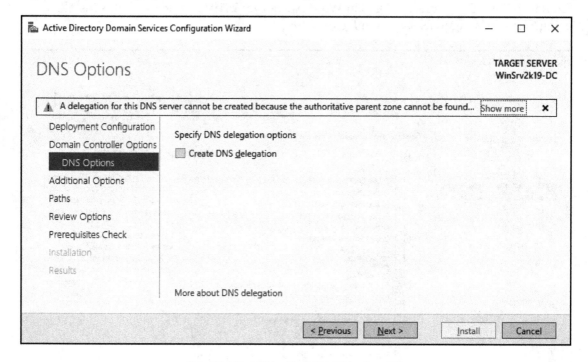

Figure 5.11: Adding DNS alongside AD DS in Windows Server 2019

As you can tell, installing DNS is a step in the process of installing the AD DS role itself. Now, let's understand what `hosts` and `lmhosts` files are.

# Understanding hosts and lmhosts files

The `hosts` and `lmhosts` files are used for name resolution and are stored in the `C:\Windows\system32\drivers\etc` directory, as shown in *Figure 5.12*. The `host` files contain the mapping of IP addresses to hostnames and are used for DNS name resolution. Unlike `hosts`, the *LAN manager hosts* (`lmhosts`) file contain the mapping of IP addresses to computer names and is used for NetBIOS name resolution. In both files, entries are inserted manually, and each entry should be kept on an individual line:

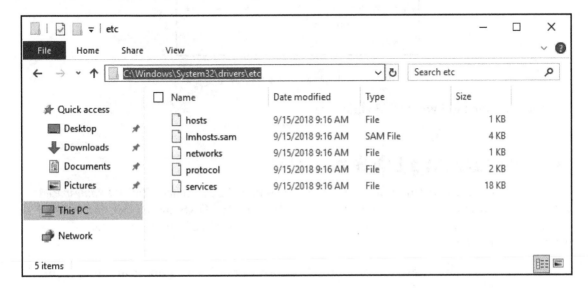

Figure 5.12: The hosts and lmhosts files in Windows Server 2019

The following table presents the examples of `hosts` and `lmhosts` entries:

| `hosts` entry | `IP address FQDN hostname #Comment` |
|---|---|
| `lmhosts` entry | `IP address FQDN hostname Extension <tag>#Comment` |

Now, let's understand what a hostname is.

# Understanding hostnames

A hostname represents a logical element that is assigned to a device, as shown in *Figure 5.13*. It is unique and it is used to identify the host in a network. Often, it is called a **domain name** too:

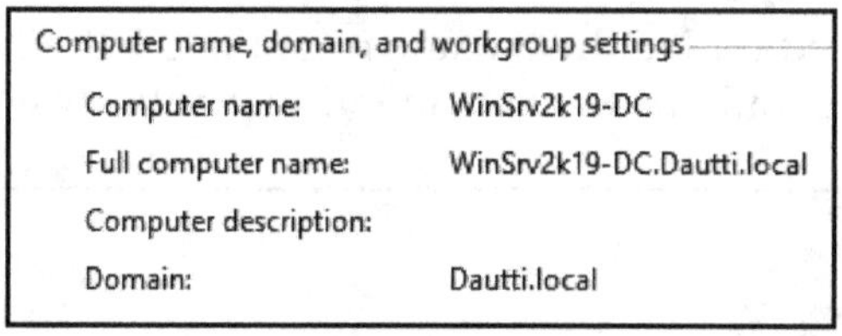

```
Computer name, domain, and workgroup settings

    Computer name:           WinSrv2k19-DC

    Full computer name:      WinSrv2k19-DC.Dautti.local

    Computer description:

    Domain:                  Dautti.local
```

Figure 5.13: Assigning a hostname in Windows Server 2019

Now, let's understand what DNS zones are.

# Understanding DNS zones

It is the hierarchical structure that enables the existence of *DNS zones*. The *AD namespace* is very much related to the *DNS namespace*. That is because the DNS namespace can be divided into zones which can store information about domains. In this way, a DNS provides three types of zones:

- The **primary zone** stores the primary copy of the DNS database and maintains all DNS zone records.
- The **secondary zone** acts as a backup of the primary zone, meaning that whenever the *primary zone* is unavailable, it then resolves DNS queries.
- The **stub zone**, in principle, represents the secondary zone with no editable primary copy of the database and contains sufficient information to identify the authoritative DNS.

*Authoritative DNSes* can either be configured manually by a system administrator or dynamically by other DNSs. It represents the DNS server, which contains the DNS records of the actual domain. In contrast, a *non-authoritative DNS* contains the cached information that has been constituted by previous DNS lookups.

Now, let's understand **Windows Internet Name Service** (**WINS**).

# Understanding WINS

To automate *NetBIOS name resolution*, you can use Microsoft's WINS server. A *WINS server* maps the IP addresses to NetBIOS names. The NetBIOS names are the names that are used when your computer is connecting to a shared folder or printer. WINS is a feature in Windows Server 2019 and can be added through Server Manager using the **Add Roles and Features Wizard**, as shown in *Figure 5.14*:

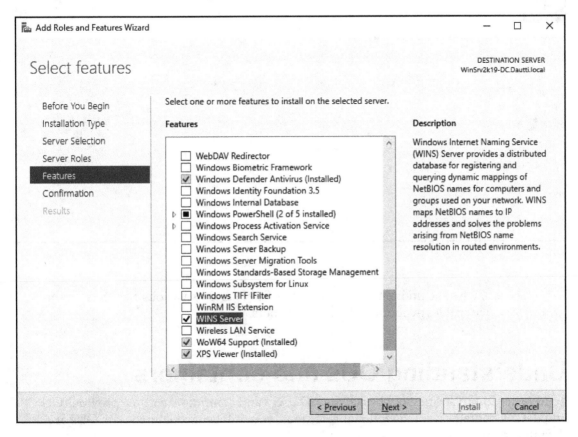

Figure 5.14: Setting up the WINS feature in Windows Server 2019

Now, let's understand the **Universal Naming Convention** (**UNC**).

# Understanding UNC

**UNC**, originally used in Unix, is a standard to identify a share in a computer network. Its format (see *Figure 5.15*) uses double backslashes to precede the name of the server, for example, \\servername\folder:

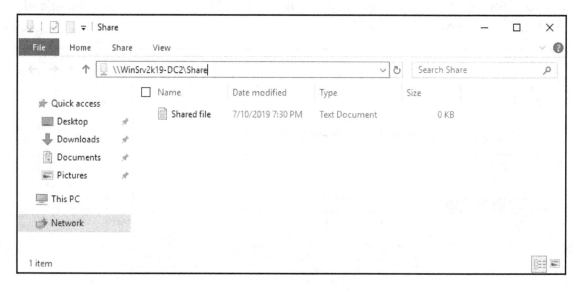

Figure 5.15: A UNC path in Windows Server 2019

In this section, we have understood the concept of DNS and its various elements. In the next section, we will learn about OUs and containers.

# Understanding OUs and containers

To ease the administration of objects, the AD users and computers console provides OU and default containers. In the following sections, you will get acquainted with OUs and default containers.

# What are OUs?

As mentioned earlier, to ease the administration of its objects, AD uses OUs. In general, users, groups, computers, and other *organizational units* are placed within OUs. Usually, organizations create OUs to mirror their organizational business structures. Regardless of the number of tree domains in a forest, each domain can have its own OU hierarchy (see *Figure 5.16*):

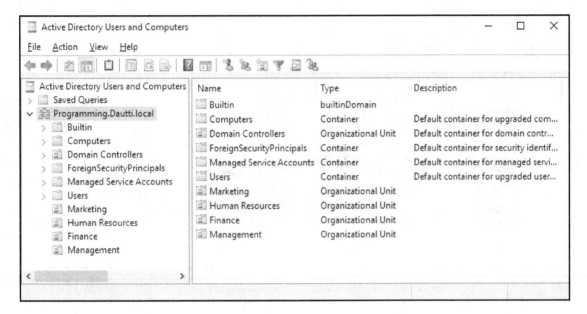

Figure 5.16: An example of OU hierarchy in Windows Server 2019

To make it clear what the OUs are, try associating them with the concept of folders in File Explorer. Now, let's understand what default containers are.

# Understanding default containers

Once the server gets promoted to a DC, several *default containers* are created, as shown in *Figure 5.17*. These *default containers* are unique because they cannot be renamed, deleted, created, or associated with a **Group Policy Object** (**GPO**):

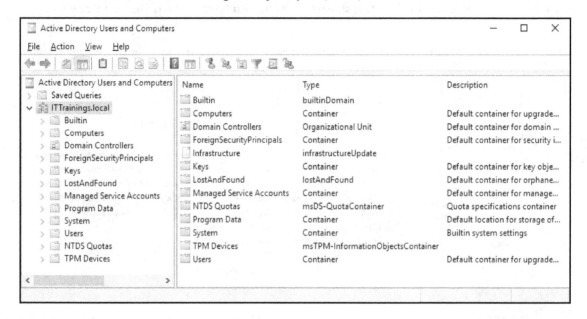

Figure 5.17: Default containers in Windows Server 2019

Now, let's understand what hidden default containers are.

# Understanding hidden default containers

Not every default container is needed for a system admin day-to-day job! Because of that, by default, there are *hidden containers* too. One reason why these containers are hidden is to stop the AD users and computer consoles from looking messy. However, it may seem that the security part is the biggest reason why there are hidden containers in AD.

To unhide these hidden default containers, enable the **Advanced Features** option from the **View** menu, as shown in *Figure 5.18*:

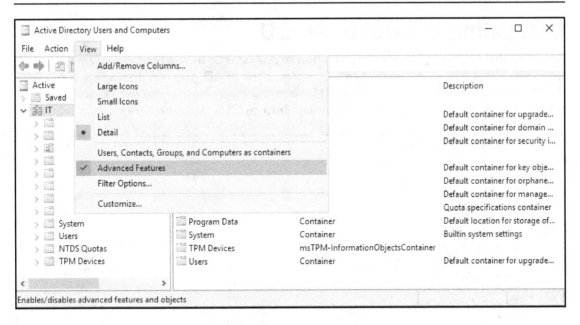

Figure 5.18: Default hidden containers in Windows Server 2019

Now that we have learned about default containers, let's take a look at some of their uses.

# Uses of the default containers

The following are simple uses for some of the default containers in Windows Server 2019:

- `Computers` is a default container for upgraded computer accounts.
- `Domain Controllers` is a default container for DCs.
- `ForeignSecurityPrincipals` is a default container for **Security Identifiers (SID)**.
- `Keys` is a default container for key objects.
- `LostandFound` is a default container for orphaned objects.
- `Managed Service Accounts` is a default container for managed service accounts.
- `Users` is a default container for upgraded user accounts.

Now, let's learn how to delegate control to an OU.

# Delegating control to an OU

Knowing that OUs facilitate the organization of AD objects, then whenever you want to grant permissions to a certain user or a group of users in AD, you can do that via the *delegation of control* to an OU. However, it is required that, before assigning permissions to a user or group of users, they need to be moved into an OU (see *Figure 5.19*):

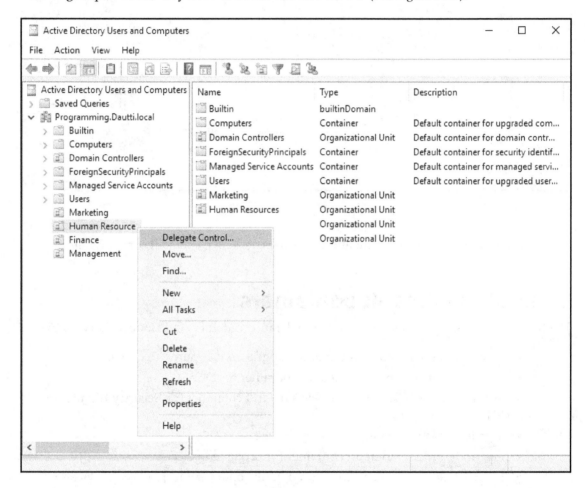

Figure 5.19: Delegating control to an OU in Windows Server 2019

In this section, we have learned the various aspects of OUs and containers. In the next section, we will understand user and computer accounts and groups.

# Understanding accounts and groups

To access network services, user and computer accounts are used. In a Windows Server-based network, both users and computer accounts reside in an AD. In such a centralized environment, groups are used to facilitate the process of assigning rights and permissions. In the following sections, you will get to know the different accounts and groups.

## Understanding domain accounts

Technically, the *domain account* is part of an AD and as such, it is authenticated by the same entity (that is, the AD). The domain account is authorized to access both local and network services based on the access that is granted to the account or a group that an account belongs to.

To create a domain account in Windows Server 2019, complete the following steps:

1. From Windows Administrative Tools, open the **Active Directory Users and Computers** console.
2. Right-click the **Users** container and select **New | User**.
3. Enter the user's required information (see *Figure 5.20*), and then click **Next**:

Figure 5.20: Creating a domain account in Windows Server 2019

4. Provide a temporary password, confirm, and click **Next**.
5. Click **Finish** to close the **New Object - User** window.

The next type of accounts that we are going to look at are local accounts.

# Understanding local accounts

Unlike domain accounts, local accounts are the part of computers where that account has been created, and as such, it is authenticated by the Windows SAM. The local account is authorized to access local services based on the access that is granted to the account. Additionally, the local account can access shared resources in a P2P network if it has the permissions to do so.

To create a local account in Windows Server 2019, complete the following steps:

1. From Windows Administrative Tools, open the **Computer Management** console.
2. Expand **System Tools | Local Users and Groups**, right-click the **Users** container, and select **New | User**.
3. Enter the user's required information (see *Figure 5.21*), and then click **Create**:

Figure 5.21: Creating a local account in Windows Server 2019

To create a local account in Windows Server 2019, the server doesn't need to be a DC. So, do not install AD DS.

Keep in mind that the local account is an account that is stored on the local computer and is also authenticated by the SAM of the OS on that computer. Now, let's take a look at the various user profiles.

# Understanding user profiles

In general, in Windows Server-based networks, the following user profiles are used:

- The **local user profile** is created when the user logs on to a computer for the first time and is stored on a local computer (see *Figure 5.22*).
- The **roaming user profile** is a local profile copied and stored to a network share.
- The **mandatory user profile** is a kind of roaming profile where a user logs off and no changes in a profile are saved:

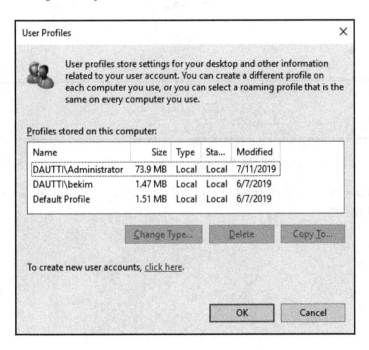

Figure 5.22: User profiles in Windows Server 2019

From the preceding explanation it can be concluded that the local user profile is stored on the local computer, the roaming user profile is stored in the network share, and the mandatory user profile is not saved at all, in fact, it is using the fixed profile from the network share too. Now, let's understand what a computer account is.

# Understanding computer accounts

In an AD, a *computer account* identifies a computer in a domain. Before joining a computer to a domain, its hostname is required to be unique in a network. Once a computer joins a domain, it continues to use its computer name for communication with other computers and servers in a network. Computer accounts are managed through the **Active Directory Users and Computers** console, as shown in *Figure 5.23*:

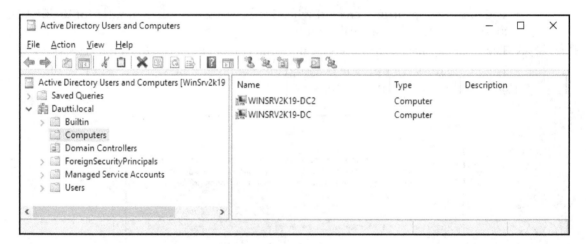

Figure 5.23: Computer accounts in Windows Server 2019

So far in this section, we have learned about various user and computer accounts. Now, let's learn about groups.

# Understanding group types

In an AD, a group represents a collection of AD objects. Instead of assigning permissions and rights to each AD object individually, groups are used for a more structured administration. Note that a group is an object too, meaning that it can also be moved to an OU.

Groups (see *Figure 5.24*) are managed through the **Active Directory Users and Computers** console. In an AD, there are two types of groups:

- **Security groups** are explicitly used to assign permissions to shared resources on a network.
- **Distribution groups** are particularly used to distribute email lists in an organization's network:

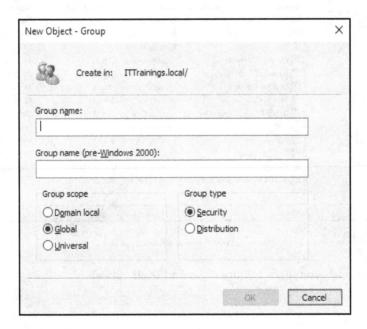

Figure 5.24: Group types in Windows Server 2019

Now, let's understand what default groups are and how to create them.

# Understanding default groups

As discussed in the previous section, groups are used to facilitate the administration of AD objects. Hence, once the server gets promoted to a DC, a significant number of default groups are created, as shown in *Figure 5.25*:

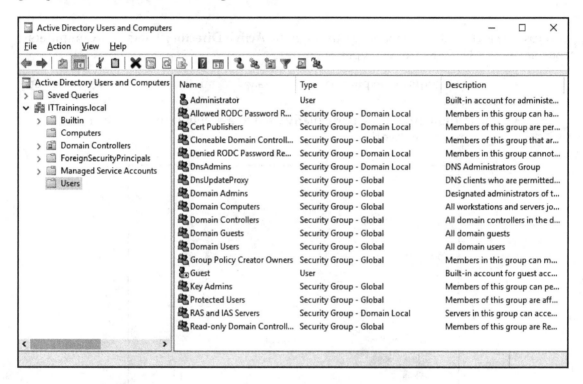

Figure 5.25: Default groups in Windows Server 2019

Now, let's understand what group scopes are and their types.

# Understanding group scopes

Regardless of whether it is a security or universal group, try to understand the group scope as an extension option of the group in a forest, tree domain, or child domain. In an AD, there are three group scopes (see *Figure 5.26*):

- The **domain local group** includes accounts, domain local groups, global groups, and universal groups from the parent's domain local group domain.
- The **global group** includes accounts and global groups from the parent's global group domain.
- The **universal group** includes accounts, global groups, and universal groups from any domain in the forest where a universal group belongs:

Figure 5.26: Group scopes in Windows Server 2019

Moving forward, let's understand what group nesting is.

# Understanding group nesting

As we have learned so far, AD groups are objects that can be organized in a group nesting. That way, adding groups to other groups minimizes the number of individually assigned permissions to users or groups.

## Understanding AGDLP and AGUDLP

Both **Accounts, Global, Domain Local, Permissions (AGDLP)** and **Accounts, Global, Universal, Domain Local, Permissions (AGUDLP)** are Microsoft's recommendations for effectively using *group nesting* when assigning permissions.

The following are the ways of assigning permissions using AGDLP group nesting:

- Add the accounts to the global group.
- Add the global group scope to the domain local group.
- Assign permissions to the domain local group.

The following are the ways of assigning permissions using AGUDLP group nesting:

- Add the accounts to the global group.
- Add the global group to the universal group.
- Add universal group to the domain local group.
- Assign permissions to the domain local group.

So far, we have learned about the AD infrastructure, DNSes, and their various elements. We have also seen what OUs and containers are. Lastly, we have understood computer accounts and groups and their types. Now, it is time to install the AD DS and DNS roles.

# Chapter exercise – installing the AD DS and DNS roles and promoting the server to a DC

In this chapter exercise, you will learn how to install the AD DS and DNS roles and promote the server to a DC.

# Installing the AD DS and DNS roles, and promoting the server to a DC

To install the AD DS role in Windows Server 2019, complete the following steps:

1. Click the **Start** button, and then, in the **Start** menu, click the **Server Manager** tile.
2. In the **Server Manager** window, in the **WELCOME TO SERVER MANAGER** section, click **Add roles and features**, as shown in *Figure 5.27*:

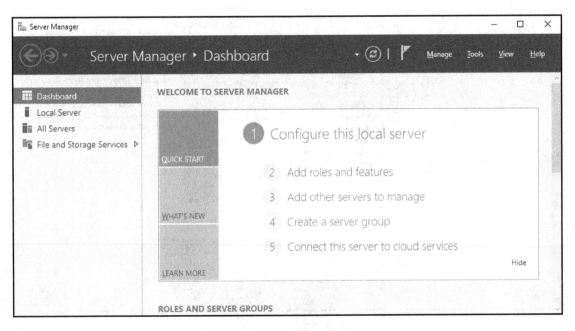

Figure 5.27: Adding roles and features to the server using Server Manager

3. With the **Add Roles and Features Wizard** open, click **Next**.
4. Select the **Role-based or feature-based installation** option and click **Next**.
5. With the **Select a server from the server pool** option checked, click **Next**.

6. Select the **Active Directory Domain Services** role, as shown in *Figure 5.28*, and then click **Next**:

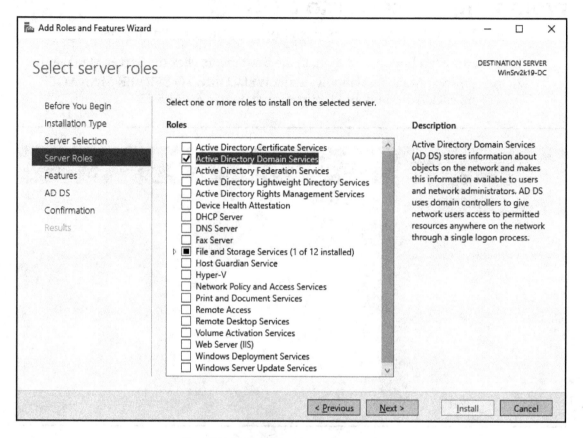

Figure 5.28: Add Roles and Features Wizard in Windows Server 2019

7. Click the **Add Features** button when the **Add features that are required for Active Directory Domain Services?** window is displayed. Click **Next**.

8. Accept the default settings in the **Select features** step and click **Next**.

9. Take your time to read the AD DS description and the things to note regarding AD DS installation. Then, click **Next**.

10. Confirm the installation selections for the AD DS role and click the **Install** button.

11. Either hit **Close** or wait until the installation progress reaches its end.

12. Click **Close** to close the **Add Roles and Features Wizard**.

13. In **Notifications**, click **Promote this server to a domain controller**.
14. In the AD DS configuration wizard, select the **Add a new forest** option, as shown in *Figure 5.29*, and then enter **Root domain name**. Click **Next**:

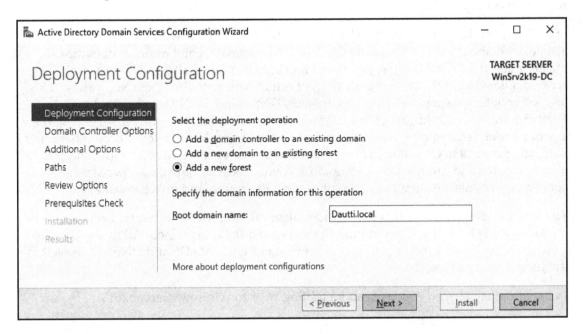

Figure 5.29: AD DS configuration wizard

15. Accept the defaults for the forest and domain functional levels, and enter the **Directory Services Restore Mode (DSRM)** password. Click **Next**.
16. If you have an existing DNS on your network, manually create a delegation for that DNS server to enable reliable name resolution from outside of your domain. Otherwise, no action is required. Click **Next**.
17. Either accept the default NetBIOS entry or change it accordingly. Click **Next**.
18. Either accept the default paths or change them accordingly. Click **Next**.
19. Review your options and click **Next**.
20. Since the prerequisites are met, click **Install**.
21. The server will restart to complete promoting itself to a DC.

# Summary

In general, in this chapter, you have learned about the directory services and naming resolution concepts.

Specifically, in the first part of this chapter, you became familiar with the AD DS role. You also learned about topics such as the DC forest, tree domain, child domain, operations master roles, trust relationships, functional levels, namespaces, site, replication, and schema. Likewise, in the second part, you got acquainted with the DNS role. Also, you learned about `hosts` and `lmhosts`, hostnames, DNS zones, WINS server, and UNC. Furthermore, in the third part of this chapter, you became familiar with OUs. Here, you got a better understanding of what OUs are, default containers, hidden default containers, and delegating control to OUs. Finally, in the fourth part, you got acquainted with concepts about accounts and groups such as domain accounts, local accounts, user profiles, computer accounts, group types and scopes, default groups, and group nesting.

To make things interesting, this chapter has taken care to provide a chapter exercise where installing a AD DS role and promoting the server to a DC is explained. All that you have learned in this chapter has helped you to understand what AD DS and DNS are, as well as the process of installing them.

In the next chapter, you will learn about adding roles to Windows Server 2019.

# Questions

1. An AD is a distributed database that stores objects in a hierarchical, structured, and secure format. (True | False)
2. _____ minimizes the number of individually assigned permissions to users or groups.
3. Which of the following user profiles are used mostly in Windows Server-based networks?
    - Domain user profile
    - Security user profile
    - Roaming user profile
    - Mandatory using profile
4. The WINS server maps the IP addresses to BIOS names. (True | False)
5. _____ is a set of communication paths through which the DC's replication data travels.

6. Which of the following are AD's group scopes?
    - OU
    - Security group
    - Global group
    - Universal group

7. UNC is a standard to identify a share in a computer network. (True | False)

8. _____ is a server that is responsible for securely authenticating requests to access resources in your organization's domain.

9. Which of the following snap-ins for **Microsoft Management Consoles** (**MMC**) consoles are used to manage AD?
    - Active Directory Administrative Center
    - Active Directory Users and Computers
    - UNC
    - OU

10. The best example of a domain is a client/server network where a dedicated server on the network is used to provide services. (True | False)

11. _____ stores the primary copy of the DNS database and maintains all DNS zone records.

12. Which of the following are forest-wide operations master roles?
    - Master schema
    - Domain naming master
    - LAN manager hosts
    - Default containers

13. Discuss AD DS and DNS roles and their implementations.

14. Discuss Microsoft's recommendations, AGDLP and AGUDLP, for assigning permissions.

# Further reading

- *AD DS Deployment*: https://docs.microsoft.com/en-us/windows-server/identity/ad-ds/deploy/ad-ds-deployment
- *What's New in DNS Server in Windows Server*: https://docs.microsoft.com/en-us/windows-server/networking/dns/what-s-new-in-dns-server
- *Creating an Organizational Unit Design*: https://docs.microsoft.com/en-us/windows-server/identity/ad-ds/plan/creating-an-organizational-unit-design
- *Managing Groups*: https://docs.microsoft.com/en-us/windows/win32/ad/managing-groups

# 6
# Adding Roles to Windows Server 2019

Now that you have had a chance to get to know the two most important roles of Windows Server 2019, AD DS and DNS, and you have learned how to install them, it is time to get acquainted with the other roles and features of Windows Server 2019. Adding roles to the server will help you to define the function of the servers in the organization's network.

This chapter will provide a broader explanation of what a role is, as well as the importance of roles in determining the server's function when providing network services. Also, you will get to know the majority of the roles and features that Windows Server 2019 supports. You will also learn how to add roles to the server and set them up properly whenever such is required. In that way, you will be able to understand what application servers, web services, remote access, and file and print services are.

In addition to learning roles, features will also be explained along with the steps it takes to add them to a server. This chapter also includes the exercise installing web server (**Internet Information Services (IIS)**) and PDS roles.

The following topics will be covered in this chapter:

- Understanding server roles and features
- Understanding application servers
- Understanding web services
- Understanding remote access
- Understanding file and print services
- Chapter exercise—installing web server (IIS) and PDS roles

# Technical requirements

In order to complete the exercises in this chapter, you will need the following equipment:

- A PC with Windows 10 Pro, at least 16 GB of RAM, 1 TB of HDD, and access to the internet
- Virtual Machine 1 (file server) with Windows Server 2019 Standard (Desktop Experience), at least 4 GB of RAM, 100 GB of HDD, and access to the internet
- Virtual Machine 2 (web server) with Windows Server 2019 Standard (Desktop Experience), at least 4 GB of RAM, 100 GB of HDD, and access to the internet
- Virtual Machine 3 (print server) with Windows Server 2019 Standard (Desktop Experience), at least 4 GB of RAM, 100 GB of HDD, and access to the internet

# Understanding server roles and features

To functionalize a server, you must determine its role. To do that, the proper role needs to be installed on the server. That being said, in the following sections, you will get acquainted with Windows Server roles, role services, and features.

## Understanding server roles

When you add a role, as in *Figure 6.3*, to Windows Server 2019, actually, you are assigning a task that the server needs to perform. That way, the server role is the server's primary function. In the best-case scenario, the server should have only one role. However, the server can have multiple roles too. Remember, always try to understand the exact role that your server needs to perform so that you can then choose the right hardware for it as well.

## Understanding role services

Other than adding roles to the server and, with it, determining the server's primary function, there are situations when you need to also add role services. That said, the question is: what are role services? Let's try to understand role services with the following example. Assume that you want to have an internet print server so that employees can print from outside the company's network (that is, via, extranet). To do that, you add the **Print and Document Services** (**PDS**) role to your server and then you add **Internet Printing** as a role service, as in *Figure 6.21*. That way, you augment the functionality of the role.

# Understanding server features

From what has been discussed so far, other than roles and role services, features (see *Figure 6.2*) are added to the server to support a given role too. For example, there are situations where you are asked to install .NET Framework 3.5 features so that you can complete the role you are adding, you need to install an **IP Address Management** (**IPAM**) server to support the DHCP or DNS roles in your network infrastructure, or maybe you want to have a WINS server alongside DNS so you can solve problems arising from NetBIOS name resolution in routed environments. All of these examples present situations where you may need to add a feature to the server.

# Understanding Server Manager

In general, to add roles in Windows Server 2019, you will use Server Manager. Introduced with Windows Server 2008, Server Manager is an administrative tool used by system administrators to add, set up, and manage server roles. Its user interface is simple and easy to navigate. Usually, the scope pane lists the installed roles whereas the details pane contains the details of a selected role in a scope pane. Like that, it can be concluded that Server Manager (see *Figure 6.1*) is the main console for adding roles, configuring services, managing resources, and administering tasks in Windows Server 2019:

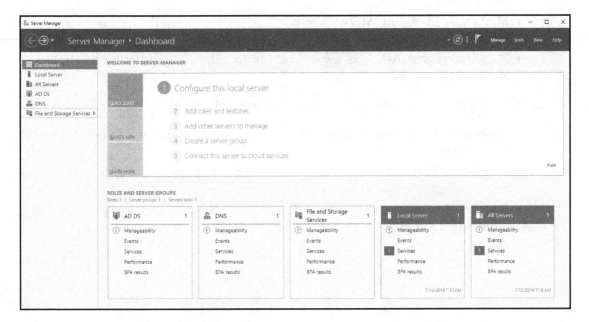

Figure 6.1: Server Manager's user interface in Windows Server 2019

So far, we have understood what are server roles and server features. The next section will take us through the concept of application features and their types.

# Understanding application servers

When searching for the meaning of the word *application* in the Merriam-Webster dictionary, one of the definitions presented is also *an act of putting something to use*. From that, it can be said that an application server is a server that provides usable services on the network. In the following sections, you will get acquainted with some of the well-known application servers that are in use today.

Let's begin by understanding what mail servers are and how to set them up.

## Understanding mail servers

A mail server is a server that sends and receives emails. The main components of a mail server are as follows:

- **Mail Transport Agent** (**MTA**) is responsible for transporting the mail between mail servers.
- **Mail Delivery Agent** (**MDA**) is responsible for delivering the mail from the server into a user's inbox.
- **Mail User Agent** (**MUA**) is responsible for providing a platform for composing and reading emails.

Additionally, the mail server utilizes the following protocols:

- **Simple Mail Transfer Protocol** (**SMTP**) uses port 25 and powers the MTA in transferring the mail between servers.
- **Post Office Protocol** (**POP**) uses port 110 and is responsible for downloading emails from the server to the user's local computer.
- **Internet Message Access Protocol** (**IMAP**) uses port 143 and is responsible for retrieving emails from the mail server and sending them to a user's mail application.

To set up a mail server in Windows Server 2019, you must add the SMTP server feature to the server, as shown in *Figure 6.2*:

1. Click **Add roles and features** in the Server Manager **WELCOME TO SERVER MANAGER** section.
2. In the **Before you begin** option, click **Next**.
3. Click **Next** in the **Installation Type** option.
4. In the **Select destination server** option, click **Next**.
5. There is no role to add, so click **Next**.
6. Select **SMTP Server** from the **Features** list:

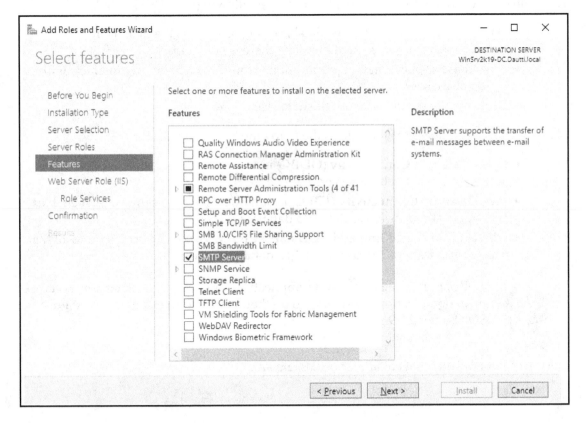

Figure 6.2: Adding the SMTP Server feature in Windows Server 2019

7. There is no **role service to add**, so click **Next**.
8. In the **Confirm installation Selections** option, click **Install**.

Exchange Server 2019 is Microsoft's application for setting up a mail server in an organization's network. To do that, you should install and configure Exchange Server 2019.

Now, let's understand what database servers and their access protocols are.

# Understanding database servers

In its simplest definition, the database server is the server that provides database services. The main components of the database server are the following:

- Data is the raw material of the database and, as such, is the main component of a database server because, without data, there is no database.
- A database application is an application through which the user interacts with the database server.
- Users are the people who use the database.

Additionally, the database server utilizes the following access protocols:

- **Open Database Connectivity (ODBC)** is a protocol that enables applications to access data in a database server.
- **Java Database Connectivity (JDBC)** is Sun Microsystem's protocol that enables Java applications to access data in a database server.
- **Object Linking and Embedding Database (OLEDB)** is Microsoft's protocol that enables applications to access data in a database server.

 SQL Server 2019 is Microsoft's application for setting up a database server in an organization's network. To do that, you need to install and configure SQL Server 2019.

Now, let's understand what collaboration servers are.

# Understanding collaboration servers

As you may know, since this book is talking about Windows Server 2019, which is an NOS, it is understood that a collaboration server is also a client/server application that is installed on a server powered by Windows Server 2019. As such, the collaboration server is the server that brings people together for a common project. This means that members of the same project from different offices within the organization can access the same collaborative server without the need to be in a single office.

 SharePoint Server 2019 is Microsoft's application for setting up a collaboration server in an organization's network. To do that, you need to install and configure SharePoint Server 2019.

Now, let's understand what monitoring servers are.

# Understanding monitoring servers

The general concept of a monitoring server can involve anything from monitoring a server's health to monitoring its performance. From this, we understand that server monitoring is a process that, in addition to monitoring key server components such as CPU, memory, disk usage, and network interface, enables other components to be monitored on the server as well. Some of them may be input/output components, services, processes, and so on.

 System Center 2019 Operations Manager is Microsoft's application for setting up a monitoring server in an organization's network. To do that, you need to install and configure System Center 2019 Operations Manager.

Now, let's understand what threat management servers are.

# Understanding threat management servers

As the name suggests, the threat management server is a server that acts as a router, firewall, antivirus program, VPN server, proxy server, and other threat management roles. That necessarily determines the importance of such client/server application in many segments such as network interconnection, network security, protection from malware, secure remote access, and controlled internet access.

System Center 2019 Endpoint Protection is Microsoft's application for setting up a threat management server in an organization's network. To do that, you need to install and configure System Center 2019 Endpoint Protection.

In this section, we have learned about some of the well-known application servers used today. Aside from helping us to get to know some of the most used client/server applications nowadays, it will help us to learn their components as well. In the next section, we will learn about the various web services.

# Understanding web services

A web service represents the means of communication between two devices, which is based on the request/response methodology using the **Hypertext Transfer Protocol** (**HTTP**).

# What is IIS?

IIS is Microsoft's web server, which provides reliable, manageable, and scalable web applications. IIS supports communication protocols such as HTTP, HTTPS, FTP, FTPS, SMTP, and NNTP for communication between the browser and the web server. For dynamic content on the server side, Microsoft has developed scripting technology called **Active Server Pages** (**ASP**).

In IIS version 10, Microsoft has significantly increased security with the support for scripts that take a long time to execute, including HTTP/2. Add to this Microsoft Edge, a new browser introduced with Windows 10. Other key features introduced with IIS 10 on Windows Server 2019 include upgraded HTTP/2 server-side cipher suite negotiation, IIS administration PowerShell cmdlets, wildcard host headers, and so on. These and many other improvements have established IIS firmly in second place in the market share, right behind Apache.

To set up a web server in Windows Server 2019, you need to add IIS as a role to the server, as shown in *Figure 6.3*:

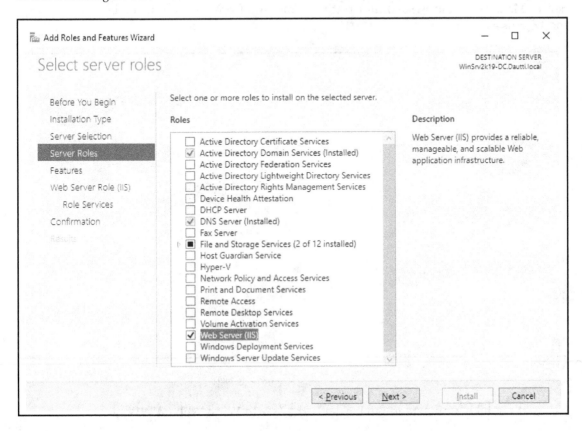

Figure 6.3: Adding the web server (IIS) role in Windows Server 2019

The **Internet Information Service (IIS) Manager** is a console that is used to manage the web server in Windows Server 2019 (see *Figure 6.4*). The IIS Manager can be accessed from Server Manager, Windows Administrative Tools, and from the **Run** dialog box by running the `inetmgr` command:

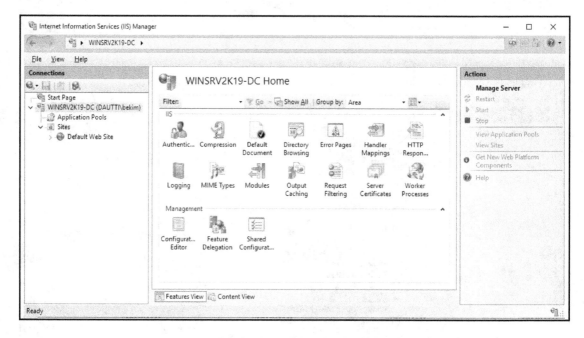

Figure 6.4: IIS Manager in Windows Server 2019

Now, let's quickly understand what exactly the **World Wide Web** (**WWW**) is.

# What is WWW?

Often, people confuse the internet with the **WWW**. Perhaps using the WWW while connected to the internet means they get the feeling that the WWW is actually the internet! Who knows? However, like many other internet services, WWW too is an internet service, accessed through the HTTP protocol, and consisting of electronic documents compiled with **Hypertext Markup Language** (**HTML**), as shown in *Figure 6.5*:

Figure 6.5: A website and its source code

Now, let's understand what **File Transfer Protocol** (**FTP**) is and how to set it up.

# What is FTP?

FTP does exactly what its name indicates. FTP transfers files from computer to computer, computer to server, or vice versa, on a LAN or WAN (or the internet).

To set up an FTP server in Windows Server 2019, first, you need to add **Web Server Role (IIS)** as a role and then **FTP Server** as a role service (see *Figure 6.6*):

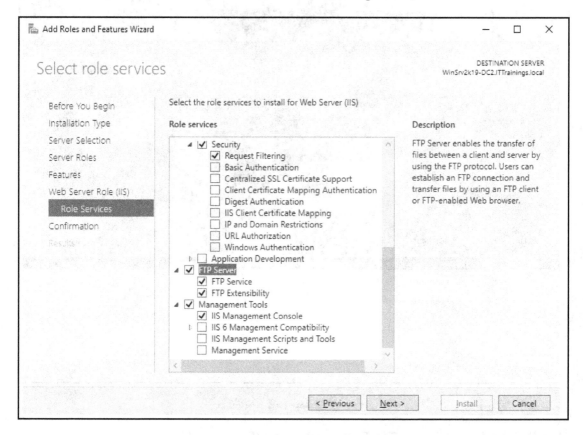

Figure 6.6: Adding FTP Server as a role service in Windows Server 2019

Now, let's understand what worker processes are and how to access them.

# Understanding separate worker processes

From an IIS perspective, a web directory represents a website that has an application pool. As we are talking about a pool of applications, then it is understood that there is more than one application. From there, each application in the application pool is supported by the same worker process. This means that a worker process that serves an application pool is separated by another worker process that serves another application pool. Hence, if a certain web application does not work, then that it does not affect the applications that are running in other application pools.

To access an application's pool worker processes, select **Application Pools** then, from the **Actions** pane on the right-hand side of the IIS Manager, select **Advanced Settings...**, as shown in *Figure 6.7*:

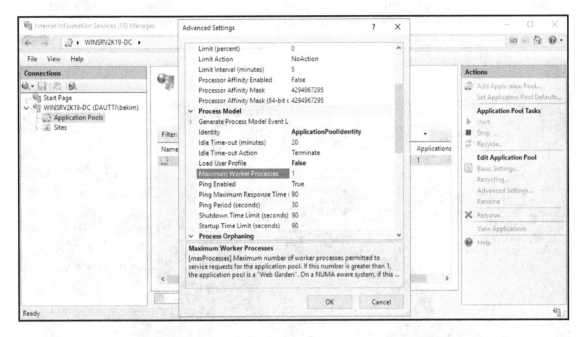

Figure 6.7: An application's pool worker process in IIS

Now let's learn how to add additional components to Windows Server's IIS.

# Adding components to the IIS

In the process of adding the web server (IIS) role, you will encounter the **Role Services** step (see *Figure 6.6*) in the *What is FTP?* section, from where you will add the required components for the IIS. Also, you can add the required components even after you have added the web server (IIS) to the server. That means you must use the **Add Roles and Features Wizard** from the Server Manager to add additional components to Windows Server's IIS.

Now, let's understand what a site or website is.

# Understanding sites

A site, often called a **website**, is a collection of web pages that are grouped together to represent the content on the intranet or internet, via web services. When you add a web server (IIS) as a role to the server, the default website is created as in *Figure 6.8*:

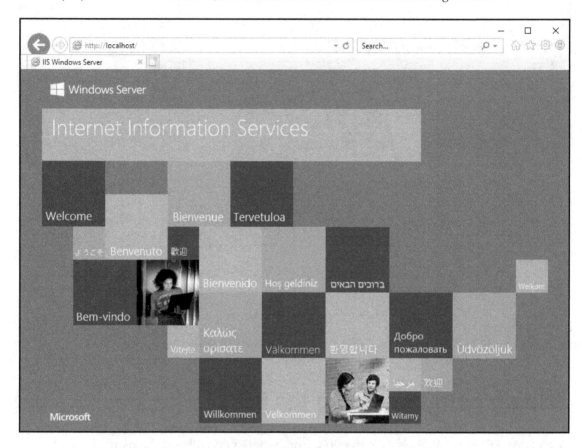

Figure 6.8: Localhost in Windows Server 2019 powered by IIS

However, if you right-click `Sites` and select **Add Website...**, as in *Figure 6.9*, you can add additional websites to Windows Server's IIS:

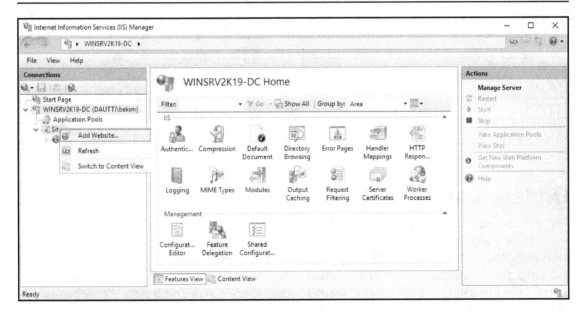

Figure 6.9: Adding website via IIS Manager in Windows Server 2019

Now, let's understand what software ports are.

# Understanding ports

In general, there are hardware and software ports. In a narrower context, a *hardware port* is any physical interface in a computer, peripheral device, or network device that allows interconnection for communication purposes. By contrast, a *software port* (often known as an *application port*) is any logical endpoint where applications from your computer communicate with other applications on other computers, both on LAN and WAN (or the internet). A web server uses ports 80 and 443 for the HTTP protocol and HTTPS protocol respectively.

The following table lists the well-known application ports:

| Protocol | Port | Transportation protocol |
|---|---|---|
| FTP | 21 | TCP |
| SSH | 22 | TCP |
| Telnet | 23 | TCP |
| SMTP | 25 | TCP |
| HTTP | 80 | TCP and UDP |

| POP3 | 110 | TCP |
|------|-----|-----|
| NNTP | 119 | TCP |
| NTP | 123 | TCP |
| IMAP4 | 143 | TCP |
| HTTPS | 443 | TCP |

Now, let's understand what the **Secure Sockets Layer** (**SSL**) is.

# Understanding SSL

SSL is a communication technology that encrypts the communication channel between a website on a web server and a browser on a computer. The browser connects to a secured website with SSL through the HTTPS protocol that operates on port 443. In such a secure infrastructure, certificates play an important role in encrypting all transmitted data. Certificates are used mutually by the website and browser in negotiating a secure session between browser-to-server or server-to-server communication, as shown in *Figure 6.10*:

Figure 6.10: Secured communication between browser and website

# Understanding certificates

As discussed in the previous section, a certificate is responsible for securing the communication channel between a website and a browser. As such, the certificate, also known as a **digital certificate**, is an electronic document that ensures that entities can exchange data securely on the internet. Usually, certificates are issued by a secure entity known as a **Certificate Authority** (**CA**) as shown in *Figure 6.11*. This infrastructure uses **Public Key Infrastructure** (**PKI**), which uses certificates to prove the ownership of the public key:

Figure 6.11: Certificate issued by a CA

You can learn more about PKI at `https://docs.oracle.com/cd/B10501_01/network.920/a96582/pki.htm`.

In this section, we have learned about the many different web services and elements. The next section will introduce us to the Remote Access role in Windows Server 2019.

# Understanding Remote Access

The Remote Access role in Windows Server 2019 enables remote access to resources inside an organization's network. To understand it better, remote access consists of a logical grouping of the following network access technologies:

- **DirectAccess**: Introduced in Windows Server 2008 R2 is using IPsec to encrypt communication between the DirectAccess client and the DirectAccess server. It encapsulates IPv6 traffic over IPv4 to reach the intranet from the internet. Access to a corporate intranet is enabled without **Virtual Private Network** (**VPN**).
- **Routing and Remote Access Service** (**RRAS**): The successor to the **Remote Access Service** (**RAS**) in Windows NT, it was introduced in Windows 2000 and represents a combined service that establishes links between remote locations via VPN and dial-up, as well as traffic paths between the sub-networks.
- **Web Application Proxy**: Web Application Proxy in Windows Server 2019 replaced the Microsoft Forefront **Unified Access Gateway** (**UAG**) and acts as a recursive proxy. Web Application Proxy uses **Active Directory Federation Services** (**AD FS**) to authenticate corporate users so they can access web applications on the corporate intranet through an extranet.

To set up a remote access server in Windows Server 2019, you need to add **Remote Access** as a role to the server, as in *Figure 6.12*:

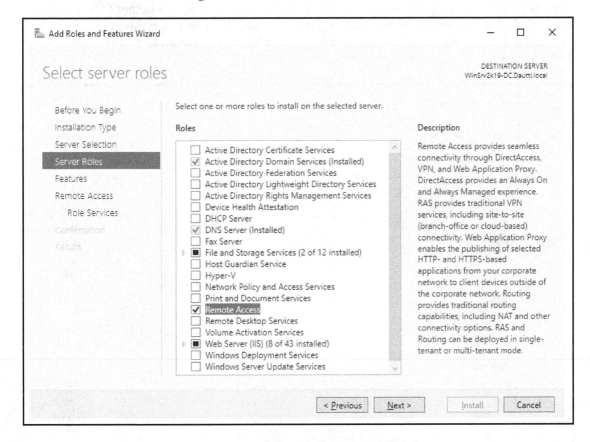

Figure 6.12: Adding the Remote Access role in Windows Server 2019

Now, let's understand the Remote Assistance feature and how to add it to the server.

# Understanding Remote Assistance

Remote Assistance in Windows Server 2019 is a feature that enables a helper to access the invitee's desktop remotely for the sake of providing assistance in troubleshooting the issues. To do that, you must use the **Add Roles and Features Wizard** to add the **Remote Assistance** feature to the server, as shown in *Figure 6.13*:

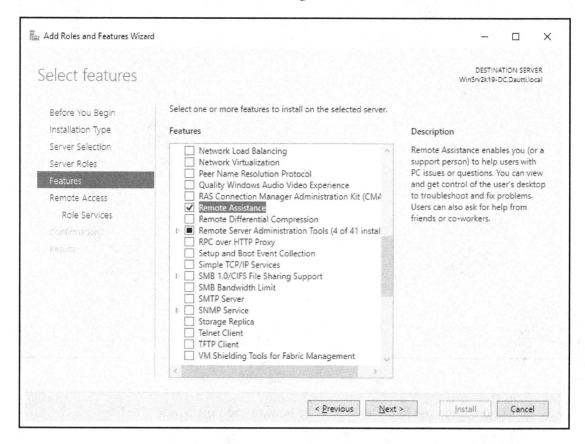

Figure 6.13: Adding the Remote Assistance feature in Windows Server 2019

Now, let's understand what the **Remote Server Administration Tools** (**RSAT**) feature is and learn how to enable it.

# Understanding RSAT

RSAT in Windows Server 2019 is a feature that enables managing server roles and features of remote servers that are running Windows Server 2019 (both in GUI and CLI modes). Additionally, RSAT is available for client computers running Windows 10 too.

To enable the **Remote Server Administration Tools** feature in Windows Server 2019, use the **Add Roles and Features Wizard**, as shown in *Figure 6.14*:

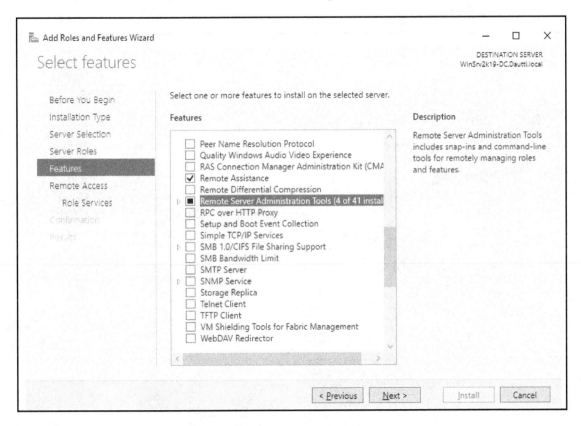

Figure 6.14: Adding the RSAT feature in Windows Server 2019

Now, let's understand what the **Remote Desktop Services** (**RDS**) server is and how to set it up.

# Understanding RDS

Known as **Terminal Services** (**TS**) until Windows Server 2008, RDS earned its name and identity with the release of Windows Server 2008 R2. This role enables to set up a GUI with remote access to computers within an organization's network and over the internet. Additionally, RDS delivers individual, virtualized applications to users' desktops.

To set up an RDS server in Windows Server 2019, you need to add the RDS role to the server, as in *Figure 6.15*:

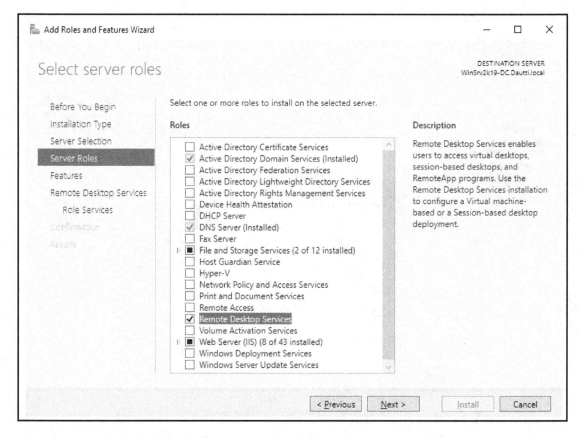

Figure 6.15: Adding the RDS role in Windows Server 2019

Now, let's understand what an RDS Licensing server is and how to set it up.

# Understanding RDS Licensing

The RDS Licensing server manages RDS **Client Access Licenses** (**CAL**). RDS CALs are used by users and computers to access a **Remote Desktop Session Host** (**RDSH**) server. By default, the RDS Licensing server provides two concurrent connections free of cost. If you need additional RDS CAL, then you need to purchase them.

To set up an **RDS Licensing** server in your organization's network with Windows Server 2019, you first need to add the **Remote Desktop Services** role and then add **Remote Desktop Licensing** role services, as in *Figure 6.16*:

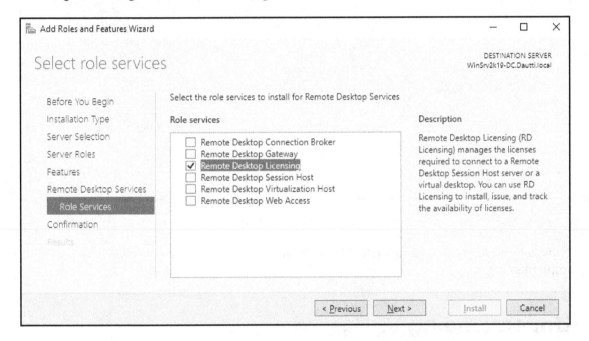

Figure 6.16: Adding Remote Desktop Licensing role services in Windows Server 2019

Now, let's understand what the **Remote Desktop Gateway** (**RDG**) server is and how to set it up.

# Understanding RDG

An RDG server, part of the RDS role, is a role service in Windows Server 2019 that enables authorized users to connect to computers within an organization's network and over the internet using a **Remote Desktop Connection** (**RDC**) client.

To set up an RDG server in your organization's network with Windows Server 2019, you first add the RDS role and then add **Remote Desktop Gateway** role services, as in *Figure 6.17*:

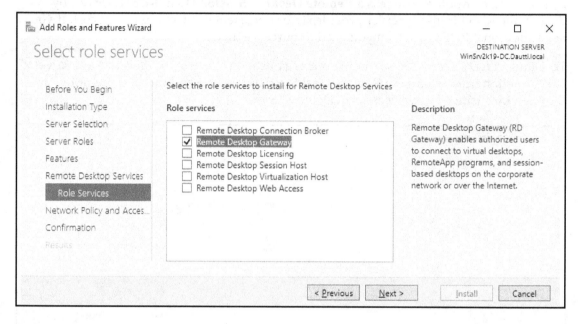

Figure 6.17: Adding RDG role services in Windows Server 2019

Now, let's understand what a **Virtual Private Network** (**VPN**) is and the ways of implementing it.

# Understanding VPN

As you may know, a VPN is a logical connection on the internet for transmitting data securely. As its name suggests, a VPN creates a virtual point-to-point link between two computers on the WAN (that is, the internet). That way, by utilizing tunneling protocols and data encryption algorithms, the VPN enables remote users to get connected to an organization's network over the internet infrastructure. This kind of network is usually implemented in two ways, remote access VPN and site-to-site VPN:

- The *remote access VPN* connects remote users (telecommuters) with the server on their organization's private network
- The *site-to-site VPN* enables organizations to connect two separate networks over the internet.

To set up a VPN server in Windows Server 2019, first add the Remote Access role and then add **DirectAccess and VPN (RAS)** role services, as in *Figure 6.18*:

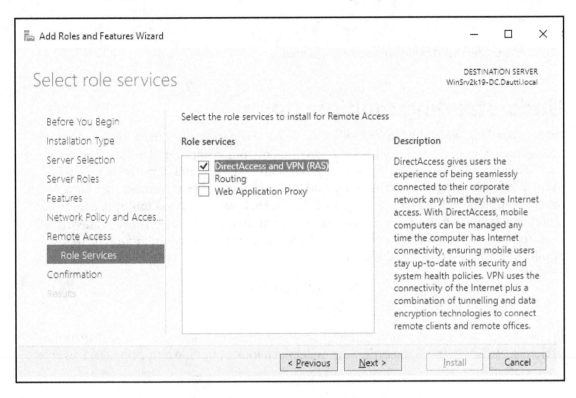

Figure 6.18: Adding DirectAccess and VPN (RAS) role services in Windows Server 2019

Now, let's understand what an **Application Virtualization (App-V)** server is.

# Understanding App-V

Microsoft App-V delivers virtualized applications to users. These virtualized applications are installed on a server and are provided to users in the format of a service. From a user's perspective, users interact with the virtualized applications as if they were installed locally.

To set up an App-V server, you should download the **Microsoft Desktop Optimization Pack (MDOP)** from Microsoft's website.

You can learn more about MDOP from `https://technet.microsoft.com/` `en-us/windows/mdop.aspx?`.

Now, let's understand what multiple ports are.

# Understanding multiple ports

As discussed earlier in the *Understanding RDS* section, port `3389` is used by RDS to send and receive data. However, that is for accessing only one computer at a time. The question is, what happens when you try to access more than one computer simultaneously with RDS? While the first computer is using port `3389`, sequential port numbers are assigned to other computers on the LAN starting with `3390`. That way, to access multiple computers simultaneously from a remote location over the internet, an IP socket is used. Having said that, an **IP socket** is a combination of an IP address and a port number that tells the application where to deliver the data:

- **Syntax**: `Public_IP_address:Port_number`
- **Example**: `192.168.2.10:8080`

In this section, we learned about the Remote Access role in Windows Server 2019 and its various features. In the next section, we will take a look at the file and print services role.

# Understanding file and print services

The *file and print services* are as old as computer networks themselves! I say that because computer networks were born out of the need to share resources. Hence, file and print services were among the pioneering services in computer networks. Nowadays, these two services have been transformed into essential services, whether at home or in business networks. That is because, these days, every **Network Operating System** (**NOS**) on the market is capable of providing file and print services, including Windows Server 2019.

# Understanding the File Services role

In Windows Server 2019, the File Services role is automatically added (see *Figure 6.19*) upon completing the installation of an operating system. Does that surprise you? Maybe not, if you remember the fact that you have just installed a NOS on the server! As mentioned earlier, file services have always been essential network services. From simple file sharing to work folders or from DFS Namespaces to BranchCache for Network Files, it is all about the availability of the data and being able to be accessed *anytime/anywhere*:

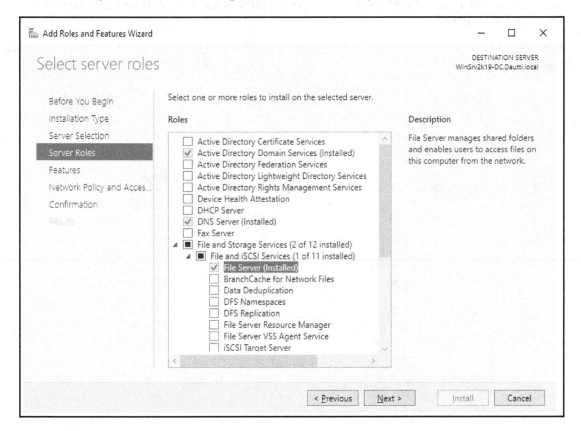

Figure 6.19: File Services role in Windows Server 2019

Now, let's take a look at the **Print and Document Services** (**PDS**) role and the various role services that can be installed as a part of it.

# Understanding the PDS role

PDS is a service that enables centralized printing on the network. Obviously, as its name indicates, PDS offers more than just the network printing service. It also provides the service for document scanning. With scanning service, users receive scanned documents from the network scanner and send them to the network shared resources. Usually, PDS is added as a role in Windows Server 2019 as in *Figure 6.20*.

Hence, to set up a print server in Windows Server 2019, select the **Print and Document Services** role and add Print Server role services:

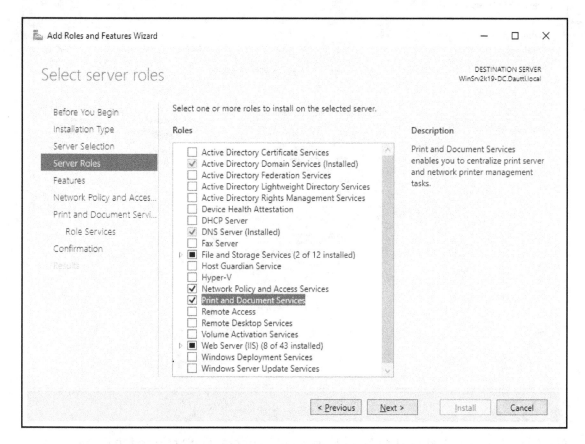

Figure 6.20: Adding PDS role in Windows Server 2019

The following role services can be installed as part of PDS (see *Figure 6.21*):

- **Print server**: This enables the management of printing queues as well as the deployment and migration of print servers.
- **Internet printing**: This enables the setting up of a website from where users, through **Internet Client Printing** (**ICP**), can print.
- **Line Printer Daemon (LPD) service**: This enables Unix-based computers and other non-Windows OSes to use **Line Printer Remote** (**LPR**) to print:

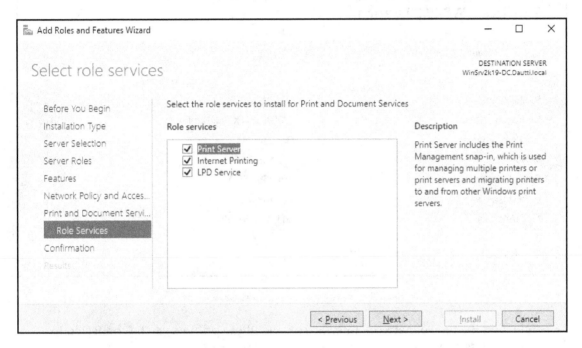

Figure 6.21: Adding PDS role services in Windows Server 2019

Now, let's quickly understand the various concepts related to a printer. Let's begin with the local printer.

# What is a local printer?

A local printer, as the name implies, is a printer that is physically connected to the computer through the parallel port (known as the **printer port**) or USB port. This printer primarily serves the computer to which it is connected. However, if the printer is shared by a host computer, then it also serves other computers on the network.

# What is a network printer?

A network printer (see *Figure 6.22*), unlike a local printer, is a dedicated printer on the computer network that provides printing services:

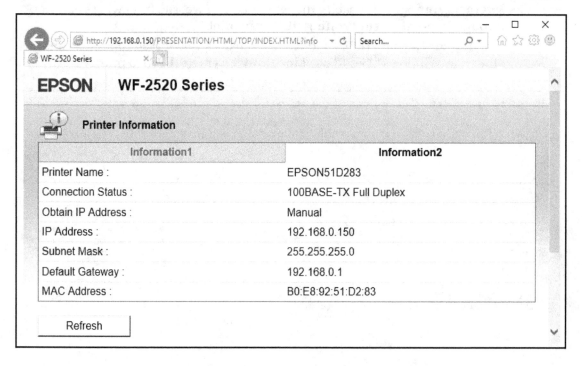

Figure 6.22: Adding Print Server role services in Windows Server 2019

Depending on the type of network interface owned, these printers can be connected to a wired or wireless network.

# What is printer pooling?

Printer pooling in Windows Server 2019 is a feature that helps to configure two or more physical printers into one logical printer. To do that, printers installed on the print server are required to be almost identical or be able to use the same driver. From the client's perspective, though there are several physical network printers available at the backend, in the frontend, it looks like it is a single printer. This logical connection of printers balances their load, hence increasing their usability and, at the same time, providing users with rational printing.

You can set up printer pooling, as in *Figure 6.23*, in Windows Server 2019 by adding the PDS role and Print Server role services:

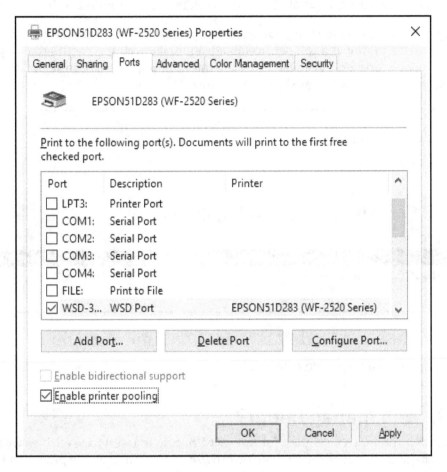

Figure 6.23: Setting up printer pooling in Windows Server 2019

Then, it requires the installation of printers and configuration of printer pooling via the **Print Management** console.

# What is web printing?

Web printing enables users to print files to network printers through a web browser.

Prior to setting up web printing in your organization's network, make sure to add the PDS role and Internet Printing as a role service. In addition, the web server (IIS) role required. To access available printers via a web browser, enter `http://servername/printers` in the browser's web address bar, as shown in *Figure 6.24*:

Figure 6.24: Web printing in Windows Server 2019

Now, let's understand what web management is.

# What is web management?

In addition to printing, web printing (or Internet Printing role services) enables web printing management too. Through the web browser, users can manage print jobs in a similar way to the traditional method of managing print jobs (for example, to see what's printing option).

To manage printers through a web interface, enter `http://servername/printers` in your browser's address bar and then select the printer. The next page (see *Figure 6.25*) lists the print jobs, which can be managed:

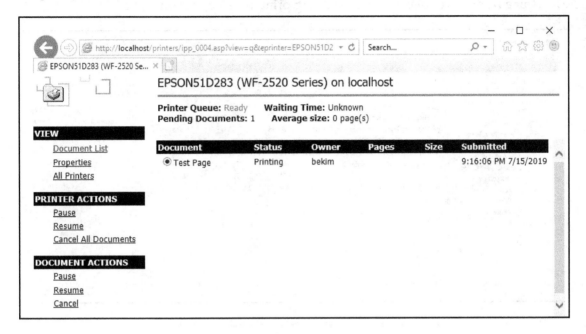

Figure 6.25: Web printing management in Windows Server 2019

Moving forward, let's now understand what driver deployment is.

# Understanding driver deployment

When it comes to managing printers from the **Print Management** console (see *Figure 6.26*), everything from driver deployment to adding printers can be accomplished:

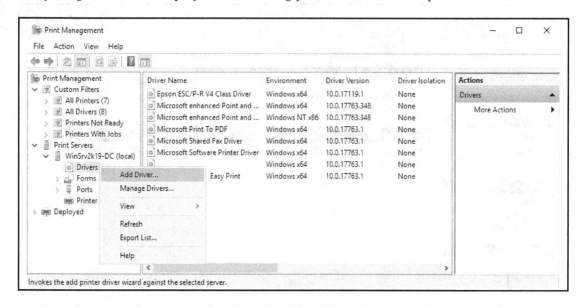

Figure 6.26: Deploying print drivers with the Print Management console in Windows Server 2019

Now, let's understand what user rights, NTFS permissions, and share permissions are.

# Understanding user rights, NTFS permissions, and share permissions

First things first, let's try to understand what user rights and permissions are. If you open the properties of a folder in any Windows OS and then click on the **Security** tab, you will notice that, under the *group and usernames* section, you can see the permissions for the <user> section. That section lists the following permission types:

- **Full control**: Allows reading, writing, modifying, executing, changing attributes and permissions, and deleting files and sub-folders
- **Modify**: Allows viewing, modifying, adding, and deleting files and sub-folders

- **Read & execute**: Allows running and executing files
- **List folder contents**: Allows viewing data files and a list of a folder's content
- **Read**: Allows viewing files and file properties
- **Write**: Allows writing in a file
- **Special permissions**: Additional advanced permissions

However, from the same section, we note that each permission may be allowed or denied (see *Figure 6.27*). In the broader context, users can be allowed or denied access to the files and folders, and that relates to user rights. While in the narrower context, every allow or deny setting contains a certain permissions that determine the type of access to the objects:

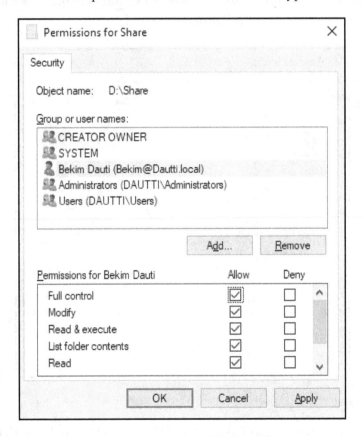

Figure 6.27: NTFS permissions in Windows Server 2019

Another consideration is the comparison of **New Technology File System** (**NTFS**) permissions with share permissions. Starting from the fact that NTFS is a native Windows Server native filing system, then when we talk about NTFS permissions, we are actually dealing with file and folder access to the local server, exactly on the server's storage. By contrast, share permission has more to do with accessing files and folders that are shared across the network. Since NTFS permissions were previously mentioned, then shared permissions are listed as follows (see *Figure 6.28*):

- **Full Control**: Allows reading, modifying, and editing permissions, and taking ownership
- **Change**: Allows reading, executing, writing, and deleting files and sub-folders
- **Read**: Allows listing and viewing the content

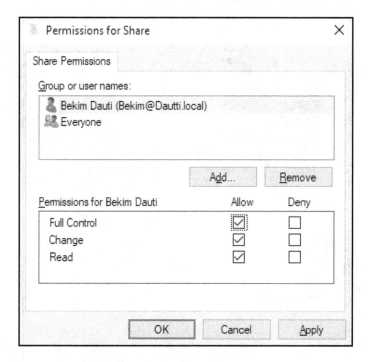

Figure 6.28: Share permissions in Windows Server 2019

Another perspective on user rights has to do with their assignment through the **Local Group Policy Editor** (gpedit.msc), Local Security Policy, or Default Domain Policy, by navigating to the Computer Configuration\Windows Settings\Security Settings\Policies\User Rights Assignment path. If the server is a domain member, then you will notice that some policies are already configured (see Figure 6.29):

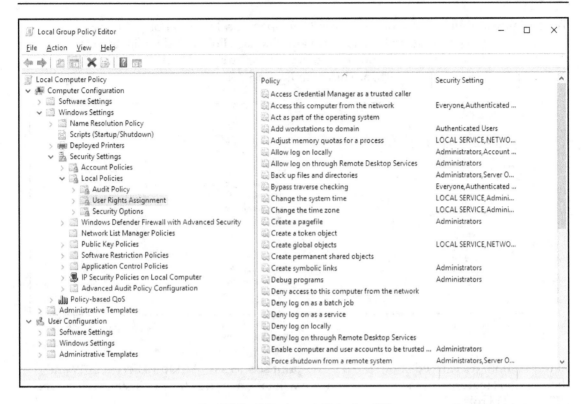

Figure 6.29: User Rights assignment in Windows Server 2019

In conclusion, from what we have learned so far in this section, there is a clear difference between user rights and permissions. While user rights have to do with user accounts, the permissions have to do with objects (that is, files and folders).

# Understanding the auditing of file servers

Given the fact that a file server stores very important and sensitive data for an organization, then auditing is a very important activity in assessing management controls in an organization's IT infrastructure. For that reason, auditing the file server represents a necessary measure to keep track of who has done what and when with the data.

To configure auditing in Windows Server 2019, open Local Group Policy Editor (`gpedit.msc`), Local Security Policy, or Default Domain Policy and navigate to the `Computer Configuration\Windows Settings\Security Settings\Local Policies\Audit Policy` path, as shown in *Figure 6.30*:

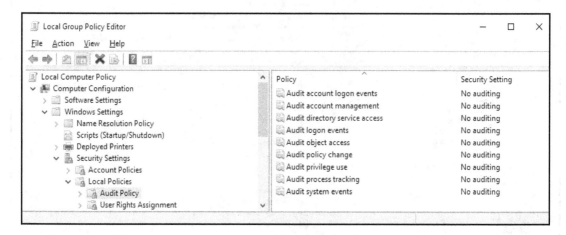

Figure 6.30: Auditing in Windows Server 2019

In this section, we learned about the file and print services in Windows Server 2019 and their various features. In the next section, we will take a look at how to install web server (IIS) and PDS roles.

# Chapter exercise – installing web server (IIS) and PDS roles

In this chapter exercise, you will learn how to do the following:

- How to install a web server (IIS) role
- How to install a PDS role

## Installing the web server (IIS) role

To install the web server (IIS) role in Windows Server 2019, complete the following steps:

1. Click the **Start** button and then, in the **Start** menu, click on **Server Manager**.
2. In the Server Manager window, click on the **Add roles and features** hyperlink.

3. Shortly, the **Add Roles and Features Wizard** will open, as shown in *Figure 6.31*:

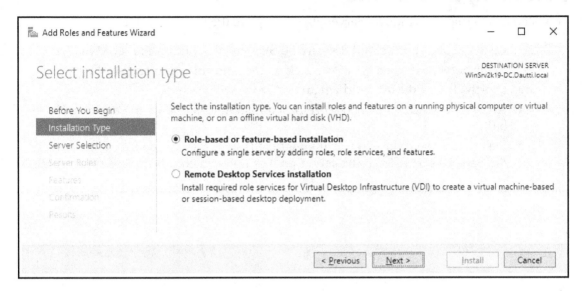

Figure 6.31: Add Roles and Features Wizard in Windows Server 2019

4. Accept the **Role-based or feature-based installation** option and click the **Next** button.
5. Ensure that the right server is highlighted from the server pool, then accept the **Select a server from the server pool** option and click **Next**.
6. From the list of the roles, select the **Web Server (IIS)** role.
7. Click the **Add Features** button when the **Add features that are required for Web Server (IIS)?** popup appears.
8. There is no feature required for adding the web server (IIS) role at this stage, so just click the **Next** button.
9. In the web server (IIS) definition and the things to note regarding web server (IIS) installation, click **Next** to proceed.
10. Either accept the web server (IIS) role services or customize them to your needs.
11. Confirm installation selections for the web server (IIS) role by clicking the **Install** button.
12. When installation progress reaches the end, click the **Close** button to close the *Add Roles and Features Wizard*.
13. A server restart is not required.

The web server (IIS) role will now get installed.

# Installing a PDS role

To install a PDS role in Windows Server 2019, complete the following steps:

1. Click the **Start** button and then, in the **Start** menu, click on **Server Manager**.
2. In the Server Manager window, click on the **Add roles and features** hyperlink.
3. Shortly, the **Add Roles and Features Wizard** will open.
4. Accept the **Role-based or feature-based installation** option and click the **Next** button.
5. Ensure that the right server is highlighted from the server pool, and then accept the **Select a server from the server pool** option and click **Next** (see *Figure 6.32*):

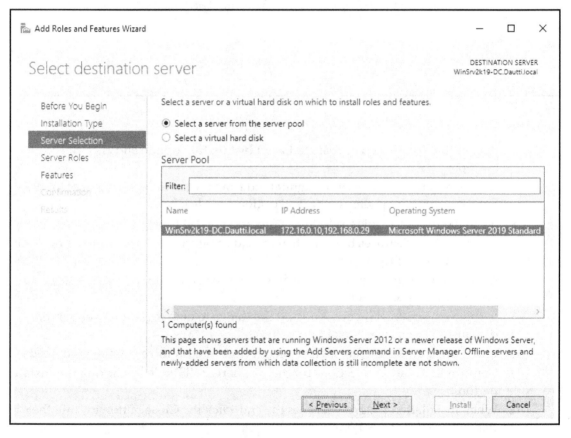

Figure 6.32: Accepting the defaults

6. From the list of the roles, select the **Print and Document Services** role.

7. Click the **Add Features** button when the **Add features that are required for Print and Document Services?** dialog pops up.
8. There is no feature required for adding PDS role at this stage, so just click the **Next** button.
9. In the PDS definition and the things to note regarding PDS installation, click **Next** to proceed.
10. Either accept the PDS role services or customize it to your needs.
11. Confirm the installation selections for the PDS role by clicking the **Install** button.
12. When installation progress reaches the end, click the **Close** button to close the **Add Roles and Features Wizard**.
13. A server restart is not required.

The PDS role will now get installed.

# Summary

In this chapter, you have learned about the Windows Server roles, role services, and features. In addition, you have learned about user rights, NTFS permissions, share permissions, and the auditing of file servers. Then, you got acquainted with some of the well-known application servers that are in use today. Likewise, you have learned about the mail server, database server, collaboration server, monitoring server, and threat management server.

Then, in the third part of this chapter, you became familiar with web services. Here, you got a better understanding of key web components such the web server (IIS), FTP, separate worker processes, sites, application ports, SSL, and digital certificates. Similarly, in the fourth part of this chapter, you have learned about the remote access services. There, Remote Assistance, RSAT, RDS, RDS Licensing, RDG, VPN, App-V, and multiple ports were mentioned. All that you have learned in this chapter will help you to understand what a role is and how it is added in Windows Server 2019. You have also learned about user rights, NTFS permission, and share permissions.

From all of the services mentioned in this chapter, alongside the theoretical aspect, you got acquainted with the steps of installing some of the services. In that way, web server (IIS) and PDS represent the chapter exercise of this chapter.

In the next chapter, you will learn about Group Policy in Windows Server 2019, which will help to add more controls to user and computer accounts.

# Questions

1. A server role is a primary task that a server should perform. (True | False)
2. _____ transfers files from computer to computer, computer to server, or vice versa both on a LAN and WAN.
3. Which of the following are NTFS permissions in Windows Server 2019? (Choose three)
   - Modify
   - Write
   - Change
   - Read
4. A web service is a communication between two devices based on the request/response methodology using the FTP protocol. (True | False)
5. _____ is any logical endpoint where applications from your computer communicate with other applications on other computers both on a LAN and WAN.
6. Which of the following protocols are utilized by mail servers? (Choose two)
   - File Transfer Protocol (FTP)
   - Hypertext Transfer Protocol (HTTP)
   - Simple Mail Transfer Protocol (SMTP)
   - Post Office Protocol (POP)
7. Remote Assistance is a feature that enables a helper to access the host's desktop remotely to assist with resolving issues. (True | False)
8. _____ is responsible for securing the communication channel between a website and a browser.
9. Which of the following ports is used by RDS?
   - 25
   - 110
   - 443
   - 3389
10. Web printing enables users to print files to network printers through Windows Explorer. (True | False)
11. _____ have to do with user access to shared folders and drives on the network.

12. Which of the following are share permissions? (Choose two)
    - Read
    - Change
    - Write
    - Modify
13. Discuss the Remote Access and RDS roles.
14. Discuss user rights, NTFS permissions, and share permissions.

# Further reading

- *IIS Web Server Overview*: https://docs.microsoft.com/en-us/iis/get-started/introduction-to-iis/iis-web-server-overview
- *DirectAccess*: https://docs.microsoft.com/en-us/windows-server/remote/remote-access/directaccess/directaccess
- *User Rights Assignment*: https://docs.microsoft.com/en-us/windows/security/threat-protection/security-policy-settings/user-rights-assignment

# Section 3: Configuring Windows Server 2019 3

The third section covers Group Policy (GP) and virtualization. Upon completion of this section, you will be able to configure GPOs and virtual machines. Also, you will get to know about storage technologies and be able to configure them.

This section comprises the following chapters:

- Chapter 7, *Group Policy in Windows Server 2019*
- Chapter 8, *Virtualization with Windows Server 2019*
- Chapter 9, *Storing Data in Windows Server 2019*

# 7
# Group Policy in Windows Server 2019

So far, you have learned how to set up Windows Server 2019, including installation, post-installation tasks, and adding roles and features. In this chapter, you will learn about **Group Policy** (**GP**) in Windows Server 2019, which is advanced configuration that limits the user's ability to change settings. Then, you will get to know how GP is managed, both on a local server and on a domain controller. In addition, you will learn about **Group Policy Object** (**GPO**) configuration values, and how GPOs are processed.

In the second part of this chapter, you will get acquainted with the Local Group Policy Editor, which enables you to manage GPOs on a local server. At the same time, you will learn how to update local GPOs. Additionally, you will get a better understanding of computer and user configurations. The chapter concludes with the chapter exercise providing a few examples of GPOs for system admins.

The following topics will be covered in this chapter:

- Understanding GP
- Types of GP editors
- Chapter exercise—examples of GPOs for system admins

## Technical requirements

In order to complete the exercises in this chapter, you will need the following equipment:

- A PC with Windows 10 Pro, at least 16 GB of RAM, 1 TB of HDD, and access to the internet
- A virtual machine with Windows Server 2019 Standard (Desktop Experience), at least 4 GB of RAM, 100 GB of HDD, and access to the internet

# Understanding GP

You may need to configure the home page of a company's website to open when the browser is launched on the organization's computers, deny access to all removable media drives on the organization's computers, or block Microsoft accounts from being used on the organization's Windows 10 computers. All of these things and many other advanced configurations can be accomplished via GP in a Windows Server domain-based network without the need to use third-party applications. It enables you to set up advanced configurations that will limit the user's ability to change settings both on local computers and on domain-joined computers.

That being said, GP is a Windows Server 2019 feature that applies restrictions at the user and computer level, whereas GPOs are administrative templates that enable system administrators to configure what users can and cannot do on computers, peripheral devices, and network applications across the organization's network. By default, the configured GPOs are stored in the C:\Windows\SYSVOL\sysvol\<domain>\Policies path in the domain controller, as shown in *Figure 7.1*:

Figure 7.1: GPOs' default location in Windows Server 2019

Now that we have a fair understanding of GPs and GPOs we will learn to manage them.

# Managing GPOs

**Group Policy Management** (**GPM**), as shown in *Figure 7.2*, is a system administrator's favorite tool for managing GPOs. GPM is a console in the domain controller that enables configuring and deploying GPOs across the organization. It is a one-stop place where system admins can configure a variety of Windows Server settings for every user and computer on the domain-based network. The GPM console consists mainly of the **Forest pane** and the **GPOs pane**. The Forest pane displays the hierarchical structure of the domain, whereas the GPOs pane contains the **Status**, **Linked Group Policy Objects**, **Group Policy inheritance**, and **Delegation** tabs.

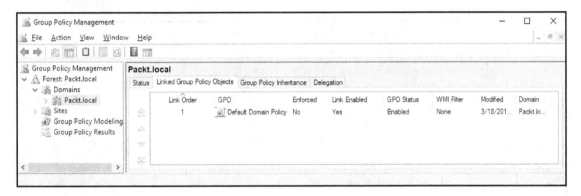

Figure 7.2: The GPM console in the domain controller

The GPM console in Windows Server 2019 can be accessed in several ways. We will study more about accessing GPM consoles in the following sections.

# Accessing the GPM console from the Administrative Tools

To access the GPM console from the **Administrative Tools** menu in the Start menu, complete the following steps:

1. Click the Start button.
2. From the Start menu, select **Windows Administrative Tools**.
3. In the **Administrative Tools** window, select **Group Policy Management**, as shown in *Figure 7.3*:

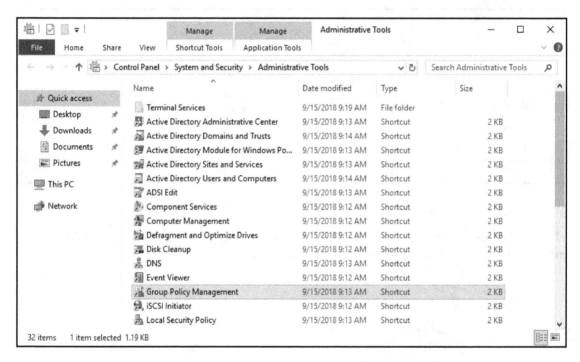

Figure 7.3: Accessing the GPM console from Windows Administrative Tools

Besides access the GPM console from the **Administrative Tools** menu in the Start menu, we can also access it from the Run dialogue box as follows.

# Accessing the GPM console from the Run dialog box

To access the GPM console from the **Run** dialog box, complete the following steps:

1. Press the Windows key + *R* to open the **Run** dialog box.
2. In the **Run** dialog box, enter gpmc.msc, as in *Figure 7.4*, and press **OK**:

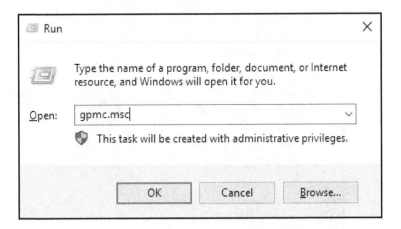

Figure 7.4: Accessing the GPM console from the Run dialog box

Finally, let's learn how to access the GPM console from the **Server Manager** menu.

# Accessing the GPM console from the Server Manager

To access the GPM console from the **Server Manager** menu in the Start menu, complete the following steps:

1. Click the Start button.
2. From the Start menu, select **Server Manager**.

3. In the **Server Manager** window, click **Tools** and select **Group Policy Management** from the menu (see *Figure 7.5*):

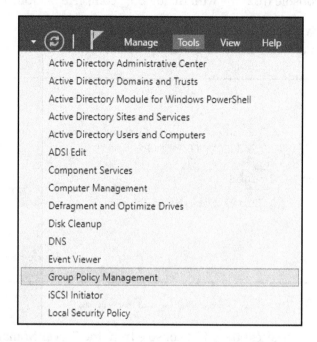

Figure 7.5: Accessing the GPM console from the Server Manager

Moving forward, let's understand the various GPO configuration values.

# GPO configuration values

As mentioned earlier, GPOs are administrative templates that are configured by system administrators. As such, they can have configuration values that determine the applicability of the policy, equivalent to registry keys in the Registry Editor. Hence, GPO settings can be configured to certain values, which affect both users and computers. Thus, GPO settings contain the following three configurable values, as shown in *Figure 7.6*:

- **Not configured**: The default setting for GPOs, meaning that the registry value has not been manipulated.
- **Enabled**: A configured setting that indicates that a GPO is enabled, meaning that the registry value has been set to 0x1.
- **Disabled**: A configured setting that indicates that a GPO is disabled, meaning that the registry value has been set to 0x0:

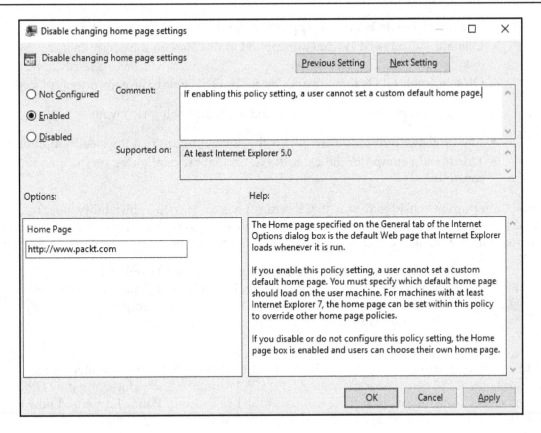

Figure 7.6: GPO settings configuration values

Once you have configured GPOs then comes their deployment. Therefore, it is good to know what is the order of GPOs processing. So let us understand how GPO processing takes place.

# Processing GPOs

Since GPOs are applied at the user and computer level, this means that these settings can be enforced and as such users cannot change them. Hence, GPOs can be used to configure settings on a local computer via the Local Group Policy Editor, and settings on a domain controller via the GPM console. For that reason, **GPO processing** takes place in the following order:

1. **Local** indicates GPOs that are applied to the computer's local policy for each user.

2. **Site** indicates GPOs that are applied to the site where the computer belongs.
3. **Domain** indicates GPOs that are applied to the domain the computer is a member of.
4. **OUs** indicates GPOs that are applied to the OUs where the computer is placed.

From a computing perspective, GPOs are applied in the following two ways:

- **The local computer** indicates GPOs that are configured on the local computer.
- **The domain computer** indicates the GPOs that are configured on the domain controller.

Another important consideration with GP settings has to do with applicability. Bear in mind that GPOs assigned to user accounts are applied when the user logs on to a computer, whereas GPOs assigned to computer accounts are applied when the computer is turned on.

 Microsoft has developed new GPs for Windows 10 version 1809 and Windows Server 2019. These new policy settings are included in the Administrative template of both computer and user configurations. They can be downloaded from this URL: `https://www.microsoft.com/en-us/ download/details.aspx?id=57464`.

In this section, you got acquainted with the Windows Server 2019 Group Policy feature, including the GPM console for managing GPs, GPO configuration values, and how GPOs are processed. The following section will cover the Local Group Policy Editor and how to update local GPOs, as well as configuration policies such as user configuration and computer configurations.

# Types of GP editors

In addition to the Group Policy Management Editor, which is used in the domain controller, there is also the Local Group Policy Editor, another **Microsoft Management Console** (**MMC**) snap-in that enables you to manage GPO settings on a local computer. With the Local Group Policy Editor, a system admin can configure local GPOs by enabling or disabling configurable settings in Local Group Policy at the user and computer level. Unlike the GPM console, which becomes available once you have installed **Active Directory Domain Services** (**AD DS**) on the server and set up a domain controller, by default, the Local Group Policy Editor can be found in Windows Server 2019.

# Local Group Policy Editor

While the **Group Policy Management** console is used to deploy GPOs in domain environments, **Local Group Policy Editor** is used to deploy GPOs on local servers that are not yet domain members.

To access the Local Group Policy Editor in Windows Server 2019, complete the following steps:

1. Press the Windows key + R to open the **Run** dialog box.
2. In the **Run** dialog box, enter gpedit.msc and press **OK**.
3. The **Local Group Policy Editor** opens up, as shown in *Figure 7.7*:

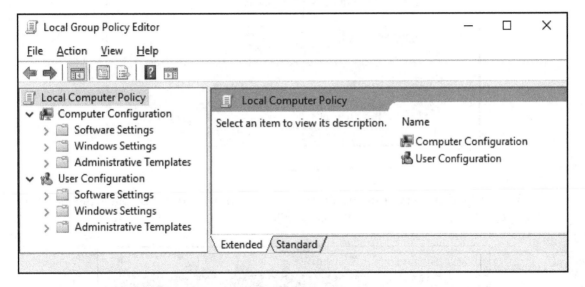

Figure 7.7: The Local Group Policy Editor in Windows Server 2019

Besides learning to access the GPO, we must also learn how to update local GPOs. Let us learn how to do this next.

# Updating local GPOs

Once you have completed the configuration of the GPOs, you can enforce the GPOs on your local server as follows:

1. Press the Windows key + *R* to open the **Run** dialog box.
2. In the **Run** dialog box, enter `gpupdate /force`, as in *Figure 7.8*, and press **OK**:

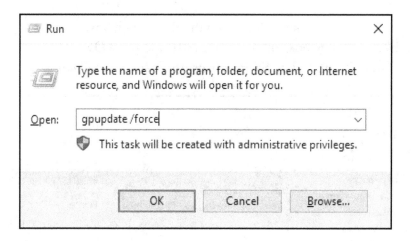

Figure 7.8: Running the gpupdate /force command via the Run dialog box

3. Shortly after, the Command Prompt window opens up and displays the message `Updating policy...` (see *Figure 7.9*):

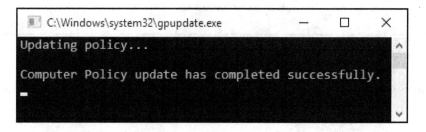

Figure 7.9: The process of deploying the policy

4. Once the computer policy update completes, the Command Prompt window closes automatically.

Typing `gpedit.msc` also works in Cortana/search box (Start menu), Windows PowerShell, and Command Prompt (`cmd.exe`). Also, it is recommended that we should not use the `gpupdate/force` command when updating GPOs. Instead, we need to use just the `gpupdate` command, because the `gpupdate/force` command causes administrative overhead on clients and servers, and causes all GPOs to be reprocessed.

# Configuration policies

As you know, there are two types of configuration policies that implement GPOs. They are user configuration and computer configuration policies that you will get acquainted with in detail in the following sections.

# Computer configuration policies

As explained in the *Processing GPOs* section earlier in this chapter, GPOs assigned to the computer level are applied when computers are turned on. **Computer configuration policies** are bound to computers regardless of the user that is logged on to the computer. That applies to both local computers and domain-joined computers.

To set up GPOs at the computer level, complete the following steps:

1. Press the Windows key + *R* to open the **Run** dialog box.
2. In the **Run** dialog box, enter `gpedit.msc` and press **OK**.
3. In the Forest pane of the GPM console, right-click the domain and select **Create a GPO in this domain, and Link it here...**, as in *Figure 7.10*:

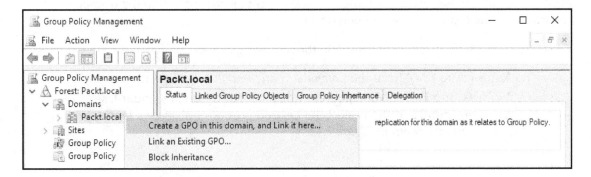

Figure 7.10: Creating a GPO in the domain controller

4. In the **New GPO** window, enter the name for the new GPO, and then click **OK**.
5. In the GPOs pane, select the **Linked Group Policy Objects** tab.
6. Right-click the newly created GPO and select **Edit** from the context menu.
7. In the **Group Policy Management Editor**, expand **Policies** under **Computer Configuration**, and then select the desired computer administrative template to configure (see *Figure 7.11*):

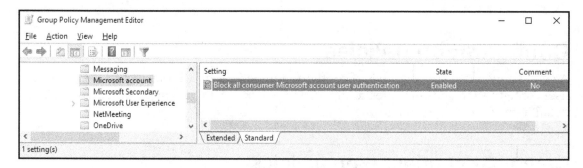

Figure 7.11: Setting up the computer configuration policies

8. Close the **Group Policy Management Editor**.
9. In the GPOs pane, right-click the recently created GPO and select **Enforced**.
10. In the **Group Policy Management** dialog box, click **OK**.

Now let's take a look at user configuration policies.

## User configuration policies

Unlike computer configuration policies, user configuration policies represent the GPOs that are assigned at the user level, meaning that these settings are applied to the user account regardless of the computer they logged on to.

To set up GPOs at the user level, complete the following steps:

1. Repeat *steps 1 to 6* from the *Computer configuration policies* section.
2. In the **Group Policy Management Editor**, expand **Policies** under **User Configuration**, and then select the desired user administrative template to configure, as shown in *Figure 7.12*:

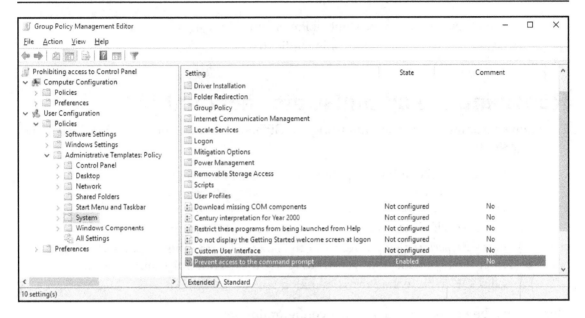

Figure 7.12: Setting up the user configuration policies

3. Close the **Group Policy Management Editor**.
4. In the GPOs pane, right-click the recently created GPO and select **Enforced**.
5. In the **Group Policy Management** dialog box, click **OK**.

In this section, you got acquainted with the Local Group Policy Editor as another way of managing GPOs. Also, you had the opportunity to get to know the different configuration policies. The following section will provide several examples of GPOs for the system administrator.

# Chapter exercise – examples of GPOs for system admins

In this chapter exercise, you will get acquainted with some GPOs that may be of interest to system admins:

- Renaming the administrator account
- Disabling the guest account
- Blocking Microsoft accounts

- Prohibiting access to the Control Panel and PC settings
- Denying access to all removable media drives

# Renaming the administrator account

To rename the administrator account using the GPO in Windows Server 2019, complete the following steps:

1. Navigate to the following path to reach the GPO: `Computer Configuration\Policies\Windows Settings\SecuritySettings\Local Policies\Security Options`
2. Double click at **Accounts: Rename administrator account**
3. In the *Properties* dialog box, check the box for **Define this policy setting**, and enter the new name that you want to use for the administrator account
4. Click **OK** to close the *Properties* dialog box

This policy is being applied to computer configuration settings.

Securing the network services in particular, and the whole network of the organization in general, are among the highest priorities. For that reason, it is recommended to rename the administrator account in Windows Server 2019 to avoid the its misuse. So let us rename the guest account using GPO.

# Renaming the guest account

To rename the guest account using the GPO in Windows Server 2019, complete the following steps:

1. Navigate to the following path to reach the GPO: `Computer Configuration\Policies\Windows Settings\SecuritySettings\Local Policies\Security Options`
2. Double click at **Accounts: Rename guest account**
3. In the *Properties* dialog box, check the box for **Define this policy setting**, and enter the new name that you want to use for the guest account
4. Click **OK** to close the *Properties* dialog box

This policy is being applied to computer configuration settings. For security reasons, to minimize the chance of misusing the guest account, you may want to change the name of the guest account. So let us block the Microsoft account using the GPO.

# Blocking the Microsoft accounts

To block the Microsoft accounts using the GPO in Windows Server 2019, complete the following steps:

1. Navigate to the following path to reach the GPO: `Computer Configuration\Policies\Windows Settings\SecuritySettings\Local Policies\Security Options`
2. Double click at **Accounts: Block Microsoft accounts**
3. In the *Properties* dialog box, check the box for **Define this policy setting**, and then select **Users can't add or log on with Microsoft accounts** from the drop-down combo list
4. Click **OK** to close the *Properties* dialog box

This policy is being applied to user configuration settings.

For security reasons, to prevent users from adding and login into organization's computers with their Microsoft accounts, system administrator have the option of blocking the usage of Microsoft accounts. So let us deny access to the Control Panel and PC settings using the GPO.

# Prohibiting access to the Control Panel and PC settings

To prohibit access to the Control Panel and PC settings using the GPO in Windows Server 2019, complete the following steps:

1. Navigate to the following path to reach the GPO: `User Configuration\Policies\AdministrativeTemplates\Control Panel`
2. Double click at **Prohibit access to the Control Panel and PC settings**
3. In the dialog box, select the **Enable** option, and then click **OK** to close the dialog box

This policy is being applied to users configuration settings.

If you wish that users in your organization's network would not be able to make changes to their computers, then you can deny their access to the Control Panel and PC settings. So let us learn to deny access to all removable media drives.

# Denying access to all removable storage classes

To deny access to all removable storage classes using the GPO in Windows Server 2019, complete the following steps:

1. Navigate the following path to reach the GPO: `User Configuration\Policies\AdministrativeTemplates\System\Removable Storage Access`
2. Double click at **All the removable storage classes: Deny all access**
3. In the dialog box, select the **Enable** option, and then click **OK** to close the dialog box

This policy is being applied to users configuration settings.

System administrators have the ability to completely restrict the use of removable storage by enabling Prohibiting access to the Control Panel and PC settings. These were examples of configuring GPOs from many that are supported by Windows Server 2019. Although only a few, these GPOs are important as they highlight some of the most commonly used GPOs in a production environment. With this we have come to an end of the chapter exercise.

# Summary

In this chapter, you have learned about GP, through which you can limit the user's ability to change the settings on a server.

In the *Understanding GP* section, you got acquainted with the Windows Server 2019 Group Policy feature, including the GPM console for managing GPs, GPO configuration values, and how GPOs are processed. Furthermore, in the *Types of GP editors* section you got acquainted with the Local Group Policy Editor as another way of managing GPOs. Also, you had the opportunity to get to know the different configuration policies. Additionally, you learned how to update GPOs on a local server and domain controller. Also, you got a better understanding of computer and user configurations.

With the skills you have acquired from this chapter, you will be able to deploy GPOs locally and in the domain. The chapter concluded with chapter exercises that contained several examples of GPOs for system admins.

In the following chapter, you will learn about virtualization in Windows Server 2019.

# Questions

1. GPOs are processed in the following order: Local, Site, Domain, **Organizational Units (OUs)**. (True | False)
2. The _____ are administrative templates that enable system administrators to configure what users can and cannot do on computers, peripheral devices, and network applications across the organization's network.
3. Which of the following represent GPO configuration values? Choose two:
     1. Enabled
     2. Disabled
     3. Allow
     4. Deny

4. The GPM is a console in the domain controller that enables configuring and deploying GPOs across an organization. (True | False)
5. The _____ displays the hierarchical structure of the domain, whereas the _____ contains the status, linked GPOs, GP inheritance, and delegation tabs.
6. Which of the following commands is used to update GPOs?
     1. gpupdate /enforce
     2. gpupdate /setup
     3. gpupdate /run
     4. gpupdate /force
7. **Not configured** is the default setting for GPOs, meaning that the registry value has not been manipulated. (True | False)
8. The _____ is another Microsoft Management Console (MMC) snap-in that enables you to manage GPO settings on a local computer.
9. GPOs assigned to the computer level are applied when computers are:
     • Turned on
     • Turned off
     • Hibernate mode
     • Sleep mode

# Further reading

- *Group Policy Best Practices*: https://www.netwrix.com/group_policy_best_practices.html
- *Windows Server: How to Create and Link a Group Policy Object Using the Group Policy Management Console*: https://www.dell.com/support/article/rs/ru/rsdhs1/sln283093/windows-server-how-to-create-and-link-a-group-policy-object-using-the-group-policy-management-console?lang=en
- *Group Policy Settings for WSUS*: https://www.itprotoday.com/windows-78/group-policy-settings-wsus

# 8
# Virtualization with Windows Server 2019

You have probably heard about cloud services, but you have probably not yet visualized what a cloud infrastructure looks like. Regardless, you should be aware that it is a complex infrastructure that is *completely* virtualized. In a data center that provides cloud services, a large number of servers are grouped to form a cluster. On top of that cluster, there are hundreds or thousands of **virtual machines** (**VMs**) running to make up the cloud's infrastructure.

So, in this chapter, you will get to know the virtualization concept, as well as become familiar with the Hyper-V software, which enables the virtualization of Windows-based servers. In addition, you will learn about the steps it takes to add the Hyper-V role to the server, get to know the Hyper-V Manager, and learn to create VMs. That way, you will be able to understand what virtualization is, how you can enable the Hyper-V role, and how to create VMs. This chapter concludes with an exercise where you will learn how to install the Hyper-V role on Windows Server 2019.

The following topics will be covered in this chapter:

- Understanding server virtualization
- Getting to know Hyper-V Manager
- Chapter exercise—installing the Hyper-V role on Windows Server 2019

# Technical requirements

In order to complete the lab for this chapter, you will need the following equipment:

- A PC with Windows Server 2019 Standard, at least 8 GB of RAM, 500 GB of HDD, and access to the internet

# Understanding server virtualization

From a technical point of view, virtualization technology should be understood as a way of creating a virtual server. In addition, virtualization also enables you to create storage devices and network resources. So, instead of having ten physical servers, you can have one physical server and nine VMs running on it. Windows Server 2019 comes equipped with a Hyper-V feature that enables virtualization. As a descendant of Windows Virtual PC, Microsoft's Hyper-V was introduced in Windows Server 2008. Since then, even though it is younger than its competition, Hyper-V has managed to attract the interest of system administrators, thereby positioning itself strongly in second place in terms of virtualization platform market share—right behind Amazon Web Services. In specific terms, Hyper-V provides the services that can be used to create and manage VMs, along with their resources.

We will now learn about various aspects of server virtualization, beginning with virtualization modes.

# Understanding virtualization modes

Generally, the following two virtualized modes are the most commonly used in today's virtualized environments:

- **Fully virtualized mode**: This enables an isolated and secure execution of one or more OSes in a single physical server where guest OSes use the host's OS resources (see *Figure 8.1*):

Figure 8.1: Windows Server 2019 running in an isolated and secure virtual environment

- **Paravirtualized mode**: This can be understood as a computer inside a computer that has an installed OS that does not simulate the hardware. Rather, it offers a special **application program interface** (**API**) so that we can modify the guest OS.

 A host OS is the OS on a physical server, whereas a guest OS is the OS on a VM. In my case, I am running Windows 10 Pro on a laptop as the host OS, and I am running Windows Server 2019 Standard as the guest OS.

Now, let's understand what we mean by Hyper-V architecture.

# Understanding Hyper-V architecture

The Hyper-V architecture is based on a hierarchical format where the first level represents the hypervisor as the main element that constitutes the Hyper-V virtual platform. Thus, a hypervisor is accommodated at the root and has direct access to hardware devices. The root component then creates branch OSes that represent isolated executable environments. Specifically, the branched OS represents a logical unit of isolation that has no access to hardware devices. Then, on these parts, it will be possible to run guest OSes. Components such as the **virtualization service provider** (**VSP**) and **virtualization service consumer** (**VSC**), through logical channels for communication known as the **virtual machine bus** (**VMBus**), enable communication between the root portion and the branch OSes (see *Figure 8.2*):

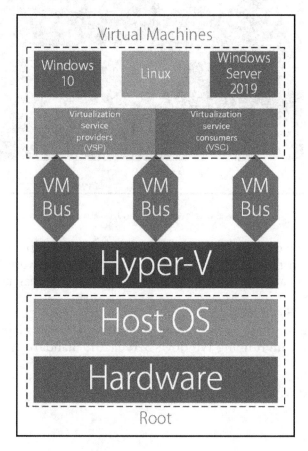

Figure 8.2: Hyper-V architecture

By correlating the *Understanding virtualization modes* and *Understanding Hyper-V architecture* sections, we understand that *Figure 8.2* represents an example of a fully virtualized mode. Now that you are familiar with the architecture of Hyper-V, it would be great to become familiar with Hyper-V installation requirements.

# Hyper-V installation requirements

First things first: to accommodate the hypervisor, the server must support virtualization. To fulfill this requirement, it must be based on an Intel or AMD processor with Intel **Virtualization Technology** (**VT**) or AMD Virtualization enabled.

Now, let's understand what we mean by nested virtualization.

# Understanding nested virtualization

Nested virtualization refers to a VM that runs inside another **VM**. In other words, it is the ability of the server's hardware to run the Hyper-V inside a VM, which itself runs on a Hyper-V too. The concept of a VM inside a VM allows us to effectively nest one Hyper-V within another.

To set up nested virtualization in Windows Server 2019 using Windows PowerShell, complete the following steps:

1. Right-click the Start button, and then select **Windows PowerShell (Administrator)** from the admin's menu.
2. In the Windows PowerShell window, run the following two commands:

```
Set-VMProcessor -VMName <VMname> -ExposeVirtualizationExtensions
$true
Get-VMNetworkAdapter -VMName <VMname> | Set-VMNetworkAdapter -
MacAddressSpoofing On
```

3. Then, proceed with the installation of the Hyper-V (refer to the *Chapter exercise – installing Hyper-V on Windows Server 2019* section later on in this chapter).

In this section, we have learned about server virtualization concepts such as virtualization modes, Hyper-V architecture, Hyper-V installation requirements, and nested virtualization. In the next section, we will learn about Hyper-V Manager.

# Getting to know Hyper-V Manager

Hyper-V Manager is an administrative tool that is used to manage VMs. Some of the operations that can be carried out with Hyper-V Manager are as follows:

- Creating, importing, and deleting VMs
- Creating a virtual switch
- Creating the SAN manager
- Inspecting and editing disks
- Stopping services

The Hyper-V Manager user interface consists of a server pane, a VM pane, a checkpoint pane, selected VM details, and an **Actions** pane (see *Figure 8.3*):

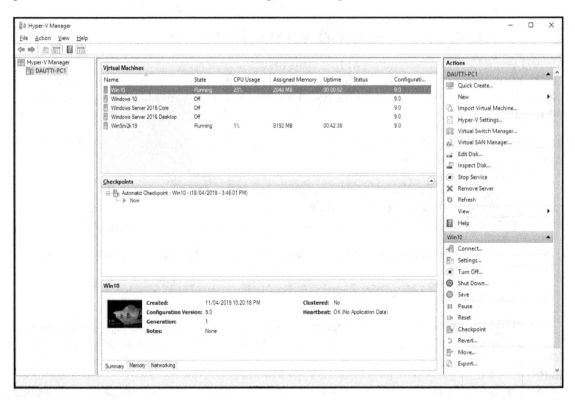

Figure 8.3: The Hyper-V Manager in Windows Server 2019

Now, let's learn how to configure Hyper-V settings.

# Configuration settings in Hyper-V

Once you install the Hyper-V role in the server, it is recommended that you spend a little time getting to know the Hyper-V settings. You can set up the Hyper-V settings by clicking on **Hyper-V Settings...** in the **Actions** pane. The settings (see *Figure 8.4*) that you can establish include the following:

- **Virtual hard disks (VHD)**: This specifies the location on your server for storing virtual hard disk files.
- **VMs**: This specifies the location on your server for storing VM configuration files.
- **Physical GPUs**: This specifies the **graphical processing unit (GPU)** to be used by VMs.
- **NUMA spanning**: This provides VMs with additional computing resources, thereby allowing you to run more VMs at the same time.
- **Storage migrations**: This specifies how many storage migrations can be performed at the same time on your server.

- **Enhanced session mode policy**: This allows the redirection of local devices and resources from servers running a **Virtual Machine Connection** (**VMConnect**):

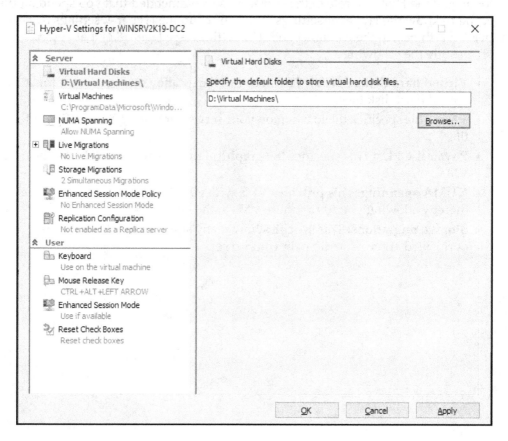

Figure 8.4: Hyper-V Settings in Windows Server 2019

Now that you are familiar with the configuration settings of Hyper-V, the next step is to find out how to create and configure VHDs.

# Creating and configuring VHDs

To create a VHD in Windows Server 2019 using Hyper-V Manager, complete the following steps:

1. Click the Start button, and then, in the Start menu, click **Windows Administrative Tools**.

2. In the **Windows Administrative Tools** window, click the **Hyper-V Manager** hyperlink.

3. In the **Hyper-V Manager** window, click **New**, and then click **Hard Disk...** from the **Actions** pane, as shown in *Figure 8.5*:

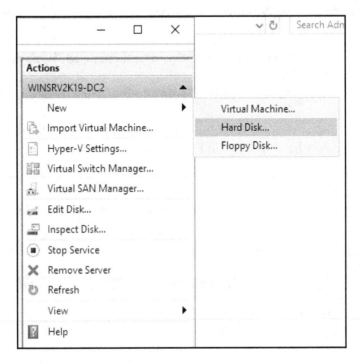

Figure 8.5: Creating a virtual hard disk

4. Click **Next** in the **Before You Begin** option of the **New Virtual Hard Disk Wizard**.

5. Select the format that you want to use for the virtual hard disk, and then click **Next**.

6. Select the type of virtual hard disk that you want to create, and then click **Next**.

7. Specify the name and location of the virtual hard disk file, and then click **Next**.

8. Create a blank virtual hard disk or copy the contents of an existing physical disk, and then click **Next**.

9. Click **Finish** to create the virtual hard disk and close the **New Virtual Hard Disk Wizard**.

Now, let's learn how to manage the virtual memory of VMs.

# Managing a VMs' virtual memory

Through Hyper-V Manager, you have the option to manage the virtual memory of VMs. Therefore, VMs need to be turned off prior to establishing the memory settings.

To manage virtual memory in Windows Server 2019 using Hyper-V Manager, complete the following steps:

1. Click the Start button, and then, in the Start menu, click **Windows Administrative Tools**.
2. In the **Windows Administrative Tools** window, click the **Hyper-V Manager** hyperlink.
3. In the **Hyper-V Manager** window, right-click any of the VMs with an off state, and then select **Settings...**, as in *Figure 8.6*:

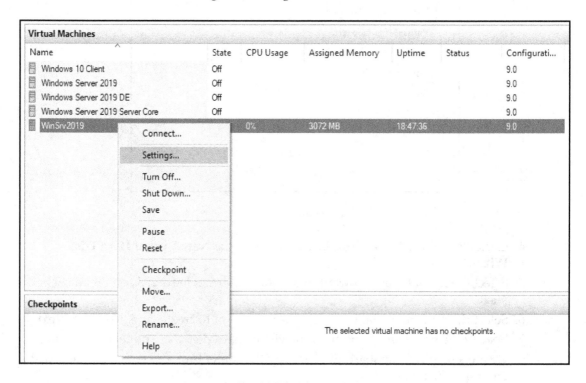

Figure 8.6: VM settings in Hyper-V

4. In the left-hand pane, under **Hardware**, click **Memory**.
5. You have the option to set a fixed or dynamic amount of memory (see *Figure 8.7*):
   - To set a fixed amount of memory, enter the amount in MB within the **RAM:** text box.
   - To set a dynamic amount of memory, tick the **Enable Dynamic Memory** checkbox, and then set the amount of memory for **Minimum RAM** and **Maximum RAM**:

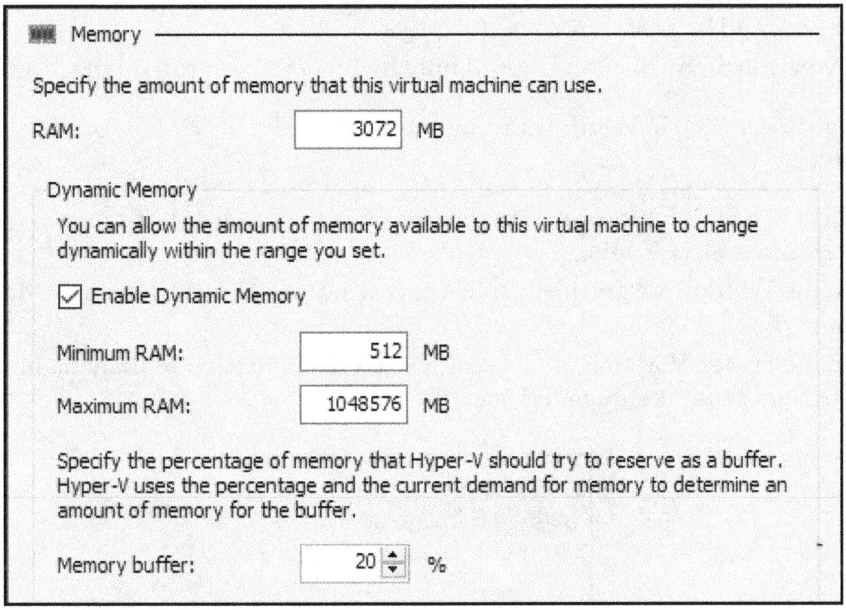

Figure 8.7: Managing virtual memory in Hyper-V

6. Click **OK** to close the **VM Settings** window.

Now, let's learn how to set up virtual networks.

# Setting up virtual networks

Similar to a physical network in which a physical switch is required to connect hosts, even in the virtual network, a virtual switch is required to connect VMs. There are three types of virtual switches available in Hyper-V:

- **External switch**: This binds the physical network adapter so that the VMs can access the physical network.
- **Internal switch**: This can only be used by the VMs that run on the physical server, and between VMs and the physical server.
- **Private switch**: This can be used only by the VMs that run on the physical server.

To create a virtual switch in Windows Server 2019 using Hyper-V Manager, complete the following steps:

1. Click the Start button, and then, in the Start menu, click **Windows Administrative Tools**.
2. In the **Windows Administrative Tools** window, click the **Hyper-V Manager** hyperlink.
3. In the **Hyper-V Manager** window, click **Virtual Switch Manager...** in the **Actions** pane, as shown in *Figure 8.8*:

Figure 8.8: Creating a virtual switch

4. Select the type of virtual switch that you want to create, and then click **Create Virtual Switch**:
    1. Enter the name for the new virtual switch (see *Figure 8.9*).
    2. Enter notes for the new virtual switch.
    3. Select the connection type that you want the virtual switch to connect to.
    4. Enable virtual LAN identification:

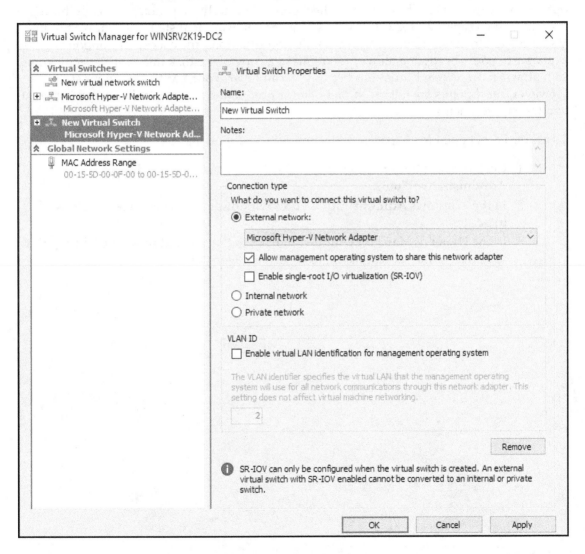

Figure 8.9: Virtual switch properties

5. Click **OK** to close the **Virtual Switch Manager** window.

Now, let's understand what we mean by checkpoints.

# Understanding checkpoints

In order to facilitate the administration of virtual environments, Hyper-V offers a variety of options and capabilities. These include checkpoints (formerly snapshots). Checkpoints are also called the **Hyper-V's restore point**. Whenever you want to install a new app on your VM and want to avoid unwanted post-installation situations, the checkpoint option is available to you. This option allows you to make a copy of the disk image at a specific time so that, when unexpected situations occur, you can revert your VM to a previous state. However, checkpoints are not recommended for production use, and only for development and test environments.

To create a checkpoint for a specific VM, complete the following steps:

1. Click the Start button, and then, in the Start menu, click **Windows Administrative Tools**.
2. In the **Windows Administrative Tools** window, click the **Hyper-V Manager** hyperlink.
3. In the **Hyper-V Manager** window, right-click the VM and select the **Checkpoint** option from the context menu, as shown in *Figure 8.10*:

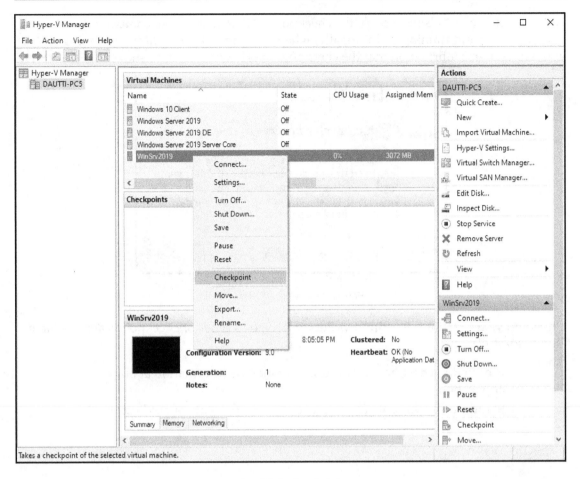

Figure 8.10: Creating a checkpoint

4. Shortly, you will notice that the checkpoint has been created within the **Checkpoints** section.

Note that, if your VM is turned off, the checkpoint will take less time compared to when your VM is up and running. Additionally, when creating a checkpoint for a running VM, you will receive confirmation that the checkpoint has been created, as shown in *Figure 8.11*:

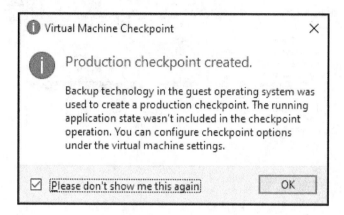

Figure 8.11: Checkpoint creation confirmation

Unlike previous versions, in Windows Server 2019, two types of checkpoints are available (see *Figure 8.12*):

- **Production checkpoint**: This does not include information about running applications.
- **Standard checkpoint**: This captures the current state of applications:

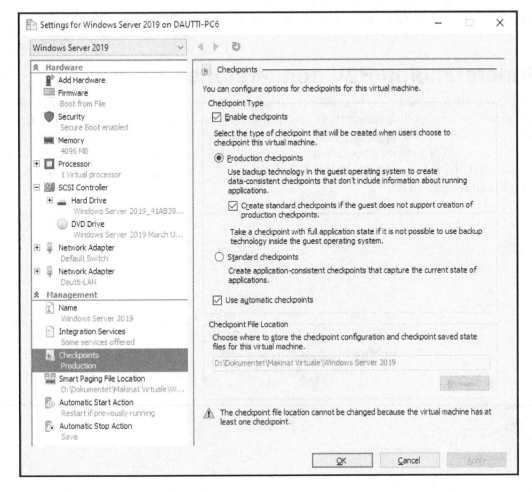

Figure 8.12: Checkpoint types

Now, let's understand what is meant by VHD and VHDX formats.

# Understanding VHD and VHDX formats

When Hyper-V was introduced in Windows Server 2008, it supported the VHD format with a disk storage capacity of up to 2 TB. Due to this, VHD became the *native disk storage* of Hyper-V. But with the introduction of Windows Server 2012, Microsoft introduced another new Hyper-V feature – VHDX format – with a disk storage capacity of up to 64 TB. Just like that, VHDX replaced VHD by making the latter become a **legacy disk storage** format that is still being supported by Hyper-V on Windows Server 2019.

Now, let's understand what we mean by **physical to virtual (P2V)** conversions.

# Understanding P2V conversions

Nowadays, virtualization has become an important network service driver and, because of that, organizations are migrating their physical servers to virtual servers (P2V) for reasons such as cost, ease of management, and future expansion. Thus, knowing that VMs are using VHDs, Microsoft engineers have developed the `Disk2vhd` app (see *Figure 8.13*) to convert a physical disk drive into a VHD. Due to this, with Hyper-V Manager, you can create a VM using the converted VHD:

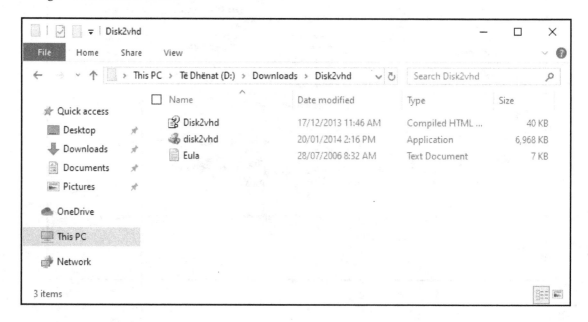

Figure 8.13: The Disk2vhd app facilitates the conversion of a physical disk drive into a VHD

 You can download the Disk2Vhd app from `https://docs.microsoft.com/en-us/sysinternals/downloads/disk2vhd` to run the conversion of P2V.

Now, let's understand what we mean by **virtual to physical (V2P)** conversions.

# Understanding V2P conversions

Despite the reasons we may have for V2P conversion, it is good to remind ourselves that, because of the technological era that we live in, the trend is P2V conversion. That being said, hypervisor manufacturers, including Microsoft, will not encourage you to conduct V2P conversion. I guess that might be the reason why hypervisor manufacturers are now offering tools for P2V conversion. However, you might find adequate tools for V2P conversion from hardware vendors. Another option for V2P conversion would be a migration. In this instance, you would want to install Windows Server 2019 on a physical server, and then migrate settings and applications from a virtual server to a physical server.

 You can download the EZ Gig IV cloning software from `https://www.apricorn.com/upgrades/ezgig` to perform the V2P conversion. It works in three simple steps: select your source drive, select your destination drive, and press the **Start Clone** button.

Now, let's learn how to configure VM settings.

# Configuring VM settings

To set up VM settings, right-click the desired VM and select **Settings** from the context menu. Among the VM settings (see *Figure 8.14*) that you can set are the following:

- **Add Hardware**: This enables devices to be added to your VM.
- **BIOS**: This enables the boot order to be set.
- **Security**: This enables state and VM migration traffic to be encrypted.
- **Memory**: This enables the VM memory to be specified.
- **Processor**: This enables the number of virtual processors to be set up.
- **IDE Controller 0**: This enables hard drives and CD/DVD drives to be added to the first IDE controller.
- **IDE Controller 1**: This enables hard drives and CD/DVD drives to be added to the second IDE controller.
- **SCSI Controller**: This enables hard drives to be added to/removed from an SCSI controller.
- **Network Adapter**: This enables the configuration of the network adapter to be specified.
- **COM 1**: This enables the first virtual COM port to be configured.
- **COM 2**: This enables the second virtual COM port to be configured.

- **Diskette Drive**: This enables the virtual floppy disk file to be specified:

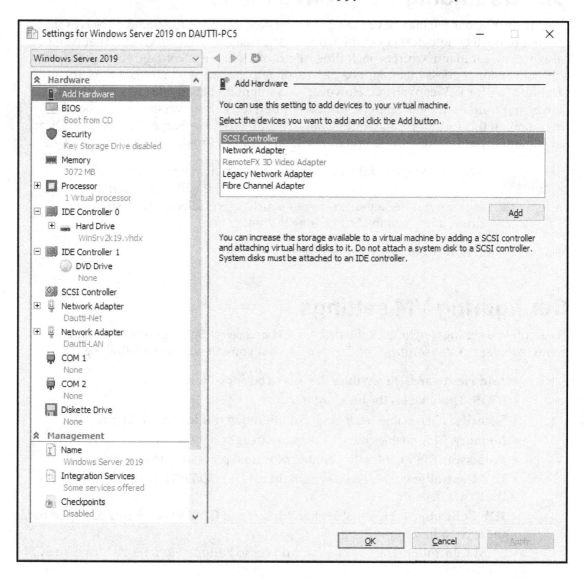

Figure 8.14: Establishing VM settings

Now, let's learn how to manage VMs.

# Managing VMs

When it comes to managing VMs, the **Actions** pane and the VM's context menu offer plenty of options. From **Quick create** to **Help**, the **Actions** pane acts as a one-stop resource when it comes to creating VMs, establishing Hyper-V settings, creating virtual switches and virtual SANs, editing and inspecting disks, stopping services, removing servers, and refreshing, as shown in *Figure 8.15*:

Figure 8.15: Actions pane in Hyper-V Manager

Unlike the **Actions** pane, options from the VM's context menu are focused only on VMs. From **Connect...** to **Rename...**, you can select options to manage the selected VM, as shown in *Figure 8.16*:

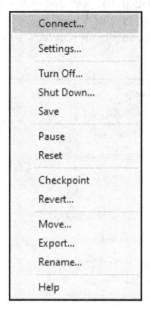

Figure 8.16: Context menu in Hyper-V Manager

In this section, we got acquainted with Hyper-V Manager and learned about its various features. Now, it is time to install the Hyper-V role.

# Chapter exercise – installing Hyper-V on Windows Server 2019

In this exercise, you will learn how to install the Hyper-V role on Windows Server 2019.

# Installing the Hyper-V role on Windows Server 2019

To install the Hyper-V role on Windows Server 2019 using the Server Manager, complete the following steps:

1. Click the Start button, and then, in the Start menu, click **Server Manager**.
2. In the **Server Manager** window, click the **Add roles and features** hyperlink.
3. In the **Before You Begin** option, click **Next**.
4. In the **Installation Type** option, click **Next**.
5. In the **Server Selection** option, click **Next**.
6. Select the **Hyper-V** role, as shown in *Figure 8.17*:

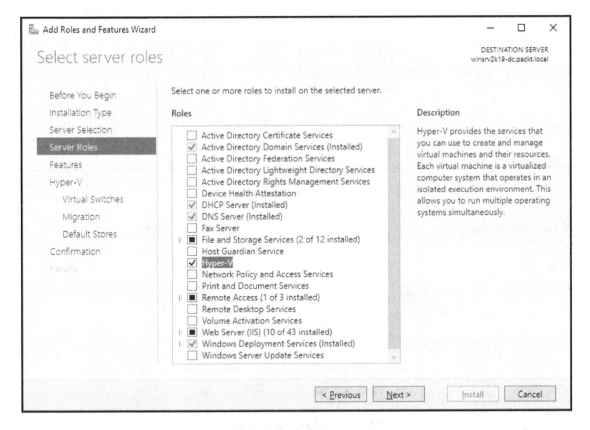

Figure 8.17: Selecting the Hyper-V role

7. Click the **Add Features** button to add features that are required for Hyper-V.

8. There is no feature to add, so click **Next**.

9. In the Hyper-V definition option, click **Next**.

10. Select the available network adapter, and then click **Next**.

11. Select **Allow this server to send and receive live migrations of virtual machines** and click **Next**.

12. Set up the path where you will store the VMs and click **Next**.

13. Confirm the installation selections for the Hyper-V role by clicking **Install**.

14. When the installation process completes, click **Close** (see *Figure 8.18*). The server will restart automatically:

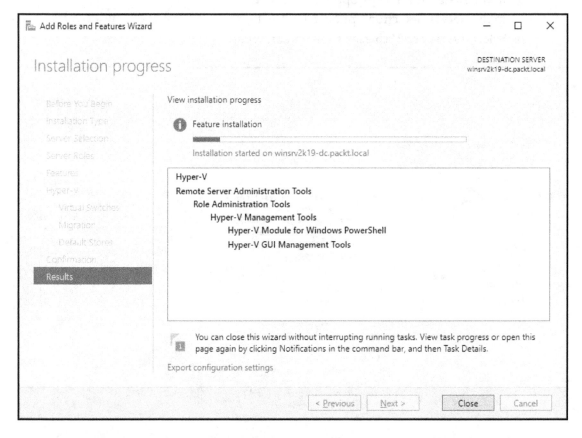

Figure 8.18: Installing the Hyper-V role on Windows Server 2019

The Hyper-V role will now be installed and is ready to use.

# Summary

In this chapter, you have learned about server virtualization, and the Hyper-V manager, through which you will enable virtualization on a server and be able to run VMs.

In the *Understanding server virtualization* section, you learned about virtualization concepts, such as virtualization modes, Hyper-V architecture, Hyper-V installation requirements, and nested virtualization, while in the *Getting to know Hyper-V Manager* section, you learned about how to configure Hyper-V settings, create and configure VHDs, manage a VMs' virtual memory, set up virtual networks, understand checkpoints, understand VHD and VHDX formats, learn about P2V conversions, understand V2P, configure VM settings, and manage VMs. This chapter concluded with an exercise that provided instructions on how to install the Hyper-V role.

In the following chapter, you will learn about storing data in Windows Server 2019.

# Questions

1. Hyper-V provides services that you can use to create and manage VMs and their resources. (True | False)
2. _____ is based on a hierarchical format where the first level represents the hypervisor as the main element that constitutes the Hyper-V virtual platform.
3. Which of the following are virtualization modes in Hyper-V? (Choose two)
     - Fully virtualized mode
     - Paravirtualized mode
     - Production checkpoints
     - Standard checkpoints
4. Checkpoints enable you to make a backup of the disk image at a specific time so that when unexpected situations arise, you can revert your VM to a previous state. (True | False)
5. Components such as _____and _____, through logical channels for communication known as VMbus, enable communication between the root portion and the branch OSes.
6. Which of the following are checkpoint types in Hyper-V? (Choose two)
     - Production checkpoints
     - Standard checkpoints
     - Inspect disk
     - Edit disk

7. Organizations are migrating their physical servers to virtual servers (P2V) for reasons such as cost, ease of management, and future expansion. (True | False)

8. _____ is an administration tool that you can use to manage the VMs.

9. Which of the following are elements of the Hyper-V architecture? (Choose two)
   - Hypervisor
   - Root
   - Branch
   - Snapshot

10. Discuss nested virtualization.

11. Discuss P2V conversion.

12. Discuss V2P conversion.

# Further reading

- *Virtualization*: https://docs.microsoft.com/en-us/windows-server/virtualization/virtualization
- *Hyper-V Virtual Hard Disk Format Overview*: https://docs.microsoft.com/en-us/previous-versions/windows/it-pro/windows-server-2012-r2-and-2012/hh831446(v%3Dws.11)
- *Disk2vhd v2.01*: https://docs.microsoft.com/en-us/sysinternals/downloads/disk2vhd

# 9
# Storing Data in Windows Server 2019

From a technical point of view, storage technologies represent a broad topic that an entire book could be written about. A disk is considered to be one of the server's core hardware components. This and many other components show how important these technologies are in the computer world. With that being said, this chapter is designed to give you a brief understanding of storage technologies and related topics.

You will learn about physical interfaces and disk controllers, how data is stored in a storage medium, storage system types that are used in network environments, various storage concepts and protocols such as **data deduplication (dedup)**, **Storage Spaces Direct (S2D)**, **software-defined storage (SDS)**, **Small Computer System Interface (SCSI)**, **Internet Small Computer System Interface (iSCSI)**, **Fibre Channel (FC)**, **Fibre Channel over Ethernet (FCoE)**, and many more. In addition, you will learn how to manage a server's storage using both Server Manager and Windows PowerShell. We will also mention volatile and non-volatile storage technologies such as RAM, ROM, **hard disk drive (HDD)**, **solid state drives (SSD)**, optical drives, and flash memory drives and cards. Last but not least, you will get to know the concepts and types of RAID too.

This chapter will conclude with an exercise on how to enable dedup in Windows Server 2019.

The following topics will be covered in this chapter:

- Understanding storage technologies
- Understanding RAID
- Understanding disk types
- Chapter exercise—enabling dedup on Windows Server 2019

# Technical requirements

In order to complete the exercise for this chapter, you will need the following equipment:

- A PC with Windows 10 Pro, at least 16 GB of RAM, 1 TB of HDD, and access to the internet
- A virtual machine with Windows Server 2019 Standard, at least 4 GB of RAM, 100 GB of HDD, and access to the internet

# Understanding storage technologies

Can you imagine an application server without RAM, or a file server without an HDD? Perhaps these questions may sound a little bit odd because of the fact that both RAM and HDD are an inseparable part of today's computer systems. The purpose of this section is to show you how important storage technologies are to computers and that they come in a variety of types, shapes, and sizes, and for different purposes. Having said that, besides the fact that storage technologies are an objective of the certification exams, their importance is absolute in the world of **information and communications technology** (**ICT**), and that is why these technologies have a whole chapter in this book dedicated to them.

Besides high processing power, a sufficient amount of RAM memory, and several network connections, your server will likely require a large amount of *storage space* too. Regardless of whether it is a single server or a cluster of servers, technologies such as IDE, SAS, SCSI, DAS, NAS, SAN, and RAID represent a wide range of storage technology options at your disposal.

Let's begin by understanding what the different storage types are.

# Different storage types

Storage technologies are numerous, and there are numerous opportunities in which to use them too. As such, different types of storage technologies exist. Let's take a look at some of these devices:

- **Optical discs**: They offer large capacities and read-and-write accepted speeds. However, they continue to play the role backup media for data.
- **HDDs:** They offer large capacities and high read-and-write speeds. They continue to maintain the number one spot in the secondary storage category.

- **SSDs**: With their growing capacities and extraordinary read-and-write speeds, they are becoming a popular storage technology. Only time will tell if they can take the top spot from HDDs.

Now that you are familiar with data storage technologies, let's get acquainted with **Advanced Technology Attachment (ATA)**, **Parallel ATA (PATA)**, **Serial ATA (SATA)**, and SCSI interfaces, which connect storage technologies.

# ATA, PATA, SATA, and SCSI interfaces

When acronyms such as ATA, PATA, SATA, and SCSI are mentioned, then we are opening a discussion about the interfaces that are used to connect storage devices and peripherals to computers. ATA, also known as **Integrated Drive Electronics (IDE)**, is a legacy interface that is used to connect HDDs, optical disc drives, floppy disk drives, and related storage technologies to computers. The two most popular types of ATA interfaces are as follows (see *Figure 9.1*):

- **PATA** uses a 40-pin connector and cable for data transfer in order to connect the storage device to the computer's motherboard and uses Molex as a power connector to connect the storage device to the computer's power supply. The disk controller resides on a drive itself.
- **SATA** represents a replacement for the PATA interface and is widely used in personal computers. It uses a 7-pin cable for data transfer to connect the storage device to the computer's motherboard and a 15-pin power supply connector to connect the storage device to the computer's power supply. Like PATA, in SATA, the disk controller is located on a drive as well:

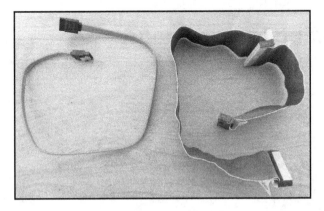

Figure 9.1: PATA and SATA data cables

SCSI, pronounced *scuzzy*, is another interface that connects storage devices and peripheral devices to computers. The two most popular types of SCSI are SPI and SAS. SPI is the early version of SCSI, whereas SAS is the modern version of SCSI that provides high data transfer rates, and is widely used in servers.

Now, let's get to know **Peripheral Component Interconnect (PCI)** and **PCI Express (PCIe)**.

## PCI and PCIe

In the mid-90s, PCI replaced IBM's **Industry Standard Architecture (ISA)**, a 16-bit built-in expansion slot on the motherboard. Unlike the ISA, Intel's PCI has a 32-bit and 64-bit built-in slot on the motherboard that enables the expansion of computer capabilities. Later on, with the increase in demand for faster speeds, PCI was replaced by **PCIe**, as shown in *Figure 9.2*. PCIe is a serial expansion bus standard that comes with four connections: PCIe x1, PCIe x4, PCIE x8, and PCIe x16. It transmits data in full-duplex mode (sending and receiving at the same time) over wires known as **lanes**:

Figure 9.2: The PCIe slot

Now, let's learn about local storage.

# Understanding local storage

**Local storage** refers to the hard drive or SSD that's directly attached to the server. In the following subsection, we will talk more specifically about *local storage*.

# Direct-attached storage (DAS)

As the name suggests, **DAS** is a group of disks that are directly connected to computers or servers. You won't be wrong if you think of your computer's HDD as a DAS. However, in addition to internal storage devices, even external storage devices that are connected to computers or servers with any of the aforementioned interfaces are considered as DAS, as shown in the *Figure 9.3*:

Figure 9.3: DAS system

Now that you are familiar with local storage, let's learn about network storage.

# Understanding network storage

In contrast to local storage, **network storage** refers to the storage device that is connected to a computer network in order to provide data access to users. In the following subsections, we will talk more specifically about network storage.

## Network-attached storage (NAS)

As the name implies, **NAS** is a network appliance that connects to computers and servers through a switch and acts as dedicated storage in an organization's network (see *Figure 9.4*):

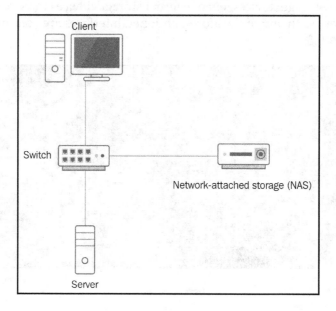

Figure 9.4: NAS system

There are manufacturers that build NAS as a file server. It brings flexibility so that organizations can rely completely on NAS for file sharing services without the need to use other servers.

## Storage area network (SAN)

As you can see from the descriptions of DAS and NAS, they are storage technologies that are distinguished by their features. Therefore, SAN, like DAS and NAS, is a storage technology too. However, unlike DAS and NAS, SAN is a standalone infrastructure. If we refer to the designation, then SAN is almost identical to LAN. While LAN connects computers on a local computer network, SAN connects storage devices in the area network. As such, a SAN cannot be accessed by other LAN devices. Just because of that, proprietary protocols or **Simple Network Management Protocols** (**SNMPs**) provide management for a SAN (see *Figure 9.5*). Usually, Ethernet or FC is used to connect SAN to servers:

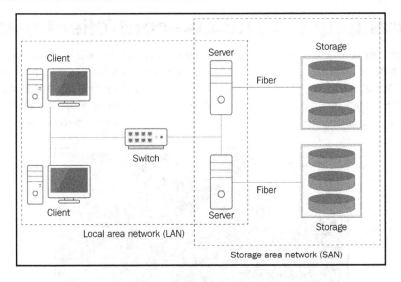

Figure 9.5: SAN system

Now that you are familiar with local and network storage, let's understand block-level storage versus file-level storage, which represents the way data is stored in storage technologies.

# Differentiating between block-level storage and file-level storage

The comparison between file-level storage and block-level storage is shown in the following table:

| File-level storage | Block-level storage |
|---|---|
| Data is stored and accessed in the form of files and folders. | Data is stored in blocks that represent volumes, which are which are then managed by the OS. |
| Used by NAS. | Used by SAN. |

Now, let's understand adapter and controller types so that we know how writing and reading are managed in storage technologies.

# Understanding adapter and controller types

The disk controller is an electronic circuit that resides on a hard disk as shown in *Figure 9.6*. It performs operations such as spinning disks, moving heads for reading and writing, and transferring data to and from RAM. Unlike the disk controller, the **Host Bus Adapter (HBA)** controller is an electronic board that is integrated with or attached to the motherboard of the server so that it can connect the storage system to the server:

Figure 9.6: Disk controller in HDD

Now, let's understand serial bus technologies so that we can understand data transmission technologies to and from storage technologies.

# Understanding serial bus technologies

For data transmission, parallel and serial transmissions are used. In parallel transmissions, a string of 8 bits is usually transmitted at a time, which is equal to 1 byte. In contrast, in serial transmissions, only 1-bit is usually transmitted at a given time. Even though more bits are transmitted through parallel transmission, serial transmission is the most widely used in storage technologies. This is because disk controllers tend to handle only 1-bit at a given time, meaning that the disk's read-and-write head reads and writes 1-bit within the given time. Thus, the serial method of transmission has proved to be more pragmatic by eliminating overhead processing, signal skewing, and crosstalk. That being said, today's most used serial interfaces in storage technologies, such as SATA, SAS, FC, and USB, utilize serial buses.

Now, let's understand storage protocols.

# Understanding storage protocols

**Storage protocols** allow us to store and retrieve data in/from storage systems. The most used storage protocols are as follows:

- **SCSI** is a storage protocol that is used heavily in block-level storage systems. The server operating system uses the SCSI protocol to read and write data on a SCSI controller that manages storage devices.
- **iSCSI** places the standard SCSI protocol in an IP packet, thus extending its functionalities throughout the organization's network.
- **FC** is another way of extending the functionalities of the standard SCSI protocol, enabling storage consolidations and longer distances.
- **FCoE** does the same for the FC protocol as iSCSI does for the SCSI protocol. That being said, FCoE extends the functionalities of the FC protocol across Ethernet networks.

 You can learn more about SCSI at `https://www.lifewire.com/small-computer-system-interface-scsi-2626002`.

Moving forward, let's learn about file sharing protocols.

# Understanding file sharing protocols

**File sharing protocols** enable data sharing over LANs, WANs, and the internet. The most used file sharing protocols are as follows:

- **Server Message Block** (**SMB**), also known as the **Common Internet File System** (**CIFS**), is a file sharing protocol used mostly by Windows OSes.
- **Network File System** (**NFS**) is a file sharing protocol used mostly by Unix and Linux.
- **File Transfer Protocol** (**FTP**) enables file sharing by transferring files from site to site.
- **Hypertext Transfer Protocol** (**HTTP**) enables file sharing over a **World Wide Web** (**WWW**) service.
- **Secure Shell** (**SSH**) enables remote file sharing over a secure connection.

 You can learn more about SSH at `https://www.ssh.com/ssh/`.

Now, let's understand FC, HBA, and FC switches, which are used to connect storage technologies.

# Understanding FC, HBA, and FC switches

The HBA is an interface standard, whereas the FC switch is a network switch. Both components are compatible with FC, a high-speed network technology that is used to connect the two, thus creating the FC fabric. FC fabric consists of one or more FC switches, and, as such, it constitutes the SAN topology.

Now, let's learn about what iSCSI hardware is, another technology for connecting storage technologies.

# What is iSCSI hardware?

iSCSI, a block-level storage, uses an IP to send the SCSI commands over TCP/IP networks. iSCSI works in such a way that the clients, known as **initiators**, use the IP protocol to send SCSI commands called **command descriptor blocks** (**CDBs**) to storage devices known as **targets**. In SANs, the **logical unit number** (**LUN**) represents a logical disk. In iSCSI, TCP port 860 is reserved for the iSCSI system port, whereas TCP port 3260 represents iSCSI's default port.

Now, let's learn about what S2D is so that we can understand what storage pools are.

# What is S2D?

**S2D**, which was introduced in Windows Server 2016, is a feature that is supported in Windows Server 2019 too. It enables the grouping of disks into storage pools (see *Figure 9.7*), thus creating software-defined storage called **storage spaces**:

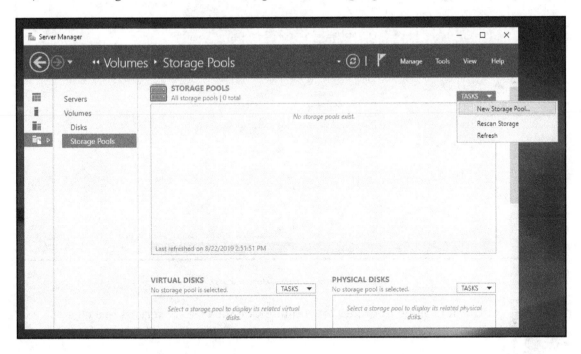

Figure 9.7: Creating a new storage pool in Windows Server 2019

Now, let's learn how duplicated data is being removed by dedup.

# What is dedup?

The idea behind the concept of **dedup** (see *Figure 9.8*) is to provide disk space savings. dedup is a technique that removes duplicated data from a dataset, thus storing a single copy of identical data on a disk. First, it analyzes the data to identify duplicated data in the dataset, and then the original file is stored in storage media while the duplicated files are replaced with a reference that points to the original file:

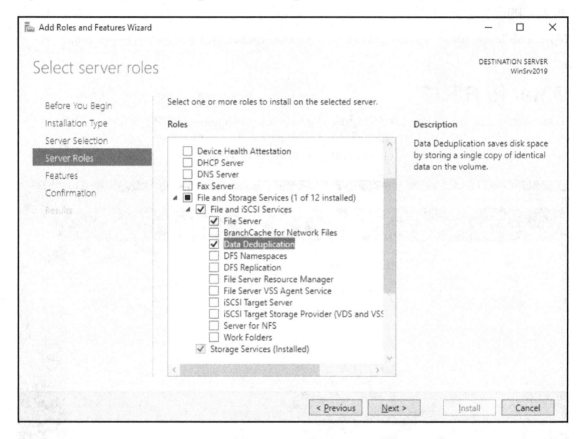

Figure 9.8: Installing dedup in Windows Server 2019

 Cluster rolling upgrades let you upgrade the OSes of servers in a cluster without the need to stop Hyper-V.

Now, let's learn how storage tiering helps us store data in high-performing storage.

# What is storage tiering?

Another interesting built-in feature in Microsoft's Windows Server is **storage tiering**, which enables the automatic transfer of the most frequently accessed files to faster storage. In simpler terms, this means it lets you combine high-performance storage with low-performance storage (for example, the HDD and the SSD) to reduce storage costs. Thus, the storage tiering agents will place the most accessed files on the faster storage, while rarely accessed files are placed in slower storage.

Now, let's learn how to manage storage with Server Manager and Windows PowerShell.

# Managing storage with Server Manager and Windows PowerShell

Prior to managing storage with **Server Manager** (servermanager.exe), ensure that the **File and Storage Services** role is added to the server. The *Figure 9.9* shows storage management using Server Manager on the local server:

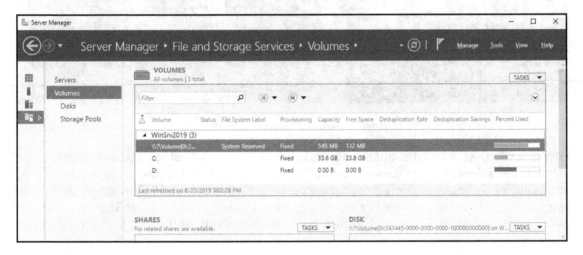

Figure 9.9: Managing storage with Server Manager

Other than Server Manager, you can manage storage with Windows PowerShell too. The *Figure 9.10* shows Windows PowerShell in action (`powershell.exe`):

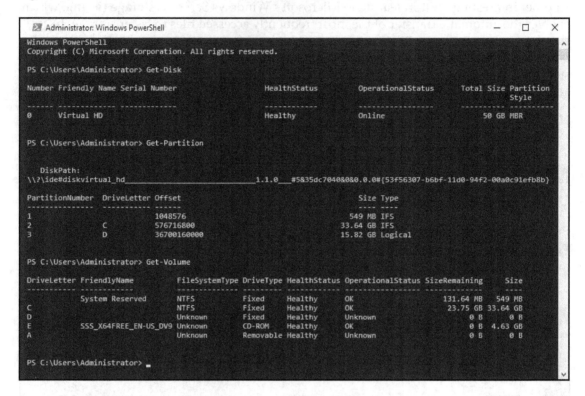

Figure 9.10: Managing storage with Windows PowerShell

In this section, we learned about storage technologies such as local storage, network storage, block-level storage versus file-level storage, adapter and controller types, serial bus technologies, storage protocols, file sharing protocols, FC, HBA, and FC switches, iSCSI hardware, S2D, dedup, storage tiering, and managing storage with Server Manager and Windows PowerShell. In the next section, we will learn about RAID.

# Understanding RAID

Regardless of whether you have come across the term **redundant array of independent disks** or **redundant array of inexpensive disks**, you should know that you are dealing with the concept of fault tolerance. RAID is a technology that combines a considerable number of physical disks into a single logical unit so that it can protect data in the case of disk failure. At the same time, note that RAID is not a backup solution and should never be considered as such.

Let's begin by learning about the different types of RAIDs.

# Types of RAID

There are a considerable number of RAID types. The most used are as follows:

- **RAID 0** is known as disk striping and offers higher read and write performance but it is not fault-tolerant. On Windows Server 2019, you can create a striped volume if you convert the disk from basic to dynamic.
- **RAID 1** is known as disk mirroring and requires at least two disks for its implementation while offering excellent read and write performance. It works in such a way that all the data that resides on disk A is mirrored on disk B. In the case of disk failure, the RAID controller uses any of the available disks.
- **RAID 5** is known as disk striping with parity and requires three disks for its implementation at a minimum. It represents the most fault-tolerant RAID that's available. The parity data is spread across all disks, meaning that RAID 5 can withstand the failure of a single disk.
- **RAID 10** is known as the stripe of mirrors and combines RAID 1 with RAID 0, thus offering disk mirroring and striping at the same time. It requires four disks for its implementation at a minimum. In the case of disk failure, the rebuild time is very fast since the striping is spread across all drives.

Now, let's compare hardware RAID with software RAID.

# Hardware versus software RAID

When it comes to deploying RAID, there are two types of RAID:

- **Hardware RAID** (see *Figure 9.11*) is an expensive solution and requires configuration prior to installing the OS. It is an electronic board that either the manufacturer of the server or you will plug into an adequate slot on the server's motherboard:

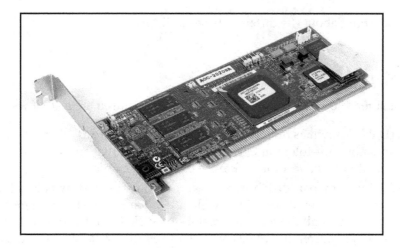

Figure 9.11: The RAID controller

- **Software RAID** is a cheaper solution and is configured after the installation of an OS. It is an application that you will end up buying from a specific vendor.

Now, let's understand SDS.

# Understanding SDS

If an organization, due to budget constraints, cannot afford to own NAS or SAN storage systems, then it can select the cheapest alternative that has to do with SDS. With Windows Server 2019, through S2D organizations can create virtualized networks with local storage. By doing this, they can build an SDS that helps separate the software that manages the storage from the storage hardware. This offers great diversity in the use of various storage technologies.

Now, let's learn how redundancy, while using S2D, enables fault tolerance and storage efficiency.

# Understanding resiliency using S2D

The fault tolerance approach in S2D is called **resiliency**. It offers mirroring with parity, and so in terms of implementation, it is similar to RAID software. However, in Windows Server 2019, S2D offers fault tolerance and storage efficiency.

Now, let's learn about today's high availability standard.

# Understanding high availability (HA)

**HA** is a characteristic of a system that never fails, thus being available at all times. However, that is only possible in an *ideal* world. In our world, the highest available standard is 99.9999%. To achieve such a standard, we need to have numerous parameters in place. Thus, from backup to fault tolerance and from resilience to reliability, all storage media is required to be operational so that the system as a whole is highly available.

The following table shows the HA standards:

| Availability (%) | Downtime per month | Downtime per year |
|---|---|---|
| 99% | 7.20 hours | 3.65 days |
| 99.9% | 43.2 minutes | 8.76 hours |
| 99.99% | 4.32 minutes | 52.6 minutes |
| 99.999% | 25.9 seconds | 5.26 minutes |
| 99.9999% | 2.59 seconds | 31.5 seconds |

In this section, we learned about types of RAID, the difference between hardware and software RAID, SDS, resiliency using S2D, and high availability. In the next section, we will learn about disk types.

# Understanding disk types

One reason why you should learn about disk types is so that you can get acquainted with their types and technical specifications. In turn, that will help you understand the real storage potential of any disk type.

Let's begin by learning about the HDD.

# Understanding HDD

The HDD, as shown in *Figure 9.12*, is considered to be a secondary storage type, right after server memory (that is, RAM memory). As such, it is a computer component that uses the electromotor to spin the disk, and it contains a magnetic read-and-write head and metal platters that permanently store data. Each platter contains tracks and sectors. The starting point for storing data in HDDs is the outer track. The read-and-write head is located above the platter at a distance of microns, thus never touching the disk. If it does, then physical damage occurs.

The data storage capacity is measured in bytes (nowadays, it is GB and TB), while the disc spinning speed is measured in **rotations per minute** (**RPM**). The most common RPM rates for PCs and laptops are from 5,400 RPM to 7,200 RPM, while for servers the most common RPM rates are from 10,000 RPM to 15,000 RPM. Usually, the HDD is located inside the computer's case and is mounted in drive bays. However, there are also external HDDs, which are mainly used for storing and backing up data. In the event of HDD disposal, it is recommended to perform disk shredding:

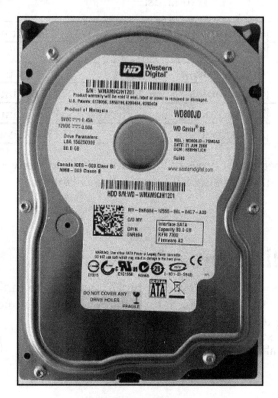

Figure 9.12: The HDD

You can learn more about HDDs at `https://www.computerhope.com/jargon/h/harddriv.htm`.

Now, let's learn about the SDD, which is a storage technology like HDD, but with a different working principle.

# Understanding SSD

The SSD (see *Figure 9.13*) is another storage technology that is considered to be secondary storage. Unlike HDDs, SSDs are memory chips with no moving parts. They use less voltage (usually 5V) than HDDs (12V for spinning the platters), are noiseless, more physically reliable, and provide faster data access. SSDs are behind HDDs in terms of capacity. However, based on current development trends in storage technologies, things might turn in favor of SSDs over HDDs. These days, many manufacturers offer their PCs and laptops with SSD disks that contain the OS and applications, as well as HDD disks to be used for data storage. Additionally, SSD drives are also encountered on servers, including NAS and SAN devices too:

Figure 9.13: The SSD

 You can learn more about SSDs at `https://www.lifewire.com/solid-state-drive-833448`.

Now, let's learn about the optical disk drive so that we can get to know the lands and pits.

# Understanding optical disk drives

Unlike HDDs, which use an electromagnetic field to read and write data to/from disk platters, **optical disk drives (ODDs)**, as shown in *Figure 9.14*, utilize laser beams with a specific wavelength to read and write data to/from **compact discs (CDs)**. Always try to differentiate between the ODDs and **optical discs (ODs)**, such as CDs or DVDs. The former is the device where the CD or DVD is inserted. CDs contain tracks in the form of a spiral. The starting point for storing data on CDs is the inner track. As is the case with HDDs, optical discs are measured by capacity in *bytes*. Usually, the capacity of common CDs is between 650 MB and 700 MB, while common DVDs range from 4.7 GB to 8.5 GB. In contrast to HDDs, the speed of optical discs is measured in KB/s and is determined by an *x* symbol that is equal to 150 KB/s. Therefore, if your optical drive has a speed of 24x, then its speed is *24 x 150 KB/s = 3600 KB/s = 3.6 MB/s*. There are three recording types of optical disks, as follows:

- **CD-ROM and DVD-RAM** are read-only optical discs.
- **CD-R and DVD-R/DVD+R** are write-once optical discs.
- **CD-RW and DVD-RW/DVD+RW** are rewritable optical discs:

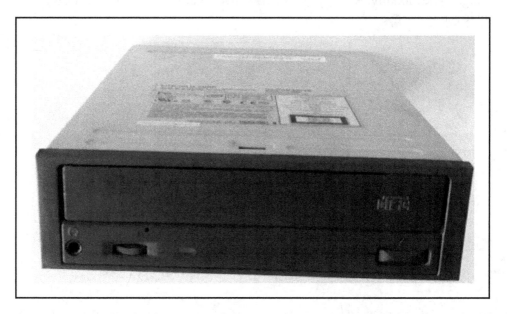

Figure 9.14: The ODD

The most common forms of optical discs at the time of writing are DVDs and Blu-ray discs. The latter has been designed to supersede DVD technologies, thus achieving tremendous capacities where a single layer holds 25 GB, a dual layer holds 50 GB, a triple layer holds 100 GB, and a quadruple layer holds 128 GB.

 You can learn more about optical disc types at `https://www.ifixit.com/ Wiki/Optical_Disc_Types`.

Now, let's learn about basic disks, which are based on the **Master Boot Record** (**MBR**) and **GUID Partition Table** (**GPT**) partition schemes.

# Understanding basic disks

Once you have installed the operating system on the server's hard disk, the hard disk structure is in its *basic configuration*. This means that the basic disk configuration is organized into partitions. As you now know (see the *Understanding partition schemes* section in `Chapter 3`, *Installing Windows Server 2019*, for more information), the basic disk is based on the MBR and GPT partition schemes, and, as such, one partition cannot be extended on one or more physical disks. Instead, a partition can be extended by adding unallocated space from the same physical disk.

Now, let's learn about dynamic disks so that we can understand how read-write performance can be increased.

# Understanding dynamic disks

To overcome the limitations of the basic disk, to be able to increase read-and-write performance with disk striping, and to operate with volumes instead of partitions, **dynamic disk** configuration was introduced. This means that volumes in dynamic disk configuration can be extended to more than one physical disk, thus allowing us to create five types of volumes: simple, mirrored, striped, spanned, and RAID-5 volumes.

In Windows Server 2019, to convert a basic disk into a dynamic disk, complete the following steps:

1. Right-click the Start button.
2. Select **Disk Management**.
3. Right-click the preferred disk, and, from the context menu, select **Convert to Dynamic Disk...** (see *Figure 9.15*):

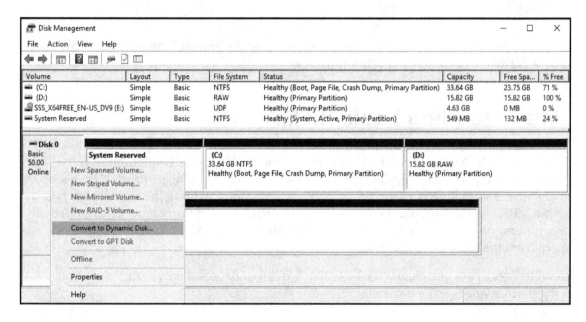

Figure 9.15: Converting a basic disk into a dynamic disk

4. If you have more than one disk, then, from the **Convert to Dynamic Disk** window, select the disks and click **OK**.
5. Click **Convert** in the **Disks to Convert** window.
6. After you have read the information in the **Disk Management** dialog box, click **Yes.**
7. Shortly after, the conversion will be completed.

Now, let's learn about mount points so that we can understand how to increase the size of the folder.

# Understanding mount points

When you attach an unallocated partition to a blank folder, what you have actually done is create a *mount point*. This allows us to increase the size of the folder if the partition where the folder is located is running out of space.

In Windows Server 2019, you can use Disk Management (`diskmgmt.msc`) to create a mount point, as shown in *Figure 9.16*:

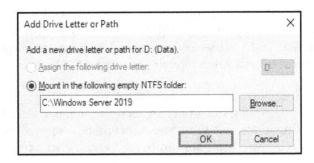

Figure 9.16: Creating a mount point with Disk Management in Windows Server 2019

Now, let's learn about filesystems so that we can understand how storing and organizing data on storage technologies is done.

# Understanding filesystems

It often happens that, when referring to the Windows OS, I think of Windows Explorer. Does that happen to you too? If so, then one rationale may be that the Windows OS is very easy to use when we're dealing with storing and organizing data on the computer—on the computer's hard disk, to be precise. This is the result of the filesystem(s) that the Windows OS is using. By taking a look at the following list, you will become familiar with the well-known filesystems that are used by the Windows OS:

- **File Allocation Table** (**FAT**) is the earliest filesystem that was used by both MS-DOS and Windows. As the name implies, it is based on a table that contains a map of clusters. A cluster is a unit of logical storage on the hard disk. FAT32 is the latest version of FAT.

- **New Technology File System** (**NTFS**) was introduced in the 1990s with Windows NT 3.1 and is still in use. Among the features that NTFS offers are disk quotas, **Encrypting File System** (**EFS**), journaling, and the **Volume Shadow Copy Service** (**VSS**). NTFS is a native filesystem on Windows Server 2019.
- **Resilient File System** (**ReFS**) was introduced in Windows Server 2012 and is supposed to be the successor of the NTFS. The new features that ReFS offers include resiliency, performance, and scalability. ReFS is available as a disk format option in Windows Server 2019.
- **Extended File Allocation Table** (**exFAT**) is a new version of FAT that was developed to be used primarily with USB flash drives and SD cards. It is interesting that exFAT is platform independent, thus enabling drives that have been formatted with this filesystem to be supported by Mac computers too.

 A journaling filesystem is an important feature that maintains data integrity by keeping track of changes being made to data in a separate log, thus making it possible to restore data whenever power outage or disk crashes occur. Microsoft has removed `Journal.dll` from Windows Server 2019.

Now, let's learn how to mount a **virtual hard disk** (**VHD**).

# Mounting a VHD

Based on the concept of the mount point, which we explained earlier, a mounted VHD drive is a mount point which, in this case, represents a drive that is mapped to an empty folder on a volume that uses the NTFS filesystem. Mostly, mounted VHD drives function like any other drives, except that instead of drive letters, they use the drive path.

In Windows Server 2019, you can attach a **VHD** to your server using Disk Management. To do so, complete the following steps:

1. Press the Windows key + *R*.
2. In the **Run** window, enter `diskmgmt.msc` and then hit *Enter*.

3. In the **Disk Management** window, click the **Action** menu and select **Attach VHD** (see *Figure 9.17*):

Figure 9.17: Attaching a VHD using Disk Management in Windows Server 2019

4. Shortly after, the attached VHD will be displayed in the **Disk Management** window.

Now, let's learn about **Distributed File System** (**DFS**).

# Understanding DFS

If you have ever wondered how you can share data from your servers in an authorized and controlled way, then look no further than DFS. With DFS, data that is stored in shared folders that's located on different servers can be grouped into logically structured namespaces. This makes it possible for users to access the data as if it were stored on local computers.

In Windows Server 2019, DFS is part of the **File and Storage Services** role. Thus, to install DFS on your server, you should expand the **File and Storage Services** role, expand **File and iSCSI Services,** and then select **DFS Namespace**, **DFS Replication**, and **File Server Resource Manager,** as shown in *Figure 9.18*:

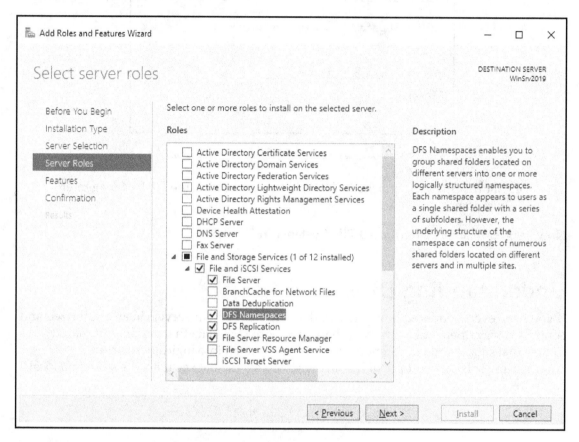

Figure 9.18: Installing DFS in Windows Server 2019

In this section, we have learned about types of RAID, the difference between hardware and software RAID, SDS, resiliency using S2D, and HA. In the next section, you will learn how to enable dedup on Windows Server 2019.

# Chapter exercise – enabling dedup on Windows Server 2019

In this chapter's exercise, you will learn how to enable dedup on Windows Server 2019.

## Enabling dedup on Windows Server 2019

To enable dedup in Windows Server 2019, complete the following steps:

1. Click **Add roles and features** within the **Server Manager** | **WELCOME TO SERVER MANAGER** section.
2. On the **Before You Begin** window, click **Next**.
3. Click **Next** on the **Installation Type** window.
4. On the **Server Selection** window, click **Next**.
5. On the **Server Roles** window, expand **File and Storage Services**.
6. Then, expand **File and iSCSI Services**.
7. Select **Data Deduplication**, as shown in *Figure 9.7*.
8. On the **Features** window, click **Next**.
9. On the **Confirmation** window, click **Install**.

10. When you see the installation has completed, click **Close**, as shown in *Figure 9.19*:

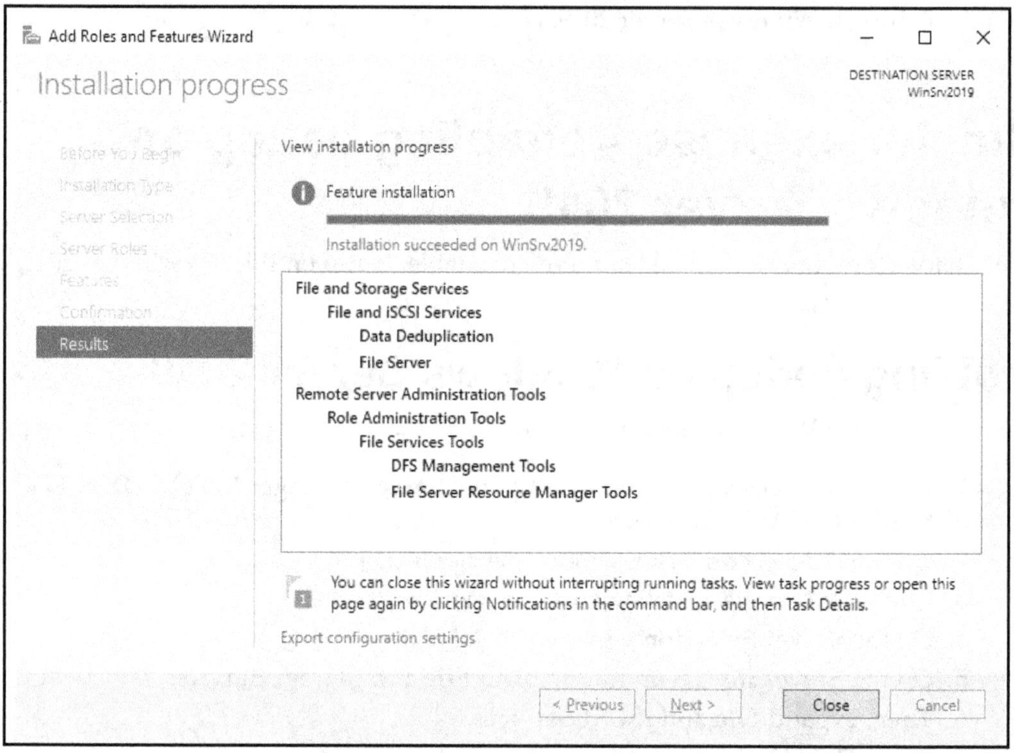

Figure 9.19: Closing the Add Roles and Features Wizard

This exercise has shown us how dedup can be installed on Windows Server 2019.

# Summary

In this chapter, you have learned about the storing technologies that are available on today's servers, as well as enhanced features in Windows Server 2019 that are related to storage technology management.

In the *Understanding storage technologies* section, you learned about storage technologies such as local storage, network storage, block-level storage versus file-level storage, adapter and controller types, serial bus technologies, storage protocols, file sharing protocols, FC, HBA, and FC switches, iSCSI hardware, S2D, dedup, storage tiering, and managing storage with Server Manager and Windows PowerShell.

Then, in the *Understanding RAID* section, you learned about types of RAID, the difference between hardware and software RAIDs, SDS, resiliency using S2D, and high availability. Finally, in the *Understanding disk types* section, you learned about HDD, SSD, ODD, basic disk, dynamic disk, mount points, filesystems, mounting a VHD, and DFS. This chapter concluded with this chapter's exercise, which provided instructions regarding how to enable dedup on Windows Server 2019.

In the next chapter, you will learn about tuning and maintaining the performance of Windows Server 2019.

# Questions

1. DFS enables the sharing of data from your server in an authorized and controlled way. (True | False)
2. _____ is a network appliance that connects with computers and servers through a switch and acts as dedicated storage in an organization's network.
3. Which of the following are network storage technologies? (Choose two)
    - DAS
    - NAS
    - RAM
    - ROM
4. Block-level storage stores data in files and folders that represent volumes that are managed by the server operating system. (True | False)
5. _____ is an electronic circuit that resides on a hard disk and performs operations such as spinning discs, moving heads for reading and writing, and transferring data to and from RAM.
6. Which of the following are storage protocols? (Choose two.)
    - SCSI
    - FC
    - PATA
    - SATA
7. The HDD is a computer component that uses the motor to spin the disc, has a magnetic read-and-write head, and has metal platters that permanently store data. (True | False)
8. _____ is a characteristic of a system that never fails, thus being available at all times.

9. Which of the following are RAID types? (Choose two)
   - RAID 1
   - RAID 5
   - RAID 15
   - RAID 20

10. The SCSI, pronounced *scuzzy*, is another interface that connects storage devices and peripheral devices to computers. (True | False)

11. \_\_\_\_\_ is a legacy interface that is used to connect HDDs, ODDs, floppy disk drives, and related storage technologies to computers.

12. Which of the following are optical discs? (Choose two)
    - CD-ROM
    - DVD-RAM
    - EPROM
    - POST

13. Discuss dedup in Windows Server 2019.

14. Discuss S2D in Windows Server 2019.

15. Discuss the DFS in Windows Server 2019.

# Further reading

- *Hard drives and partitions*: https://docs.microsoft.com/en-us/windows-hardware/manufacture/desktop/hard-drives-and-partitions
- *Overview of Disk Management*: https://docs.microsoft.com/en-us/windows-server/storage/disk-management/overview-of-disk-management
- *Storage Spaces Direct overview*: https://docs.microsoft.com/en-us/windows-server/storage/storage-spaces/storage-spaces-direct-overview
- *Basic and Dynamic Disks*: https://docs.microsoft.com/en-us/windows/win32/fileio/basic-and-dynamic-disks
- *Overview of Redundant Arrays of Inexpensive Disks (RAID)*: https://support.microsoft.com/en-gb/help/100110/overview-of-redundant-arrays-of-inexpensive-disks-raid

# 4
# Section 4: Keeping Windows Server 2019 Up and Running

The fourth section covers tuning, maintaining, update, and troubleshooting in Windows Server 2019. Upon completion of this section, you will be able to use task manager and resource monitor to tune and maintain Windows Server 2019 . Also, you will learn the troubleshooting methodology and how to use Windows Update and Event Viewer to update and troubleshoot Windows Server 2019.

This section comprises the following chapters:

- Chapter 10, *Tuning and Maintaining Windows Server 2019*
- Chapter 11, *Updating and Troubleshooting Windows Server 2019*

# 10
# Tuning and Maintaining Windows Server 2019

This chapter is designed to teach you the considerations for server hardware and best practices regarding performance monitoring methodology. Understanding the importance of a server's role in a computer network and possessing knowledge of a server's hardware components has two benefits: it helps you to select the server hardware as well as troubleshoot that hardware.

Also, this chapter teaches you server performance monitoring methodologies and procedures. Performance monitoring will help you to identify the cause of server performance issues at an early stage. In that way, you will be able to react promptly to avoid further degradation of server performance. As for the server baseline, it represents a snapshot of the server's performance under a normal workload, which enables you to compile a detailed report about the server's performance.

This chapter concludes with an exercise on performance logs and alerts.

The following topics will be covered in this chapter:

- Understanding server hardware components
- Understanding performance monitoring
- Understanding logs and alerts
- Chapter exercise—the performance logs and alerts service

# Technical requirements

To complete the lab for this chapter, you will need the following equipment:

- A PC with Windows 10 Pro, at least 16 GB of RAM, 1 TB of HDD, and access to the internet
- A virtual machine with Windows Server 2019 Standard, at least 4 GB of RAM, 100 GB of HDD, and access to the internet

# Understanding server hardware components

From a technical point of view, a server is nothing more than a computer. As you open up the computer's case, you will notice various parts that make up the internal hardware of the computer. In computer jargon, these parts are called **hardware components**—in our case, the server's hardware components. Now, the question arises: why should we pay that much attention to these hardware components? Does this sound like the right question? Let me remind you of something that you may already know: a server's primary task is not data processing; in fact, the server's role (see `Chapter 6`, *Adding Roles to Windows Server 2019*) includes providing network services and handling user requests to access services. This is the reason why you should have some knowledge of the server hardware and why you should pay attention when selecting the server's hardware.

With this in mind, let's examine server hardware components, the roles they play, and the impacts they have on the performance of a server to strengthen further the assertion that there should be considerations taken into account when dealing with server hardware.

# Understanding the processor

There is no doubt that speed is one of the determining factors in choosing the right processor. The processor's speed is measured in **Hertz (Hz)**. Today's processor speeds are given in **Gigahertz (GHz)**. However, we would be making a mistake if we relied only on the speed factor. Therefore, the following factors should also be considered:

- **Cache**: This is the processor's memory. Modern processors have three types of cache: L1, L2, and L3. While L1 and L2 are inside the processor, L3 is located outside the processor. Obviously, their numbers determine the speed of each cache memory.

- **Cores**: This is the processor's processing unit. In the past, processors had just one core. Today, there are processors with two, four, eight, or more cores. So, to understand the cores in a processor better, think about assembling two processors with a single core, each into a single package. Does that make sense? So, the more cores a processor has, the more multiprocessing is done.

- **Word size**: Word size has to do with the processor's internal architecture that defines the data bus size, the instruction size, and the address size. Today, there are 32-bit and 64-bit processors. Obviously, these numbers determine the processor's word size, that is, the amount of data that the processor receives from the RAM to be processed and then sends back to the RAM.

- **Virtualization technology**: This refers to the processor's ability in relation to the virtualization concept; that is, whether the processor supports virtualization, where many operating systems simultaneously share processor resources efficiently:

Figure 10.1: Intel's Xeon quad-core processor

No doubt, a processor plays a very important role in a server. However, it will not be able to function without memory. So now, let's learn more about memory.

# Understanding memory

The primary storage is a hardware component that is capable of temporarily storing data, allowing processors to access data faster and easier, as well as acting as a communication bridge between applications and peripheral devices to access the processor. All of these features belong to **Random Access Memory** (**RAM**). As with RAM, **Read-Only Memory** (**ROM**) is also considered primary storage. The following table lists the differences between RAM and ROM:

| RAM | ROM |
| --- | --- |
| Volatile | Non-volatile |
| The data is lost when the power goes off | The data is kept when the power goes off |
| Known as working memory as it loads the operating system and apps | Known as hardware initialization memory as it runs the **Power-On Self-Test** (**POST**) |

When it comes to RAM for servers, the physical size is almost the same as that for PCs (see *Figure 10.2*), except that RAM modules for servers have one chip more. The other difference is in functionality, so servers use a type of RAM called **Error-Correcting Code** (**ECC**) memory. ECC RAM enables you to detect and correct memory faults. Other advanced types of RAM for servers include **Single Device Data Correction** (**SDDC**) and **Double Device Data Correction** (**DDDC**), which enable multiple memory faults to be detected and corrected. With all of these advantages of RAM for servers, there is one disadvantage, too, and that is their price. In general, RAM for servers is expensive:

Figure 10.2: ECC RAM modules placed in memory banks

While RAM is considered primary memory and is volatile, the disk is considered a secondary memory and is non-volatile. Now, let's understand more about the disk.

# Understanding the disk

As you already know, servers need to be up and running all of the time. That is because the services and data stored on a disk (see *Figure 10.3*) should be available to users all of the time. For the servers to be operational all of the time, they must have hardware that enables such a requirement. In that regard, *hot-swappable* technology enables the replacement of damaged disks with new disks while servers are running. All of that enables the high availability of data:

Figure 10.3: SAS HDDs

Moving forward, let's understand the network interface.

# Understanding the network interface

Servers usually have more than one network interface (see *Figure 10.4*). If they do not, then you have to consider adding **Network Interface Cards** (**NICs**) to your server. That approach offers tremendous benefits. Some of these benefits are as follows:

- **NIC teaming**: This enables you to increase bandwidth from/to the server.
- **Network Load Balancing (NLB)**: This enables you to distribute the network load across servers.
- **Network separation**: This enables you to separate intranet traffic from internet traffic:

Figure 10.4: Server network interfaces

Simply put, a network interface represents a physical port, while network architecture represents the design of a computer network. Now, let's understand 32-bit and 64-bit architectures.

# Understanding 32-bit and 64-bit architectures

To understand the difference between 32-bit and 64-bit architecture, let's take the following example. Trucks A and B are delivering loads of 3,200 kg and 6,400 kg, respectively. Both trucks can carry these loads from city C to city D at identical traveling speeds over the same road. Which truck will bring a greater load to city D for the same distance traveled and time consumed? In computer jargon, that means a processor can exchange 64 bits of data with RAM memory in any communication. So, the recommendation is to consider 64-bit hardware for your server, without compromising 64-bit software such as the OS, applications, device drivers, and other utilities when available. All of this enables an increase in the overall performance of your server.

In general, the secondary memory in computers is fixed (that is, non-removable), However, there are also removable storage technologies. Having said that, let's now look at removable drives.

# Understanding removable drives

First things first, the removable drive is a storage technology that can be plugged into, and unplugged from, the server while the server is running. Furthering the concept of hot-swap explained earlier in the *Understanding disk* section of this chapter, removable drives for your server can be attached using USB and IEEE 1394 ports. CDs, DVDs, HDDs, floppies (an obsolete technology), USB flash drives, and backup drives are some of the types of removable drives, and some of these are shown in *Figure 10.5*:

Figure 10.5: Removable drive and USB flash drives

To process heavy data usage, the server might require a graphics card. Let's learn more about this in the next section.

## Understanding graphics cards

Generally speaking, servers are backend computing machines and, hence, they do not necessarily have advanced graphics cards. Regardless, everything depends on the purpose that the server serves. So, if it is a server involved with graphics and video processing, then it might require an advanced graphics card, as shown in *Figure 10.6*:

Figure 10.6: AMD's Radeon video graphic adapter

Sometimes, servers may heat up while performing heavy tasks. To keep this in check, cooling is required. Let's learn more about this.

# Understanding cooling

Without excluding other server components, processors and HDDs are the hardware components that generate the most thermal heat. To have optimal cooling, aside from processor coolers, servers are also equipped with multiple additional coolers known as **case coolers**, as shown in *Figure 10.7*. There are also additional coolers on top of the rack. There are often air conditioners in the server room too, which aid in the overall cooling of the environment:

Figure 10.7: Cooling system in a server's case

Moving forward, let's understand how a server uses a power supply.

# Understanding power usage

Several processors, multiple disks, several network interfaces, large motherboards, multiple ports, graphics cards, RAID cards, optical drives, backup tapes, and other server hardware make up a list of potential components that are eager to consume power. Because power supplies are considered to be a single point of failure, servers are equipped with a redundant power supply. Depending on a server's form factor, most servers are equipped with two or more **Power Supply Units (PSUs)** (see *Figure 10.8*):

Figure 10.8: PSUs

Finally, let's learn about physical ports and their relevance to a server.

# Understanding physical ports

It is a characteristic of servers to have multiple ports. This is due to the role that the servers play in computer networks. Some of the ports (see *Figure 10.9*) we encounter at the back of servers include AC power connectors, gigabit Ethernet ports, PCIe ports, USB ports, HD-15 video connectors, management ports, and (although rarely seen nowadays) legacy ports such as serial ports, parallel ports, and PS/2 ports:

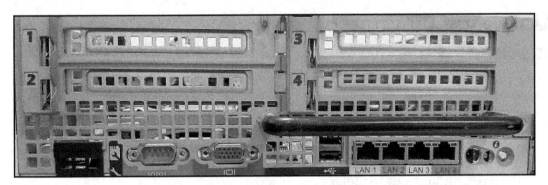

Figure 10.9: Various ports to connect a variety of devices

In this section, we have learned about processor, memory, disks, network interfaces, 32-bit and 64-bit architectures, removable drives, graphics cards, cooling, power usage, and physical ports. In the next section, we will learn about monitoring the server's performance.

# Understanding performance monitoring

There is a saying: *prevention is better than cure*. If we apply that to server administration, then we can understand how important performance monitoring is. Monitoring the server's performance helps to identify server problems at an early stage of development, and we can then take the necessary steps to prevent them from turning into costly problems, in terms of both time and business.

To have productive performance monitoring, a clear plan with the right tools is required. That also means setting up a metric by which performance monitoring will be measured. Such a metric needs baseline information. This will help to evaluate the actual performance of servers, determine when hardware and software upgrades are needed, and evaluate whether an upgraded system is working better than the previous one.

Microsoft's TechNet website, `https://technet.microsoft.com/en-us/`, provides very useful information about Microsoft products, including monitoring.

Let's begin by understanding the performance monitoring methodology.

# Understanding the performance monitoring methodology

In the previous section, we learned that the responsibility of performance monitoring is to maintain the server in a healthy state. But if there is no clear plan for its implementation, then the results obtained from performance monitoring will be based on multiple assumptions. Viewed from a business perspective, that means that the wrong data results in the wrong business decisions. Simply put, performance monitoring must be based on facts and not assumptions. To prevent that from happening, an approach known as a performance monitoring methodology comes into play.

In this regard, the methodology helps to conduct research. At that stage, a questionnaire is drawn up that helps us to understand the process and achieve a goal. For this reason, you need to make sure that your questionnaire contains questions including the following:

- What is the purpose that the server serves?
- What are the services that the server is providing?
- What components do you want to monitor?
- What is the metric of component performance?
- Which tool will you use for system analysis and data collection?

You can read more about monitoring and tuning your server at `https://msdn.microsoft.com/en-us/library/bb742410.aspx`.

Now, let's take a look at performance monitoring procedures.

# Understanding performance monitoring procedures

From what has been said previously, it can be understood that the methodology helps in the development of procedures. In this instance, we are talking about server performance monitoring procedures that are well-structured activities. In this regard, to monitor the performance of your servers, you may want to consider the following procedures:

- Document the server's hardware, software, and configuration.
- Establish the server's baseline.
- Upgrade the server's hardware and software.
- Perform the server's baseline and compare that with previous baselines.
- Identify server bottlenecks.
- Take concrete steps to fine-tune the server's performance.

Before implementing these procedures, we need to first implement a baseline. Let's understand how to do this.

# Understanding server baselines

In general, a server's performance must be monitored. As a system administrator, you should ask yourself a few questions about server performance monitoring. Some of these questions may include the following:

- How do you know when servers are working under their load?
- Do you have a sample to compare their performance against?

Questions such as these may encourage you to approach such an activity with more dedication. For that reason, before explaining how to establish a baseline, and what to consider when creating a baseline, it is good to know: what is a baseline? In short, a **server baseline** represents a snapshot of a server's performance under a normal workload. It enables you to compile a detailed report on the performance of various server components under normal workload conditions. Without neglecting other server components, the main reason for a baseline is to collect the following performance information:

- Processor utilization
- RAM utilization
- Disk read-and-write operations
- Network connection utilization

This implies that performance monitoring is not confined solely to collecting information from the previously-mentioned hardware components. The fact that many computer networks serve different purposes strengthens the opinion that the parameters that we are monitoring need to be different too.

 As was mentioned in the information box of the *Processing GPOs* section of Chapter 7, *Group Policy in Windows Server 2019,* regarding the development of new GPs for Windows 10 version 1809 and Windows Server 2019, beware that Microsoft publishes new baselines all the time. Hence, in May 2019, Microsoft released the security configuration baseline settings for Windows 10 version 1903 and Windows Server version 1903. The new security baseline can be downloaded at https://www.microsoft.com/en-us/download/details.aspx?id=55319.

# Understanding Performance Monitor

Simply put, Performance Monitor is a Windows **Microsoft Management Console** (**MMC**) that monitors the server's performance. It enables us to visualize performance information, either in real time or from a log file. The examined performance information is displayed in formats such as a line graph, histogram bar, or report.

# Running Performance Monitor

To run Performance Monitor in Windows Server 2019, complete the following steps:

1. Press the Windows key + *R*.
2. Enter perfmon.exe and press *Enter*.
3. Shortly, **Performance Monitor** will appear, as shown in *Figure 10.10*:

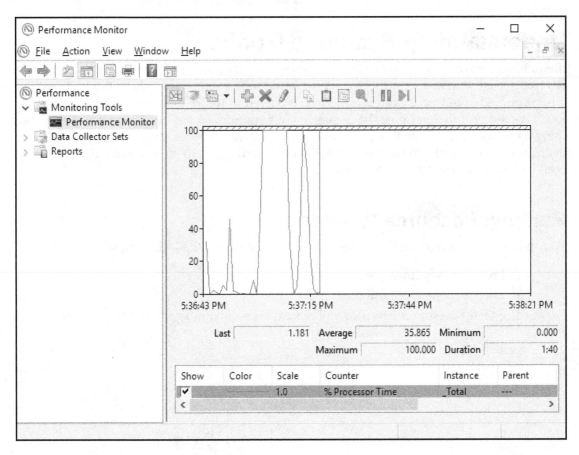

Figure 10.10: Performance Monitor in Windows Server 2019

You can open Resource Monitor from within Performance Monitor.

Next, let's understand Resource Monitor, an alternative to the aforementioned Performance Monitor.

# Understanding Resource Monitor

If you have owned a computer with a Windows operating system for a while now, it may have happened that just recently, you have started to feel that it is working slower than when you first bought it. Regardless, you do not need to worry because you can use Resource Monitor to determine the causes of your computer's slow performance. The same thing happens with servers too. So, whenever it is proven that server performance has decreased considerably, Resource Monitor is at your disposal to view the real-time usage of both hardware and software resources.

## Running Resource Monitor

To run Resource Monitor in Windows Server 2019, complete the following steps:

1. Press the Windows key + *R*.
2. Enter `resmon.exe` and press *Enter*.
3. Shortly, **Resource Monitor** will appear, as shown in *Figure 10.11*:

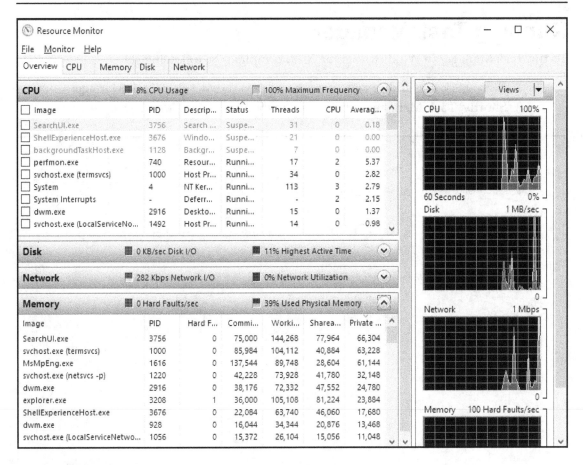

Figure 10.11: Resource Monitor in Windows Server 2019

Besides Performance Monitor and Resource Monitor, Task Manager is an important managerial tool. Let's quickly learn about it.

# Understanding Task Manager

In addition to Performance Monitor and Resource Monitor, Task Manager enables you to monitor the processes, performance, and services currently running on your server. Other than that, Task Manager allows us to start/stop applications and background processes. Regarding the performance of your server, Task Manager offers a visual representation of this. Available views are a summary and graph.

# Running Task Manager

To run Task Manager in Windows Server 2019, complete the following steps:

1. Right-click the taskbar and, from the context menu, select **Task Manager**.
2. Shortly, **Task Manager** will appear, as shown in *Figure 10.12*:

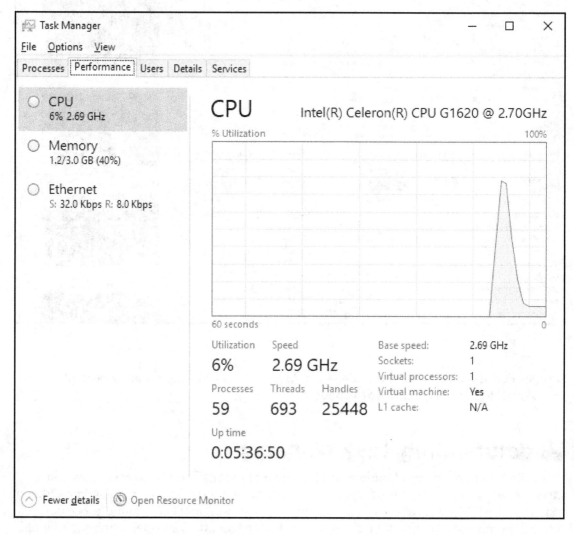

Figure 10.12: Task Manager in Windows Server 2019

You can open Resource Monitor from within Task Manager, as shown in *Figure 10.12*.

Now, let's understand performance counters and how to use them.

# Understanding performance counters

In Performance Monitor, you can use counters and instances of selected objects to collect data for the server hardware that you are keeping your eye on. Counters provide performance information on how well an operating system, application, service, or driver is working. Objects have counters to measure different aspects of performance, where each object has at least one instance that represents a unique copy of a particular type of object. That way, you can determine your server's bottlenecks and react promptly to avoid further degradation of server performance. Then, by following the necessary steps, you can fine-tune your server's performance.

## Setting up Data Collector Sets

To set up a Data Collector Set in Windows Server 2019, complete the following steps:

1. With the **Performance Monitor** open, expand **Monitoring Tools** and select **Performance Monitor**.
2. Right-click **Performance Monitor** and select **New | Data Collector Set**.
3. Enter the name for your Data Collector Set and click **Next**.
4. Specify the location where you want to save it by clicking **Browse** and then click **Next**.
5. Set the user in **Run as** and select either **Start this data collector set now** or **Save and close**.
6. Click **Finish**.
7. Right-click **Graph** and select **Add Counters...**.
8. Select counters from the **Available counters** section and click the **Add** button to add them to the list in the **Added counters** section.
9. Repeat *step 8* to add more counters, as shown in *Figure 10.13*.

10. Click **OK** to close the window:

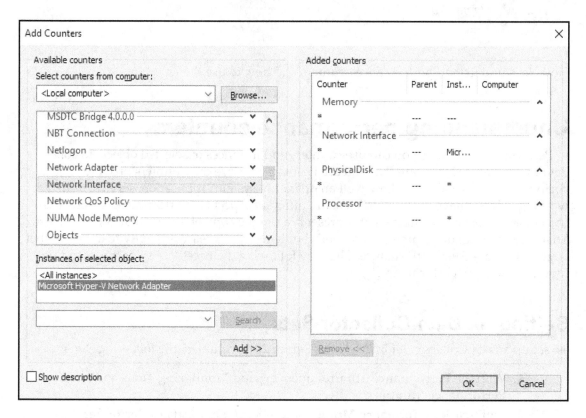

Figure 10.13: Performance Monitor counters in Windows Server 2019

 You can find information about performance monitoring thresholds and other useful monitoring information for various technologies at `https://www.manageengine.com/network-monitoring/network-performance-monitoring.html`.

In this section, we have learned about performance monitoring methodology, performance monitoring procedures, server baselines, Performance Monitor, Resource Monitor, Task Manager, and performance counters. In the next section, we will learn about logs and alerts.

# Understanding logs and alerts

As you know, performance monitoring activities are continuous. As such, it requires dedication and patience from system administrators. However, before that, it requires us to recognize the importance of the performance monitoring process as a way of maintaining the server's continuous work. To achieve this, the correct tools must be used. For this reason, tools such as logs and alerts play an important role in that process. While logs are useful for detailed analysis and archiving of records, alerts enable you to be vigilant about the performance and configuration of the servers.

## The purpose of performance logs and alerts

With Performance Monitor, you can collect performance information, log that information automatically, and set up alerts. The logged performance information can be used for analysis, or it can be exported to either a spreadsheet or database program for subsequent analysis and report generation. To configure performance logs and alerts in Windows Server 2019, use the approach outlined in the following section.

In this section, we have learned about performance logs and alerts and, in the next section, you will carry out this chapter's exercise relating to performance logs and alerts.

## Chapter exercise – the performance logs and alerts service

In this exercise, you will learn how to do the following:

- Start the performance logs and alerts service
- Access the Performance Monitor logs folder
- Create performance data logs
- Set up performance counter alerts

# Starting the performance logs and alerts service

To start the performance logs and alerts service in Windows Server 2019, complete the following steps:

1. Press the Windows key + *R*.
2. Enter `services.msc` and press *Enter*.
3. From the list of services, locate the **Performance Logs & Alerts** (see *Figure 10.14*) service to check its status.
4. If it is stopped, then right-click and select **Start**.
5. Close the **Services** window:

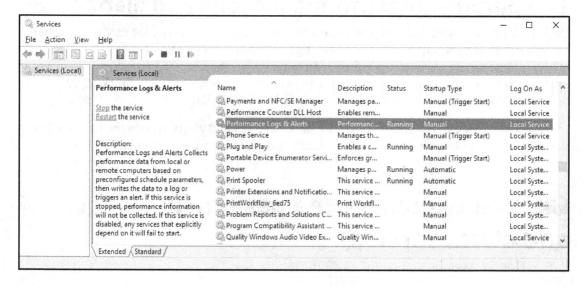

Figure 10.14: Performance logs and alerts service in Windows Server 2019

Now that we have started the performance logs and alerts service, let's move to our next task of accessing the Performance Monitor logs folder.

# Accessing the Performance Monitor logs folder

To access the Performance Monitor logs folder, `PerfLogs`, in Windows Server 2019, complete the following steps:

1. Press the Windows key + *R*.
2. Enter `C:` and press *Enter*.
3. The `PerfLogs` folder appears, as shown in *Figure 10.15*:

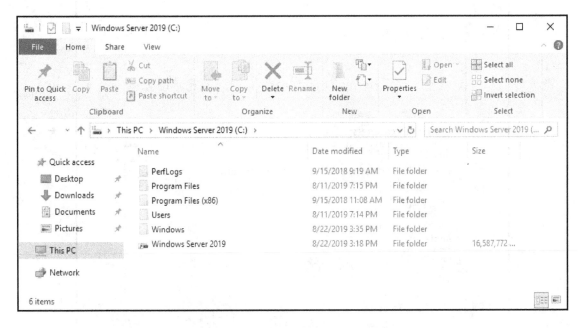

Figure 10.15: PerfLogs folder in Windows Server 2019

Moving forward, let's now create some performance data logs.

# Creating performance data logs

To create performance data logs in Windows Server 2019, complete the following steps:

1. With **Performance Monitor** open, expand **Data Collector Sets** and select **User Defined**.
2. Right-click **User Defined** and select **New** | **Data Collector Set**.

3.  Enter the name for your Data Collector Set.
4.  Choose the **Create manually (Advanced)** option and then click **Next**.
5.  Choose the **Create data logs** option and the **Performance counter** sub-option, and then click **Next**.
6.  Click the **Add** button to add counters, as shown in *Figure 10.16*, specify the time interval, and then click **Next**:

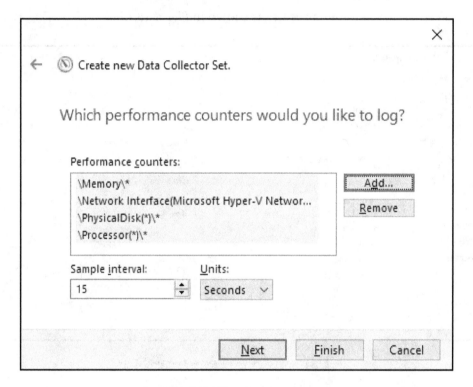

Figure 10.16: Adding performance counters

7.  Check that the default folder for saving data logs is the `PerfLogs` folder, and then click **Next**.
8.  Set the user in **Run as**, and select the **Start this data collector set now** option.
9.  Click **Finish**.

Finally, let's now set up performance counter alerts.

# Setting up performance counter alerts

To set up a performance counter alert in Windows Server 2019, complete the following steps:

1. Repeat *steps 1 to 4* from the *Creating performance data logs* section.
2. Choose **Performance Counter Alert**, and then click **Next**.
3. Click the **Add** button to add counters, as shown in *Figure 10.17*, specify an alert limit, and then click **Next**:

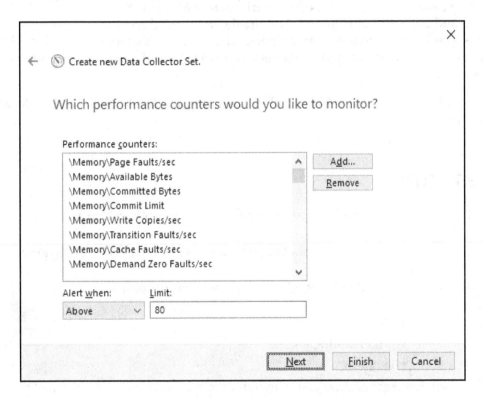

Figure 10.17: Setting up the performance counter alert

4. Set the user in **Run as**, and select the **Start this data collector set now** option.
5. Click **Finish**.

This was a nice exercise as it covered various examples of performance logs and alerts in Windows Server 2019.

# Summary

In this chapter, you have learned about a server's hardware components and how to maintain and monitor a server's performance via Windows Server 2019 features.

In the *Understanding server hardware components* section, you learned about the processor, memory, disk, network interface, 32-bit and 64-bit architectures, removable drives, graphic cards, cooling, power usage, and physical ports. Then, in the *Understanding performance monitoring* section, you learned about performance monitoring methodology, performance monitoring procedures, server baselines, Performance Monitor, Resource Monitor, Task Manager, and performance counters. And finally, in the third section, *Understanding logs and alerts*, you learned about performance logs and alerts. This chapter concluded with a chapter exercise that provided instructions about how to run the performance logs and alerts service.

In the following chapter, you will learn about updating and troubleshooting Windows Server 2019.

# Questions

1. Servers provide network services and handle user requests to access services. (True | False)
2. _____ represents a snapshot of your server's performance under a normal workload.
3. Which of the following is related to processors? (Choose two)
   - Cache
   - Cores
   - NIC Teaming
   - Hot-swap
4. Task Manager enables you to monitor the processes, performance, and services currently running on your server. (True | False)
5. _____ are the hardware that generate the most thermal heat.
6. Which of the following are the benefits of having multiple NICs on the server? (Choose two)
   - Network Load Balancing (NLB)
   - Network separation
   - Word size
   - Virtualization technology

7. Because power supplies are not considered to be a single point of failure, servers are not equipped with a redundant power supply. (True | False)

8. _____ has to do with the processor's internal architecture and defines the data bus size, the size of the instructions, and the address size.

9. Which of the following Windows MMCs are used for performance and resource monitoring? (Choose two)
    - Performance Monitor
    - Resource Monitor
    - Server Manager
    - Device Manager

10. Counters provide performance information on how well an operating system, application, service, or driver works. (True | False)

11. _____ helps to identify server problems at an early stage of development, and take the necessary steps to prevent them from turning into costly problems in terms of both time and business.

12. Which of the following are considered to be a server's primary storage? (Choose two.)
    - RAM
    - ROM
    - HDD
    - USB Flash Drive

13. Discuss Performance Monitor and Resource Monitor.

14. Discuss performance logs and alerts.

# Further reading

- *System Requirements*: https://docs.microsoft.com/en-us/windows-server/get-started-19/sys-reqs-19
- *Server Hardware Performance Considerations*: https://docs.microsoft.com/en-us/windows-server/administration/performance-tuning/hardware/
- *How to: Use Performance Monitor to Collect Event Trace Data*: https://docs.microsoft.com/en-us/dynamics365/business-central/dev-itpro/administration/monitor-use-performance-monitor-collect-event-trace-data

# 11
# Updating and Troubleshooting Windows Server 2019

This chapter is designed to teach you about the hardest part of working with servers: updating and troubleshooting. Yes, this is true! However, as you progress through this chapter, you will find even the most difficult lessons have been simplified and made very easy for you. Thus, by understanding the importance of troubleshooting, updating, and maintaining servers, the potential of having a high standard of business continuity is greatly increased.

Along the same lines, this chapter introduces you to the server startup process, advanced boot options and Safe Mode, backup and restore, disaster recovery plan, and updating the OS, hardware, and software. We also mention the Event Viewer tool, which allows you to monitor different logs on your system, thus helping you to troubleshoot and solve any problems. In this way, you will be able to minimize downtime, which, from a business point of view, is expressed in money loss.

The chapter concludes with an exercise on how to use the Event Viewer tool to monitor and manage logs.

The following topics will be covered in this chapter:

- Understanding updates
- Understanding the troubleshooting methodology
- Understanding the startup process
- Understanding business continuity
- Chapter exercise—using Event Viewer to monitor and manage logs

# Technical requirements

In order to complete the exercise for this chapter, you will need the following equipment:

- A PC with Windows 10 Pro, at least 16 GB of RAM, 1 TB of HDD, and access to the internet
- A virtual machine with Windows Server 2019 Standard, at least 4 GB of RAM, 100 GB of HDD, and access to the internet

# Understanding updates

After every Windows installation, it is recommended that you check whether Microsoft Windows Update has any updates for your newly installed OS. Naturally, through Windows Update, you will add feature enhancements and, more importantly, security. Therefore, it is not good at all to neglect or, for whatever reason, compromise the OS update process.

# Understanding Windows Update

Every second Tuesday of each month, unofficially known as **Patch Tuesday**, Microsoft releases new updates, among which are cumulative updates, security patches, and other fixes for their OSes and applications. Everything is distributed through Windows Update, which is both a Windows feature and a website: `https://update.microsoft.com`. From time to time, a notification is displayed in the system tray saying **You need some updates**, as shown in *Figure 11.1*:

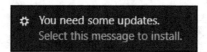

Figure 11.1: Windows Update notifications

In Windows Server 2019, Windows Update has undergone a slight change in terms of its interface and the way it accesses the updates. The following options are available (see *Figure 11.2*):

- **Change active hours**: This allows you to set up active hours so that Windows Update will not restart the server—even if it requires a restart of the server so that the installation of the updates can be completed.

- **View update history**: This displays the list of updates and their statuses. In addition to this, you can uninstall updates and access recovery options.
- **Advanced options**: This allows you to choose how updates are installed. You have two choices: **Give me updates for other Microsoft products when I update Windows** and **Defer feature updates**:

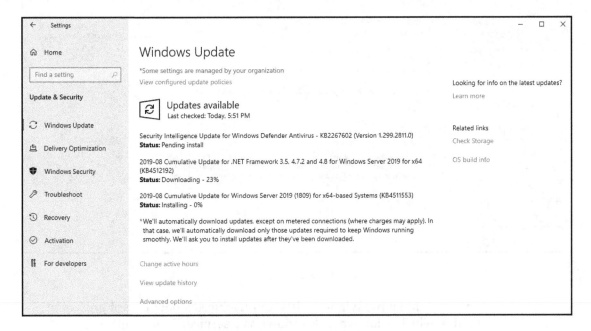

Figure 11.2: The Windows Update user interface

Now that we have a general overview of Windows Update, let's go ahead and learn how to update Windows Server 2019 by ourselves.

# Updating Windows Server 2019

To update Windows Server 2019 using Windows Update, complete the following steps:

1. Press the Windows key + *I* to open the Windows **Settings** section.
2. In the Windows **Settings** window, click on **Update & Security**.
3. Under **Update status**, click on the **Check for updates** button. **Checking for updates...** rolls on.
4. If Windows Update finds new updates, it will then prompt you to install these updates.

5. In most cases, you will need to restart the server (as shown in *Figure 11.3*) in order for the updates to take effect:

Figure 11.3: Updating Windows Server 2019

 As you might know, Windows 10 has introduced a new way of providing updates, which is known as **Windows as a service**. This means that Windows 10 will constantly evolve, and thus new releases will be delivered through Windows Update. But what if you do not want to receive these new releases? Well, the option that's offered by Microsoft is called defer feature updates. You can learn more about this interesting feature at `https://www.onmsft.com/news/mean-defer-feature-updates-windows-10`.

So, we just learned how to update Windows. Now, let's take a look at software from vendors other than Microsoft.

# Updating Microsoft programs

Regardless of whether the server is running a Microsoft OS, it is normal to use software from vendors other than Microsoft; for example, an Oracle DB, an Apache web server, a VMware virtualization platform, and so on. Because of this, we must understand the differences between the processes of updating software from Microsoft and updating software from other vendors. If we assert that each software company is unique, then it can be concluded that updating your software from vendors other than Microsoft has its own specific approach. Let's go back to the Microsoft software update process in order to find out what new things Windows Server 2019 has to offer. The steps are as follows:

1. Press the Windows key + *I* to open the Windows **Settings** section.
2. In the Windows **Settings** window, click on **Update & Security**.
3. Under the **Update settings** section, click on **Advanced options**.
4. Select the **Give me updates for other Microsoft products when I update Windows** option, as shown in *Figure 11.4*:

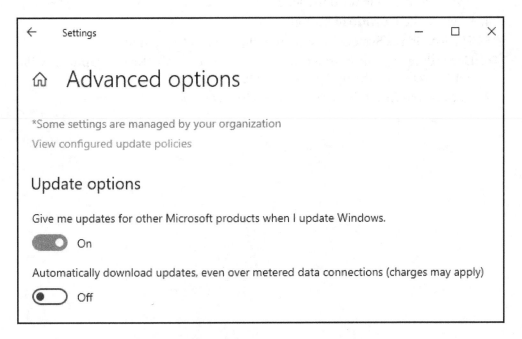

Figure 11.4: Updating Microsoft programs

5. Close the Windows **Settings** window.

As you know, in general, Microsoft programs are updated via Microsoft's Windows Update. However, that might not be the case with non-Microsoft programs. Having said that, let's demonstrate how to update non-Microsoft programs.

# Updating non-Microsoft programs

For the most part, on Windows-based servers, Windows Update is responsible for updating Microsoft OSes, applications, and utilities. Earlier in this chapter, we explained that software from vendors other than Microsoft is unique in the way that it is updated. Now, we will show you how to update a third-party application (such as Adobe Reader X) on Windows Server 2019. The steps are as follows:

1. Open Adobe Reader from the **Start** menu.
2. In the **Help** menu, select **Check for Updates...**.
3. Shortly afterward, **Adobe Reader Updater** displays a message stating that an update is available for download.
4. Click on the **Download** button.
5. The icon in the System Tray silently downloads the update.
6. Depending on your internet connection speed, **Adobe Reader Updater** will notify you when the update is ready to be installed.
7. Click on the **Install** button, as shown in *Figure 11.5*:

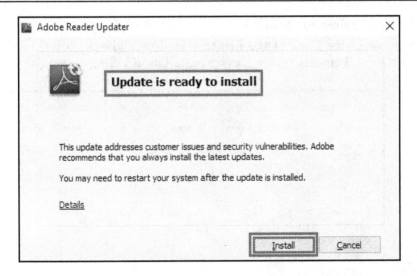

Figure 11.5: Updating non-Microsoft programs

8. You need to close Adobe Reader when prompted to do so and then click on **Retry**.
9. Click on **Yes** to confirm that you allow the app to install.
10. When the update has successfully installed, click on **Close**.

Now that we have learned how to update Microsoft and non-Microsoft programs, it's time we learned how to update our device drivers.

# Updating the device drivers

In the *Updating the device drivers* section of `Chapter 4`, *Post-Installation Tasks in Windows Server 2019*, we presented the necessary steps so that you can update your device drivers using the device manager. That is why, here, you will be shown how to configure Windows Update to check for the latest drivers and updates for your server hardware automatically. The steps are as follows:

1. Press the Windows key + *R*, enter `Control Panel`, and then press *Enter*.
2. Click on **Hardware**.

3. Click on **Devices and Printers**.

4. From within the **Devices and Printers** window, right-click on the name of the server, and then click on the **Device installation** settings (see *Figure 11.6*):

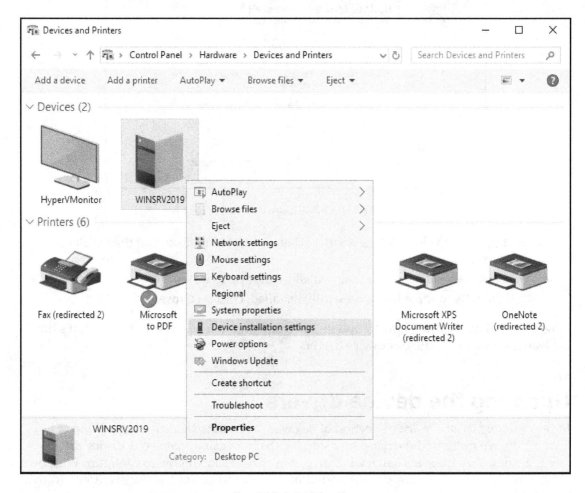

Figure 11.6: Device installation settings

5. Select the **Yes (recommended)** option, as shown in Figure *11.7*:

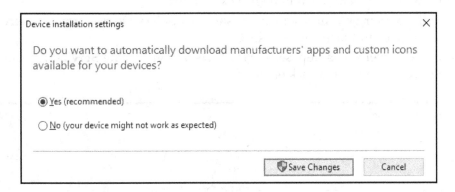

Figure 11.7: Setting up device driver update

6. Click on **Save Changes** to close the **Device installation settings** dialog box.

Microsoft's product updates need to be managed and organized. This is achieved with the help of **Windows Server Update Services** (**WSUS**). Let's learn more about this next.

# Understanding WSUS

As the successor to **Software Update Services** (**SUS**), WSUS allows system administrators to manage the distribution of Microsoft's product updates to their organization's computers. WSUS works in such a way that its infrastructure enables the downloading of updates, patches, and fixes to an organization's server. Then, the server distributes the updates to other computers. Using WSUS, system administrators can approve or cancel the updates, set the installation of updates on a given date, and generate reports to determine what updates are required for each computer. In this way, the organization's computers do not need to refer to Microsoft Update anymore, since the updates are provided by WSUS.

In Windows Server 2019, WSUS is a role that is added using Server Manager. Thus, to add the WSUS role, complete the following steps:

1. Press the Windows key + *R*, enter `servermanager.exe`, and then press *Enter*.
2. In the **Server Manager** console, select **Add Roles and Features**.
3. In the **Before You Begin** step, click on **Next**.

4. In the **Installation Type** step, make sure that role-based or feature-based installation is selected, and then click on **Next**.

5. In the **Server Selection** step, make sure that **Select a server from the server pool** is selected, and then click on **Next**.

6. In the **Server Roles** step, select **Windows Server Update Services**, as shown in *Figure 11.8*, and then click on **Next**:

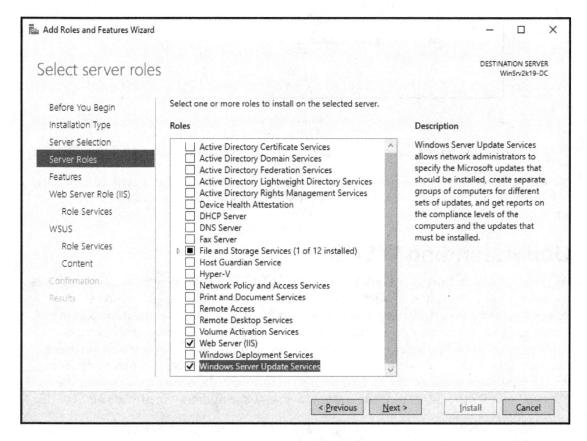

Figure 11.8: Installing Windows Server Update Services

7. In the **Features** step, there is no need to add features; therefore, click on **Next**.

8. In the **WSUS** step, the description and things to note regarding the WSUS installation are presented. Click on **Next**.

9. In the **Role Services** step, **WID Connectivity** and **WSUS Services** are selected by default. Click on **Next**.

10. In the **Content** step, enter the name of the local or network location where the updates are going to be stored. Click on **Next**.
11. In the **Confirmation** step, click on **Install**.
12. When the installation is complete, click on **Close** to close the **Add Roles and Features Wizard**.

In this section, we have learned about Windows Updates, updating Windows Server 2019, updating Microsoft programs, updating non-Microsoft programs, updating device drivers, and understanding WSUS. In the next section, we will gain an understanding of the troubleshooting methodology.

# Understanding the troubleshooting methodology

Troubleshooting in IT is a skill that you are going to master with time. This means that each time you solve a problem, you gain more confidence, become more experienced, and establish a larger knowledge base. That is why learning and practicing means a lot in IT because, while learning how to troubleshoot, you are practicing troubleshooting at the same time. With that in mind, the more you refine your mastery, the greater the chance you have to solve problems and overcome issues.

Let's begin by understanding the best practices, guidelines, and procedures of the troubleshooting methodology.

# Best practices, guidelines, and procedures

In the world of IT, best practices are well-defined methods that are applied wherever problems occur. These best practices allows you to make sure that an organization's policy and procedure management are handled effectively and efficiently. This has made best practices a feature of well-known accredited management standards such as ISO 9000 and ISO 14001. Therefore, by following best practices, servers will run more efficiently, network services will be more reliable, client/server applications will be more secure, and network infrastructures will be more scalable. In addition to this, **guidelines** represent suggestions, recommendations, or best practices for how to meet the policy standard. Finally, **procedures** are the step-by-step instructions that detail how to implement the components of the policy.

You can learn more about the ISO 9000 standard at `http://asq.org/learn-about-quality/iso-9000/overview/overview.html` and the ISO 14001 standard at `http://asq.org/learn-about-quality/learn-about-standards/iso-14001`.

Next, let's understand the troubleshooting process.

# Understanding the troubleshooting process

Among dozens of available methodologies, there exists a six-step troubleshooting model known as the detection method, which is used by Microsoft product support services engineers. The steps are as follows:

1. Discover the problem by gathering as much technical information as possible.
2. Evaluate system configuration by asking questions to determine whether any hardware, software, or network changes have been made recently.
3. List or track possible solutions by isolating the problem through removing or disabling hardware or software components.
4. Execute a plan through testing solutions, and, at the same time, ensure that you have a plan *B* too.
5. Check the results. If the problem has not been solved, go back to *step 3*.
6. Take a proactive approach by documenting any changes that you have made while troubleshooting the problem.

 You can learn more about the troubleshooting process in general, and the detection method in particular, at `https://technet.microsoft.com/en-ca`.

Besides these processes, troubleshooting is based on two approaches, which we will learn about next.

# Systematic versus specific approach

In general, the troubleshooting process and problem solving techniques recognize two methods:

- A **systematic approach** is an effective troubleshooting methodology because it is based on structured steps toward solving the problem, regardless of the type of problem.
- A **specific approach** is based primarily on having the knowledge and preliminary experience of solving the same/similar problems. In this approach, guesswork comes into play.

Now, let's examine the troubleshooting procedures.

# Understanding the troubleshooting procedures

No matter how skillful you might be, remember that troubleshooting is a skill that relies on certain guidelines. It requires an organized and logical approach to problems with servers (in particular) and computer networks (in general). The procedures that you may want to consider when involved in troubleshooting include the following:

- You may want to consider checking the documentation to see whether the problem has occurred in the past.
- You may want to check any available logs, including the Event Viewer.
- You may want to consider searching through the Microsoft **Knowledge Base (KB)** articles.
- You may want to consider running a backup prior to testing any solutions.
- You may want to consider running diagnostic programs.

The tools that you may want to consider when troubleshooting problems include the following:

- The **Advance Boot Options** menu, including **Safe Mode**
- **Windows Repair**
- **Memory Diagnostics**
- **System Information**
- **Device Manager**
- **Task Manager**

- **Performance Monitor**
- **Resource Monitor**
- **Event Viewer**

Now, let's examine the **Information Technology Infrastructure Library** (**ITIL**), which allows you to tailor your IT services to your business needs.

# Understanding the ITIL

ITIL represents the foundation for IT service management. ITIL, a well-structured framework, consists of best practices that guide IT organizations on how to design, implement, operate, and manage IT services. All of these ITIL practices are presented in the form of publications. At the same time, these publications constitute the ITIL version 3 core books. In summary, ITIL allows you to tailor IT services to business needs, thus making IT an important driver in today's economy.

 You can learn more about ITIL at `https://www.axelos.com/best-practice-solutions/itil`.

Next, let's learn about the Event Viewer and its benefits as a source of troubleshooting information.

# Understanding Event Viewer

The Event Viewer (see *Figure 11.9*), as the name suggests, is an MMC snap-in that allows system administrators to monitor events in servers. This feature also makes the Event Viewer a good source of troubleshooting information whenever software, hardware, and network-related issues impact server infrastructure. From applications to forwarded events, there are five types of logs that you can monitor with Event Viewer:

- **Application** contains applications or program events.
- **Security** contains events that are triggered by security-related activities, such as an invalid login attempt or trying to access a folder with denied permissions. It requires you to have auditing enabled.
- **Setup** contains application setup events.
- **System** contains events that are triggered by Windows' system components.

- **Forwarded Events** contains events that are triggered by remote computers. It requires you to create an event subscription:

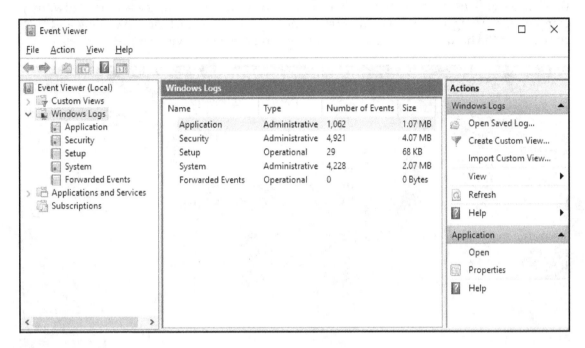

Figure 11.9: The Event Viewer

In this section, we have covered best practices, guidelines and procedures, troubleshooting processes, systematic versus specific approaches, troubleshooting procedures, the ITIL, and the Event Viewer. In the next section, we will introduce the startup process.

# Understanding the startup process

Although it is completely technical, being able to identify and understand the hardware components in general, and the steps in the startup process in particular, has tremendous benefits. This is because it helps you in troubleshooting hardware-related problems, and so keeps downtime to a minimum.

To begin, let's take a look at the **Basic Input/Output System** (**BIOS**).

# Understanding BIOS

BIOS (see *Figure 11.10*) is a program that controls the functionality of the server hardware components. Alongside this, the other important tasks of BIOS include identifying and configuring the hardware in a server and identifying the boot devices:

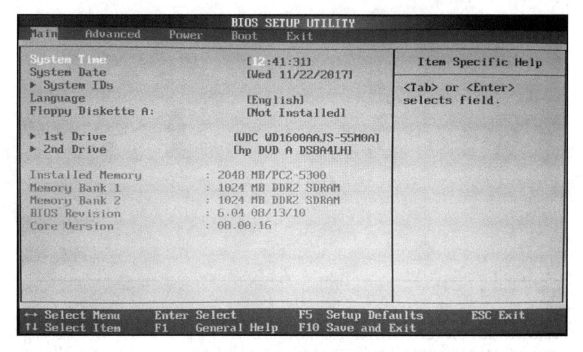

```
                        BIOS SETUP UTILITY
  Main    Advanced    Power    Boot    Exit

  System Time                 [12:41:31]              Item Specific Help
  System Date                 [Wed 11/22/2017]
  ▶ System IDs                                       <Tab> or <Enter>
  Language                    [English]              selects field.
  Floppy Diskette A:          [Not Installed]

  ▶ 1st Drive                 [WDC WD1600AAJS-55M0A]
  ▶ 2nd Drive                 [hp DVD A DS8A4LH]

  Installed Memory          : 2048 MB/PC2-5300
  Memory Bank 1             : 1024 MB DDR2 SDRAM
  Memory Bank 2             : 1024 MB DDR2 SDRAM
  BIOS Revision             : 6.04 08/13/10
  Core Version              : 08.00.16


  ↔ Select Menu      Enter  Select         F5  Setup Defaults      ESC Exit
  ↑↓ Select Item     F1     General Help   F10 Save and Exit
```

Figure 11.10: The BIOS SETUP UTILITY

 In the *Understanding boot options* section of `Chapter 3`, *Installing Windows Server 2019*, you can find additional information about BIOS, including boot options.

Over time, BIOS was eventually replaced by the **Unified Extensible Firmware Interface** (**UEFI**). We will learn more about this next.

# Understanding UEFI

Unlike computers in the past, modern computers do not have legacy BIOS; instead, they are equipped with a UEFI, as shown in *Figure 11.11*. Unlike BIOS, a UEFI is easily updated by downloading updates from the manufacturer's website. It supports 32-bit and 64-bit modes, and boots from disks with capacities that are far larger than BIOS:

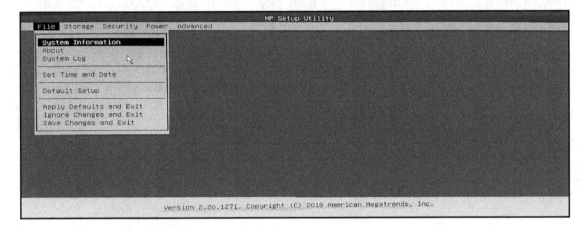

Figure 11.11: The UEFI setup utility

Now, let's take a look at the **Trusted Platform Module** (**TPM**).

# Understanding TPM

Ever since Windows Vista, when Microsoft introduced the BitLocker feature for disk encryption, TPM has been present on computers with Windows OSes. This is because TPM supports the process of encrypting disks by BitLocker by providing hardware security for the latter. From a technical standpoint, TPM is a chip on the computer's motherboard, which is used by Windows to store the encryption key whenever BitLocker encrypts the drives.

Now, let's explore the **Power-On Self-Test** (**POST**), which is a diagnostic test that verifies whether or not the server hardware is working correctly.

# Understanding POST

When a server is booted, BIOS performs a hardware test known as a **POST**. A POST is a diagnostic test that verifies that the server hardware is working correctly. Regardless of the BIOS manufacturer, it is good practice to learn the beeps that the POST produces during server hardware initialization. It is recommended that you keep an eye on the components, such as the processors, RAM, and graphics cards, as they are the first three components to be examined by a POST. If any of these components are faulty, then the server boot fails.

 You can learn more about various beep codes from different BIOS manufacturers at https://www.computerhope.com/beep.htm.

Now, let's take a look at the **Master Boot Record** (**MBR**).

# Understanding MBR

Once a POST finishes verifying that the server hardware is working correctly, BIOS then hands over control to the first boot device. This is because BIOS looks after the boot device that contains the MBR. The MBR is created when disk partitions are created; however, the MBR resides outside the disk partitions. More precisely, the MBR is located on the first disk sector. As we learned previously, the MBR contains either **NT Loader** (**NTLDR**), **Boot Manager** (**BOOTMGR**), or both, depending on the Windows OS installed on the server's disk. This then determines the progress of the programs that will be executed with the purpose of loading the OS into RAM as shown in the following table:

| NTLDR (Windows NT to Windows Server 2003) | BOOTMGR (Windows Vista to Windows Server 2019) |
|---|---|
| BOOT.INI | **Boot Configuration Data (BCD)** |
| NTDETECT.COM | WinLoad.exe |
| NTOSKRNL.EXE | NTOSKRNL.EXE |
| HAL.DLL | Boot-class device drivers |

In the *Understanding partition schemes* section of `Chapter 3`, *Installing Windows Server 2019*, you can find additional information about the MBR, including information on **GUID Partition Table** (**GPT**).

Now that we have understood the MBR, let's look at BCD.

# Understanding BCD

BCD represents a store consisting of specific files that enables control over what should happen when an OS boots. `Bcdedit.exe` (see *Figure 11.12*) is a file that is used to manage the BCD data store. In a similar fashion to `boot.ini`, `bcdedit.exe` is located inside the disk partitions. It works with OSes from Windows Vista to Windows Server 2019:

```
Administrator: Windows PowerShell                                   —    □    ×

Windows PowerShell
Copyright (C) Microsoft Corporation. All rights reserved.

PS C:\Users\Administrator> Bcdedit.exe

Windows Boot Manager
--------------------
identifier              {bootmgr}
device                  partition=\Device\HarddiskVolume1
description             Windows Boot Manager
locale                  en-US
inherit                 {globalsettings}
bootshutdowndisabled    Yes
default                 {current}
resumeobject            {660a0452-bcad-11e9-b710-00155d007501}
displayorder            {current}
toolsdisplayorder       {memdiag}
timeout                 30

Windows Boot Loader
-------------------
identifier              {current}
device                  partition=C:
path                    \Windows\system32\winload.exe
description             Windows Server
locale                  en-US
inherit                 {bootloadersettings}
recoverysequence        {660a0454-bcad-11e9-b710-00155d007501}
displaymessageoverride  Recovery
recoveryenabled         Yes
allowedinmemorysettings 0x15000075
osdevice                partition=C:
systemroot              \Windows
resumeobject            {660a0452-bcad-11e9-b710-00155d007501}
nx                      OptOut
PS C:\Users\Administrator> _
```

Figure 11.12: Running bcdedit.exe

In a multiple boot scenario, the MBR contains both NTLDR and BOOTMGR. This means that both `boot.ini` and `bcdedit.exe` are also present to display the respective OS's list. As we mentioned previously, you can use `bootsect.exe` (refer to the *Understanding Boot sector* section later on this chapter) to update the MBR for hard disk partitions in order to switch between NTLDR and BOOTMGR.

Naturally, the sections for MBR and BCD precede the bootloader. Now, let's explore the bootloader.

# Understanding bootloader

A bootloader is a program that loads the OS kernel into RAM and is located in the MBR. In Windows OSes, there are two types of bootloaders:

- NTLDR is the old Windows bootloader that was used from Windows NT to Windows Server 2003.
- BOOTMGR is the newest Windows bootloader. It can be used from Windows Vista to Windows Server 2019.

Now, let's explore the boot sector, which contains the information that is needed to boot the server (that is, the bootloader).

# Understanding the boot sector

In the *HDD* section of `Chapter 9`, *Storing Data in Windows Server 2019*, tracks and sectors are mentioned. Tracks look like concentric circles, and there are thousands of them on a disk. Sectors are the track's divisions and their size depends on the filesystem that the server's OS uses. You most likely understand what a boot sector is by now. It is the sector on a server's disk that contains the information that's required to boot the server (that is, the bootloader). Physically, the boot sector is located in the first sector of the first disk track. Usually, a boot sector contains the MBR.

Now, let's learn about the boot menu, which is used when there is more than one OS running on a computer.

# Understanding the boot menu

If you have multiple Windows OSes running on your computer, known as **multi-booting,** then every time you turn on your computer, you will see a boot menu that lists multiple OSes. If you did not know, this is boot.ini (see *Figure 11.13*), that is, a text file that enables the boot menu display. It works with OSes from Windows NT to Windows Server 2003. Unlike the MBR, boot.ini is located inside the disk partitions. The path to boot.ini is C:\boot.ini, which consists of two parts: the bootloader and the OS. The former includes a timeout value of 30 seconds and the default OS location, while the latter consists of the OSes and their respective boot entries:

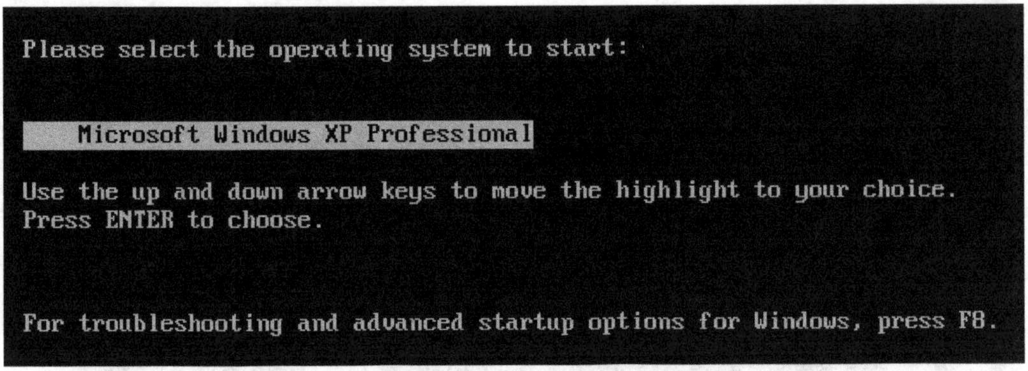

```
Please select the operating system to start:

    Microsoft Windows XP Professional

Use the up and down arrow keys to move the highlight to your choice.
Press ENTER to choose.


For troubleshooting and advanced startup options for Windows, press F8.
```

Figure 11.13: Boot.ini displays the list of OSes

Now, let's take a look at Safe Mode, which represents a diagnostic mode and uses a minimal set of drivers and services.

# Understanding Safe Mode

At some point, you may have experienced that the OS does not start when you've tried to turn on your computer. Without thinking too much about it, you might have turned your computer off and on again, and then, by pressing the *F8* key, accessed the **Windows Advanced Options Menu**, where you selected the **Safe Mode** option. The reason we do this is that Safe Mode is a diagnostic mode in Windows and uses a minimal set of drivers and services. Note that the *F8* key (see *Figure 11.14*) option can be used in the OSes from Windows NT to Windows Server 2003. For Windows Vista to Windows Server 2019, Microsoft offers **Advanced Startup Options** to recover OSes. Regardless, you can access Safe Mode with them too, but in other ways:

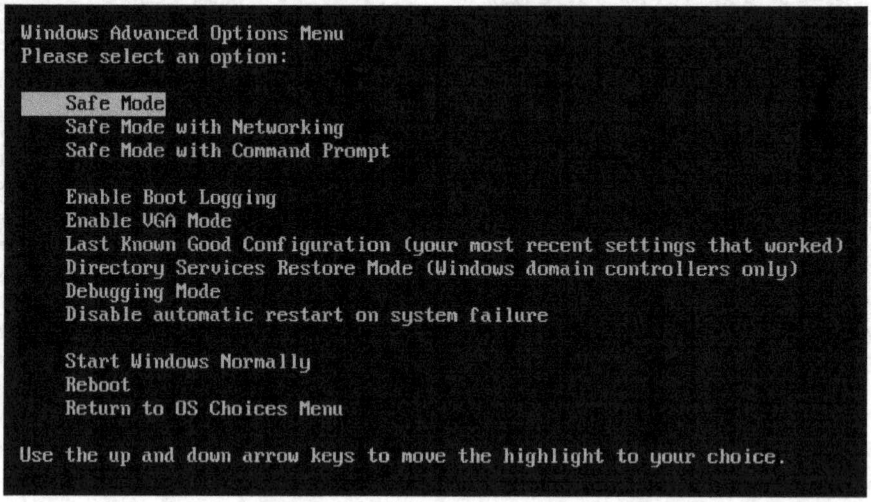

```
Windows Advanced Options Menu
Please select an option:

    Safe Mode
    Safe Mode with Networking
    Safe Mode with Command Prompt

    Enable Boot Logging
    Enable VGA Mode
    Last Known Good Configuration (your most recent settings that worked)
    Directory Services Restore Mode (Windows domain controllers only)
    Debugging Mode
    Disable automatic restart on system failure

    Start Windows Normally
    Reboot
    Return to OS Choices Menu

Use the up and down arrow keys to move the highlight to your choice.
```

Figure 11.14: Windows Advanced Options Menu in Windows XP Professional

In Windows Server 2019, complete the following steps to access the **Safe Mode** option from the **Advanced Boot Options** menu:

1. While holding down the *Shift* key, restart Windows Server 2019 by clicking on **Restart** from the **Power** option.
2. On the **Choose an option** screen, select **Troubleshooting**.
3. On the **Advanced options** screen, select **Startup Settings**.
4. Click on the **Restart** button on the **Startup Settings** screen.
5. Shortly afterward, the **Advanced Boot Options** screen will be displayed, as shown in *Figure 11.15*:

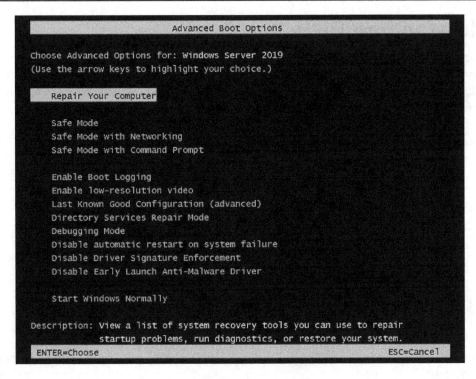

Figure 11.15: The Advanced Boot Options menu

In this section, we have learned about BIOS, UEFI, TPM, POST, MBR, BCD, bootloader, boot sector, boot menu, and Safe Mode. In the next section, we will explore business continuity.

# Understanding business continuity

As a system administrator in this digital age, you must understand that any period of downtime will mean a loss of profit for the company. Therefore, it is your primary responsibility to minimize downtime as much as possible. This can be achieved through a proper assessment of the components that have the potential to fail and taking the appropriate measures to avoid this failure.

Let's start by learning about the **Disaster Recovery Plan** (**DRP**).

# Understanding DRP

DRP is a well-structured plan that ensures an organization will continue to provide services or recover from a disastrous situation as soon as possible. If you take into account the fact that you cannot prevent the unexpected from happening, you can at least minimize any losses if you are always prepared. Therefore, in such situations, DRP is known as a proactive method for maintaining business continuity. The following is a list of things that organizations should consider when compiling DRP:

- Make an inventory of all hardware and software.
- Analyze all potential threats and vulnerabilities.
- Establish the organization's priorities.
- Define the organization's tolerance in case of a disaster.
- Review how the disaster was handled in the past.
- Acknowledge that staff matters more than data recovery and services.
- Execute DRP DRY tests regularly.
- Have management approve the DRP.
- Never forget to update the DRP.

Now, let's go on to understand data redundancy, which helps to restore services in case of a natural disaster.

# Understanding data redundancy

The idea behind data redundancy is to be able to store the same set of data in multiple locations and to be able to update it automatically. But what if the data updates are not successfully implemented? Data inconsistency problems occur, which can lead to more problems, such as data integrity. This can further multiply problems with the data and can potentially harm organizations that have a large amount of data and multiple data storage locations.

Now, let's explore clustering, which merges the processing power of several servers.

# Understanding clustering

**Clustering** refers to a group of servers that combine processor power, RAM, storage capacity, and network interfaces to achieve high availability of services. Clustering recognizes the following two most common practices:

- **Failover clustering**: This requires a minimum of two servers and works on the active-passive principle, where one server is active and the other server is passive. Usually, it is applied to databases, mail servers, and, in general, backend processing environments.
- **Load-balancing clustering**: This requires a minimum of two servers as well; however, servers are merged into one virtual server, exchanging heartbeats. As far as users are concerned, they access a single server; as far as backend processing is concerned, the loads are distributed between the servers. Usually, it is applied to web servers, and, in general, frontend processing environments.

Now, let's examine redirection, which facilitates the method of accessing documents in a network environment.

# Understanding folder redirection

System administrators can use folder redirection to redirect the folder on a local computer, or a shared folder on a network, to a new location. With folder redirection, the data that is stored on the server can be accessed by users in a similar fashion to how it would be if it was stored on a local computer.

In Windows Server 2019, you can create a **Group Policy Object** (**GPO**), as shown in *Figure 11.16*, to redirect a folder. The steps are as follows:

1. Press the Windows key + *R*, enter gpmc.msc, and then press *Enter*.
2. Expand **User Configuration**.
3. Expand **Policies**.
4. Expand **Windows Settings**.
5. Expand **Folder Redirection**.
6. Right-click on **Documents** and select **Properties**.

7. Select the **Basic - Redirect everyone's folder to the same location** setting.
8. In the **Target folder location** section, select **Redirect to the following location**.
9. Specify the root path to your redirected folder.
10. Click on **OK** to close the **Document Properties** window:

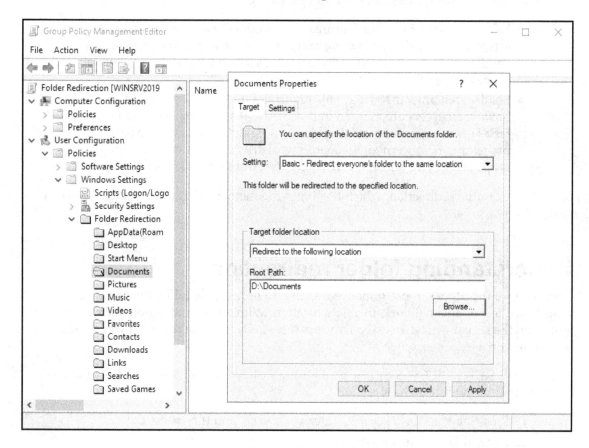

Figure 11.16: Creating a GPO for Folder Redirection

Losing your data might hamper continuity. To prevent this, you can back up your data. Let's learn more about this next.

# Understanding backup and restore

Data on a server needs to be protected from being lost. To avoid such situations, backups are usually used to make a copy of the data in case the original data is lost. In addition to a backup, a restore is the process of data recovery whenever data on a server is lost or corrupted. The following types of backups can be made:

- **Full backup**: This makes a copy of all of the data. To restore your data, you only require the last set of full backups.
- **Incremental backup**: This makes a copy of the data that has changed since the last backup, regardless of the type. Usually, incremental backups are done from Monday to Thursday, and on Friday, the full backup takes place. To restore your data, you need the last set of full backups and all of the sets of incremental backups between the full backup and the day you want to restore the data from. Because of this, it takes less time to do the backup, but more time to restore the data.
- **Differential backup**: This makes a copy of the data that has changed since the last full backup. In the same way as an incremental backup, a differential backup is done from Monday to Thursday, and on Friday, the full backup takes place. To restore your data, you need the last set of full backups and the last set of incremental backups. Because of this, it takes more time to do a backup, and less time to restore the data.

When it comes to choosing a backup media, usually, it depends on the importance of the data and its quantity. Storage technologies such as CDs, DVDs, removable HDDs, backup tapes, **network-attached storage** (**NASs**), and **storage area networks** (**SANs**) are all considered potential storage technologies for backing up. These days, organizations use online backup services too. Convenience, security, and cost are among the decisive factors for choosing online backup services. Last but not least, it is worth mentioning the most common backup rotation scheme, known as **Grandfather-Father-Son** (**GFS**). The son backup is done daily, the father backup is done weekly, and the grandfather backup is done monthly.

In Windows Server 2019, Windows Server Backup is a feature that can be added by using Server Manager. To add Windows Server Backup, complete the following steps:

1. Press the Windows key + *R*, enter `servermanager.exe`, and then press *Enter*.
2. From the **Server Manager** console, select **Add Roles and Features**.
3. In the **Before You Begin** option, click on **Next**.
4. In the **Installation Type** step, make sure that **Role-based or feature-based installation** is selected, and then click on **Next**.
5. In the **Server Selection** option, make sure that **Select a server from the server pool** is selected, and then click on **Next**.
6. In the **Server Roles** option, there is no need to add roles; therefore, click on **Next**.
7. In the **Features** step, scroll down the list of features and select **Windows Server Backup** (see *Figure 11.17*). Then, click on **Next**:

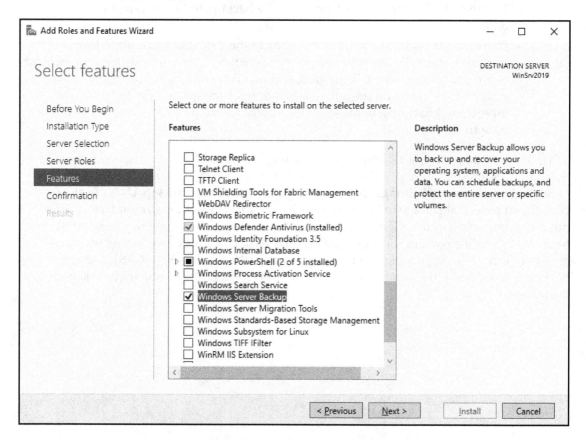

Figure 11.17: Installing the Windows Server Backup feature

8. In the **Confirmation** option, click on **Install**.
9. When the installation is complete, click on **Close** to close the **Add Roles and Features Wizard**.

Once we have created a backup, we can try and restore the data. Let's demonstrate how to do this.

# Understanding Active Directory (AD) restore

Remember that, during the process of adding the AD DS role (in the *Adding the Active Directory Domain Services role* section of `Chapter 5`, *Directory Services in Windows Server 2019*), in one of the steps of the **Active Directory Domain Services Configuration Wizard**, the **Directory Services Restore Mode** (**DSRM**) password is required (see *Figure 11.18*). That password is very important for AD restore, so you have to be careful. DSRM is to AD as Safe Mode is to the OS. It is a way of restoring AD when the latter has failed or requires restoring.

Usually, there are two methods for restoring data that is replicated on a **Domain Controller** (**DC**). The first method has to do with reinstalling the OS, reconfiguring the DC, and then, through normal replication, it will get populated from the second DC on a network. The second method takes into consideration the backup as a way of restoring the DC's replicated data. From that, the replicated data from a backup medium can be restored in the following two ways:

- **Non-authoritative restore**: This is applied in cases where a DC has failed due to hardware- or software-related problems. The AD structure is restored from a backup medium, and then it will populated from the second DC on a network through normal replication.

- **Authoritative restore**: This takes place after a non-authoritative restore, thus helping to restore the entire system to a state before the AD objects were deleted. It uses the `Ntdsutil` command, which enables an authoritative restore of the entire AD:

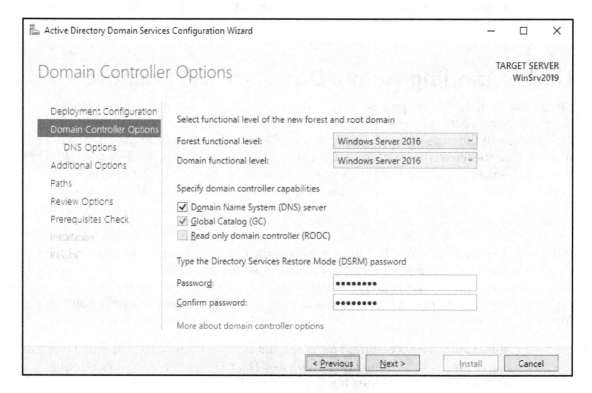

Figure 11.18: Setting up the DSRM

We cannot keep our server up and running unless we have a proper power supply. Let's learn how to overcome this problem next.

# Understanding power redundancy

Regardless of the processor power, RAM capacity, data storage space, and network interfaces that your server can have, all of this is useless if you have no power supply. This means that the power supply is very important for a server's overall well-being. That is why the **uninterruptible power supply** (**UPS**) device (see *Figure 11.19*) has an important place in the world of servers. The UPS is a device with a battery, which continues to supply the server with power when a power outage occurs. Despite the capabilities offered by the UPS, it still does not offer a solution for long power outages. For that reason, electric generators represent an alternative solution to overcome such issues:

Figure 11.19: Rack-mountable UPS

In this section, we have learned about the DRP, data redundancy, clustering, folder redirection, backup and restore, AD restore, and power redundancy. In the next section, you will run an exercise about the monitoring and managing logs via Event Viewer.

# Chapter exercise – using Event Viewer to monitor and manage logs

In this exercise, you will learn how to do the following:

- Set up centralized monitoring
- Filter Event Viewer logs
- Change the default logs location

# Setting up centralized monitoring

To set up centralized monitoring in Windows Server 2019, complete the following steps:

1. On a **Remote Server**, open the **Command Prompt** with elevated admin rights, enter `winrm quickconfig`, and then press *Enter*.
2. Right-click on the **Start** button and select **Computer Management**.
3. Expand **Local Users and Groups** and click on **Groups**.

4. Open the administrators group and add the central server.

5. On a **Central Server**, open **Command Prompt** with elevated admin rights, enter `wecutil qc`, and then press *Enter*.

6. Press **Y** (for yes) when prompted to do so.

7. From the **Command Prompt** window, enter `eventvwr.exe` to open **Event Viewer**.

8. Right-click on **Subscriptions** and select **Create Subscription....**

9. Enter the **Subscription name** and its **Description**.

10. Select **Forwarded Events** as **Destination log**.

11. Select **Remote Server** by clicking on the **Select Computers...** button, as shown in *Figure 11.20*, and then click on **OK**:

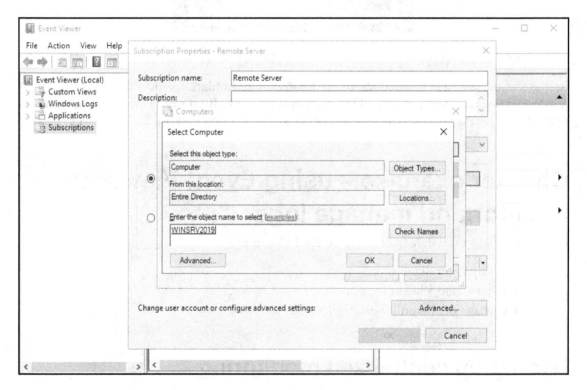

Figure 11.20: Adding Remote Server in order to collect events

12. In the **Subscription Properties** window, click on the **Select Events...** button, and select **Edit**.

13. In the **Query Filter** window, set the event logs filtering criteria that you want to collect and click on **OK**.

14. Click on the **Advanced...** button to make sure that the machine account is the chosen option, and then click on **OK**.
15. Click on **OK** to close the **Subscription Properties** window.

Now that we have set up centralized monitoring, let's filter Event Viewer logs.

# Filtering Event Viewer logs

To filter the Event Viewer logs in Windows Server 2019, complete the following steps:

1. Press the Windows key + *R*, enter `eventvwr.msc`, and then press *Enter*.
2. Expand **Windows Logs** and select the log type that you want to filter.
3. In the **Actions** pane, click on **Filter Current Log...**, as shown in *Figure 11.21*:

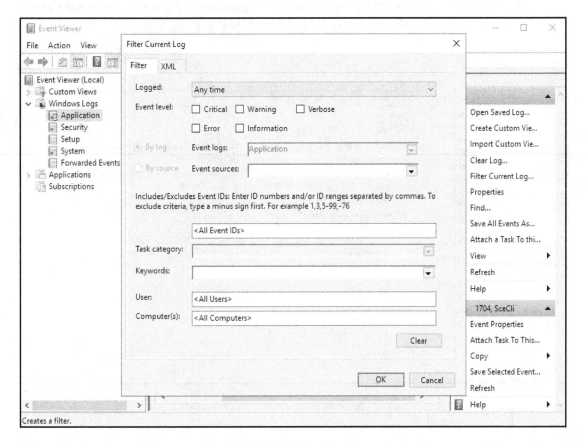

Figure 11.21: Filtering Event Viewer logs

4. In the **Filter Current Log** window, set the filtering criteria to get the desired results.

5. Click on **OK** to close the **Filter Current Log** window.

Finally, let's change the default logs location.

# Changing the default logs location

To change the default logs location in Windows Server 2019, complete the following steps:

1. Press the Windows key + *R*, enter `regedit`, and then press *Enter*.

2. Locate the following path: `HKEY_LOCAL_ MACHINE\System\CurrentControlSet\Services\EventLog\System`.

3. Within the `System` folder, open the `File` value, enter the new path in the **Value data** text box, as shown in *Figure 11.22*, and then click on **OK**:

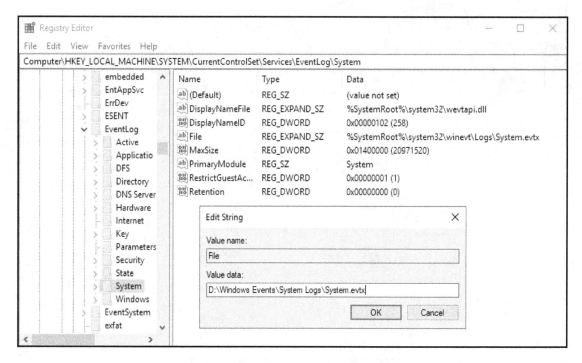

Figure 11.22: Changing the default logs location in Windows Server 2016

4. Locate `HKEY_LOCAL_`
   `MACHINE\System\CurrentControlSet\Services\EventLog\Application`
   to change the default location for application logs.

5. Locate `HKEY_LOCAL_`
   `MACHINE\System\CurrentControlSet\Services\EventLog\Security` to
   change the default location for security logs.

6. Close the **Registry Editor** window.

This was a useful exercise as it explained various ways of using Event Viewer to manage and monitor logs in Windows Server 2019.

# Summary

In this chapter, you learned about updating and troubleshooting Windows Server 2019.

In the *Understanding the updates* section, you learned about Windows Updates, updating Windows Server 2019, updating Microsoft programs, updating non-Microsoft programs, updating device drivers, and understanding WSUS. Then, in the next section, we learned about the troubleshooting methodology. Here, we learned about the best practices, guidelines and procedures, troubleshooting processes, systematic versus specific approaches, troubleshooting procedures, ITIL, and Event Viewer. Furthermore, in the *Understanding the startup process* section, we learned about BIOS, UEFI, TPM, POST, MBR, BCD, bootloader, boot sector, boot menu, and Safe Mode. Finally, in the *Understanding business continuity* section, we learned about DRP, data redundancy, clustering, folder redirection, backup and restore, AD restore, and power redundancy. This chapter concluded with an exercise that provided instructions on how to use Event Viewer to monitor and manage logs.

In the next chapter, you will learn about studying and preparing for the MTA 98-365 exam.

# Questions

1. A boot sector is a sector on a server's ROM that contains the required information so that you can boot your server. (True | False)

2. _____ is an MMC snap-in that enables system administrators to monitor events in servers.

3. Which of the following are troubleshooting methods?
   - Rational approach
   - Pragmatic approach
   - Systematic approach
   - Specific approach

4. A six-step troubleshooting model known as the detection method is used by Apple Product Support Services engineers. (True | False)

5. _____ is a device with a battery that continues to supply the server with power when a power outage occurs.

6. Which of the following are Event Viewer types of logs?
   - Application
   - Security
   - Software
   - Driver

7. The DRP is a well-structured plan that ensures the organization will continue to provide services or it will recover from situations when a disaster occurs as soon as possible. (True | False)

8. _____ is a diagnostic test that verifies whether or not the server hardware is working correctly.

9. Which of the following are Windows bootloaders?
   - NTLDR
   - BOOTMGR
   - `BOOT.INI`
   - `BCDEDIT.EXE`

10. The Basic Input/Output System, known as BIOS, is a program that controls the functionality of the server hardware components. (True | False)

11. _____ refers to a group of servers that combine processor power, RAM, storage capacity, and network interfaces to achieve the high availability of services.

12. Which of the following are backup types?
    - Incremental
    - Differential
    - Arithmetic
    - Geometric

13. Discuss the startup process.

14. Discuss the troubleshooting process.

15. Discuss Event Viewer filtering and central logging.

# Further reading

- *Get started with Windows Update*: https://docs.microsoft.com/en-us/windows/deployment/update/windows-update-overview
- *How to Troubleshoot Common Issues*: https://docs.microsoft.com/en-us/collaborate/troubleshooting
- *Advanced troubleshooting for Windows boot problems*: https://docs.microsoft.com/en-us/windows/client-management/advanced-troubleshooting-boot-problems
- *High Availability and Business Continuity*: https://docs.microsoft.com/en-us/office365/servicedescriptions/exchange-online-service-description/high-availability-and-business-continuity

# Section 5: Getting Ready for the Certification Exam

The fifth section provides information about what the MTA 98-365 exam is, as well as its objectives. Also, in this section, you will find information about what to expect, how to prepare, how to register, and what to do on the day of the MTA 98-365 exam. Of course, this section covers the post-MTA 98-365 exam certification path too.

This section comprises the following chapter:

- Chapter 12, *Preparing for the MTA 98-365 Exam*

# Preparing for the MTA 98-365 Exam

**12**

This chapter is designed to provide you with an overview of the MTA 98-365 exam, including the skills measured. In addition, this chapter contains explanations as to what the MTA 98-365 exam or Windows Server Administration Fundamentals certification is and how to register for the exam. Also, this chapter contains suggestions on how to prepare for the exam and considerations that need to be taken into account when taking the exam.

Furthermore, you will find useful resources that will help you gather as much information as possible about the exam in general, and what it takes to pass it successfully and, with it, launch a successful career. Last but not least, learn about and practice as much as you can with Windows Server 2019, because only by doing so will you be able to achieve the adequate skills to pass the MTA 98-365 exam without hitting hurdles, and become a **Microsoft Technology Associate (MTA)**.

The following topics will be covered in this chapter:

- What is the MTA certification?
- Who should take the MTA 98-365 exam?
- Which skills are measured by the MTA 98-365 exam?
- What should you expect in the MTA 98-365 exam?
- How should you prepare for the MTA 98-365 exam?
- How do you register for the MTA 98-365 exam?
- The day of the MTA 98-365 exam
- Post MTA 98-365 exam certification path
- Useful resources

# What is the MTA certification?

An MTA represents entry-level certification for candidates seeking to validate their technical skills, helping them to begin a career in technology. As opposed to Microsoft's professional certification level, where candidates aim to achieve a certain certification track, the MTA does not have a specific track. Instead, it is framed to cover three areas of technical concept: developer, database, and IT professional. An MTA is a certification designed for all those candidates making their first steps in technology who want to validate their knowledge in order to develop a professional profile by stepping up to the level of professional certificates. Thus, candidates can target **Microsoft Certified Solutions Associate** (**MCSA**) or **Microsoft Certified Solutions Developer** (**MCSD**) certifications. I think the most important thing is the fact that you need to pass one exam to earn the MTA certification, which does not expire. Thus, once you have read this book and this chapter, aim for the MTA certification by taking the MTA 98-365 exam.

The following steps will help you obtain an MTA certification:

1. **Skills**: No prerequisites.
2. **Exams**: Pass one exam to earn an MTA certification. Be sure to explore the exam prep resources.
3. **Completion**: Complete one MTA certification for every exam you pass in *step 2*.
4. **Continuing Education**: Earn an MCSA or MCSD certification to broaden your expertise.

If you cannot decide whether you should take the MTA 98-365 exam, the next section should help you out.

# Who should take the MTA 98-365 exam?

The MTA 98-365 exam is the coded name for the **Windows Server Administration Fundamentals** certification. As the name of the certification suggests, the MTA 98-365 exam is designed to assess the fundamental knowledge of candidates about server administration concepts. Therefore, candidates are required to prove that they are familiar with the concepts and the technologies necessary to administer servers. Specifically, that means that candidates must know what Windows Server is, how Windows Server is deployed, what Active Directory is, what server roles are and how they are installed, as well as how to monitor and manage server resources, account management, and system recovery tools and concepts.

Now let's take a look at the skills that are measured by the MTA 98-365 exam.

# Which skills are measured by the MTA 98-365 exam?

The **skills measured** represent a general guideline for a certain certification exam, issued by the exam client (in this case, Microsoft), of what is likely to be included in the exam. At the same time, Microsoft periodically updates the **skills measured** to better reflect the content of the exam. You will find that the following skills are measured by the 98-365 exam.

 You can find more information about 98-365 exam objectives at `https://www.microsoft.com/en-us/learning/exam-98-365.aspx`.

# Understanding server installation (10–15%)

To accomplish this objective, the candidate is required to know how to install Windows Server in general, and Windows Server 2019 in particular. Clean installation, upgrade, migration, unattended installation, and installation over a network are the installation options that you need to know about. The best way to learn these is to practice as much as you can. You must have good knowledge of operating devices and device drivers, and you should know about the Windows Registry too. When you are confident that you have gained the skills that are required for this objective, feel free to move on to the next objective.

### Understanding device drivers

This objective may include, but is not limited to, the following:

- Objective 1.1.1: Adding devices and installing device drivers
- Objective 1.1.2: Removing devices and uninstalling device drivers
- Objective 1.1.3: Managing devices and disabling device drivers
- Objective 1.1.4: Updating device drivers
- Objective 1.1.5: Rolling back device drivers
- Objective 1.1.6: Troubleshooting a device driver
- Objective 1.1.7: Plug and play
- Objective 1.1.8: **Interrupt request** (**IRQs**) and **direct memory access** (**DMA**)
- Objective 1.1.9: Driver signing
- Objective 1.1.10: Managing device drivers through Group Policy

### Understanding services

This objective may include, but is not limited to, the following:

- Objective 1.2.1: Windows services
- Objective 1.2.2: Working with the registry and services
- Objective 1.2.3: Service startup types
- Objective 1.2.4: Service recovery options
- Objective 1.2.5: Service delayed startup
- Objective 1.2.6: Run as settings for a service
- Objective 1.2.7: Starting, stopping, and restarting a service
- Objective 1.2.8: Service accounts and dependencies

### Understanding server installation options

This objective may include, but is not limited to, the following:

- Objective 1.3.1: Windows Server 2019 editions
- Objective 1.3.2: Understanding partition schemes
- Objective 1.3.3: Advanced startup options
- Objective 1.3.4: Desktop Experience, Server Core, and Nano Server installation options
- Objective 1.3.5: Performing a clean installation
- Objective 1.3.6: Performing an unattended installation
- Objective 1.3.7: Performing installation over a network using WDS
- Objective 1.3.8: VHD/VHDX installation source
- Objective 1.3.9: Upgrading and migration overview

# Understanding server roles (25–30%)

To accomplish this objective, the candidate is required to be able to identify application servers, to know about web services, to understand remote access, to know the difference between NTFS and shared permissions, and to understand the concept of virtualization in Windows Server. Specifically, you should have good knowledge of each and every role available in Windows Server 2019, and at the same time know how to add them to your server. This objective requires you to know about printers too. When you are confident that you have gained the skills that are required for this objective, feel free to move on to the next objective.

## Identifying application servers

This objective may include, but is not limited to, the following:

- Objective 2.1.1: Mail servers
- Objective 2.1.2: Database servers
- Objective 2.1.3: Collaboration servers
- Objective 2.1.4: Monitoring servers
- Objective 2.1.5: Threat management

## Understanding web services

This objective may include, but is not limited to, the following:

- Objective 2.2.1: **What is Internet Information Services (IIS)?**
- Objective 2.2.2: What is the WWW?
- Objective 2.3.3: What is FTP?
- Objective 2.3.4: Installing IIS from Server Manager
- Objective 2.2.5: Separate worker processes
- Objective 2.2.6: Adding components
- Objective 2.2.7: Sites
- Objective 2.2.8: Ports
- Objective 2.2.9: **Secure Sockets Layer (SSL)**
- Objective 2.2.10: Certificates

## Understanding remote access

This objective may include, but is not limited to, the following:

- Objective 2.3.1: Remote assistance
- Objective 2.3.2: Remote server administration tools
- Objective 2.3.3: Remote desktop services
- Objective 2.3.4: Multipoint services
- Objective 2.3.5: Licensing
- Objective 2.3.6: Remote Desktop Gateways
- Objective 2.3.7: Virtual Private Networks
- Objective 2.3.8: Application virtualization
- Objective 2.3.9: Multiple ports

## Understanding file and print services

This objective may include, but is not limited to, the following:

- Objective 2.4.1: Local printers
- Objective 2.4.2: Network printers
- Objective 2.4.3: Printer pooling
- Objective 2.4.4: Web printing
- Objective 2.4.5: Web management
- Objective 2.4.6: Driver deployment
- Objective 2.4.7: User rights, NTFS permissions, and share permissions
- Objective 2.4.8: Auditing file servers

## Understanding server virtualization

This objective may include, but is not limited to, the following:

- Objective 2.5.1: Virtualization modes
- Objective 2.5.2: Creating and configuring **Virtual Hard Disks** (**VHDs**)
- Objective 2.5.3: Managing virtual memory
- Objective 2.5.4: Setting up virtual networks
- Objective 2.5.5: Checkpoints
- Objective 2.5.6: **Physical to Virtual** (**P2V**) conversions
- Objective 2.5.7: Virtual to physical conversions
- Objective 2.5.8: VHD and VHDx formats
- Objective 2.5.9: Nested virtualization

# Understanding Active Directory (20–25%)

To accomplish this objective, the candidate is required to have good knowledge of Directory Services and **Group Policy** (**GP**) in Windows Server. Specifically, you should be able to add **Active Directory Domain Services** (**AD DS**) and promote the server to a domain controller, add **Domain Name System** (**DNS**) roles and understand DNS zones, and know how to access the GPM console and how to enable GPOs in Windows Server 2019. When you are confident that you have gained the skills that are required for this objective, feel free to move on to the next objective.

# Understanding accounts and groups

This objective may include, but is not limited to, the following:

- Objective 3.1.1: Domain accounts
- Objective 3.1.2: Local accounts
- Objective 3.1.3: User profiles
- Objective 3.1.4: Group types
- Objective 3.1.5: Group scopes
- Objective 3.1.6: Group nesting

# Understanding organizational units (OUs) and containers

This objective may include, but is not limited to, the following:

- Objective 3.2.1: The purpose of OUs
- Objective 3.2.2: Uses for different container objects
- Objective 3.2.3: Delegating control to an OU
- Objective 3.2.4: Default containers

# Understanding the Active Directory infrastructure

This objective may include, but is not limited to, the following:

- Objective 3.3.1: Domain controllers
- Objective 3.3.2: Forest
- Objective 3.3.3: Operations master roles
- Objective 3.3.4: Domain versus workgroups
- Objective 3.3.5: Child domains
- Objective 3.3.6: Trust relationships
- Objective 3.3.7: Functional levels
- Objective 3.3.8: Deprecated functional levels
- Objective 3.3.9: Namespace
- Objective 3.3.10: Sites
- Objective 3.3.11: Replication
- Objective 3.3.12: Schema
- Objective 3.3.13: Passport

### Understanding Group Policy (GP)

This objective may include, but is not limited to, the following:

- Objective 3.4.1: Group Policy processing
- Objective 3.4.2: Group Policy Management Console
- Objective 3.4.3: Computer policies
- Objective 3.4.4: User policies
- Objective 3.4.5: Local policies

# Understanding storage (10–15%)

To accomplish this objective, the candidate is required to have good knowledge of storage technologies in general, and each and every storage technology in particular. You should be able to identify different storage types, understand the concept behind RAID and know the RAID types, and have good knowledge of disk types. In addition, you must have good knowledge of filesystems, be able to perform disk formatting and disk conversion from basic to dynamic, be able to mount points and virtual disks, and be able to add DFS roles in Windows Server 2019. When you are confident that you have gained the skills that are required for this objective, feel free to move on to the next objective.

### Identifying storage technologies

This objective may include, but is not limited to, the following:

- Objective 4.1.1: Advantages and disadvantages of different storage types
- Objective 4.1.2: ATA, PATA, SATA, and SCSI interfaces
- Objective 4.1.3: Network-attached storage
- Objective 4.1.4: Storage area networks
- Objective 4.1.5: Storage protocols
- Objective 4.1.6: File-sharing protocols
- Objective 4.1.7: Local storage
- Objective 4.1.8: Network storage

### Understanding RAID

This objective may include, but is not limited to, the following:

- Objective 4.2.1: Types of RAID
- Objective 4.2.2: Hardware versus software RAID

## Understanding disk types

This objective may include, but is not limited to, the following:

- Objective 4.3.1: Basic disk
- Objective 4.3.2: Dynamic disk
- Objective 4.3.3: Mount points
- Objective 4.3.4: Filesystems
- Objective 4.3.5: Mounting a **Virtual Hard Disk** (**VHD**)
- Objective 4.3.6: The Distributed File System

# Understanding server performance management (10–15%)

To accomplish this objective, the candidate is required to be able to identify major server hardware components, understand server performance monitoring, and have good knowledge of logs and alerts. Specifically, you need to have good knowledge of each and every server hardware component in general, and redundant hardware in particular. In addition, you need to have good knowledge of operating with performance monitoring and resource monitoring consoles and understand the importance of logs and alerts in maintaining the server's performance. When you are confident that you have gained the skills that are required for this objective, feel free to move on to the next objective.

## Identifying major server hardware components

This objective may include, but is not limited to, the following:

- Objective 5.1.1: Processors
- Objective 5.1.2: Memory
- Objective 5.1.3: Disks
- Objective 5.1.4: Network interfaces
- Objective 5.1.5: 32-bit and 64-bit architecture
- Objective 5.1.6: Removable drives
- Objective 5.1.7: Graphic cards
- Objective 5.1.8: Cooling
- Objective 5.1.9: Power usage
- Objective 5.1.10: Ports

## Understanding performance monitoring

This objective may include, but is not limited to, the following:

- Objective 5.2.1: Performance monitoring methodology
- Objective 5.2.2: Performance monitoring procedures
- Objective 5.2.3: Server baseline
- Objective 5.2.4: Performance Monitor
- Objective 5.2.5: Resource Monitor
- Objective 5.2.6: Task Manager
- Objective 5.2.7: Performance counters
- Objective 5.2.8: Data Collector Sets

## Understanding logs and alerts

This objective may include, but is not limited to, the following:

- Objective 5.3.1: The purpose of performance logs and alerts

# Understanding server maintenance (15–20%)

To accomplish this objective, the candidate is required to be able to identify steps in the startup process, understand business continuity, understand the importance of updates, and have good knowledge of the troubleshooting process. Specifically, you should be able to identify and troubleshoot issues in the startup process, know how to perform a backup and restore, understand that performing updates is a proactive approach that helps you to avoid issues, and have good knowledge of the troubleshooting process. Additionally, you should be aware that downtime is the biggest enemy of a server's high availability, thus you need to equip yourself with adequate knowledge to help you maintain the healthy status of servers. When you feel confident that you have mastered all six objective domain area, you are ready to take the 98-365 certification exam. So, what are you waiting for? Go on, register for the exam, sit it, and pass it proudly. Good luck!

## Identifying steps in the startup process

This objective may include, but is not limited to, the following:

- Objective 6.1.1: **Basic Input/Output System (BIOS)**
- Objective 6.1.2: UEFI
- Objective 6.1.3: TPM

- Objective 6.1.4: Bootsector
- Objective 6.1.5: Bootloader
- Objective 6.1.6: **Master Boot Record** (**MBR**)
- Objective 6.1.7: Boot menu (`boot.ini`)
- Objective 6.1.8: Boot Configuration Data (`bcdedit.exe`)
- Objective 6.1.9: **Power-On Self-Test** (**POST**)
- Objective 6.1.10: Safe Mode

## Understanding business continuity

This objective may include, but is not limited to, the following:

- Objective 6.2.1: Backup and restore
- Objective 6.2.2: **Disaster recovery planning** (**DRP**)
- Objective 6.2.3: Clustering
- Objective 6.2.4: Active Directory restore
- Objective 6.2.5: Folder redirection
- Objective 6.2.6: Data redundancy
- Objective 6.2.7: **Uninterruptible power supply** (**UPS**)

## Understanding updates

This objective may include, but is not limited to, the following:

- Objective 6.3.1: Software
- Objective 6.3.2: Driver
- Objective 6.3.3: Operating systems
- Objective 6.3.4: Applications
- Objective 6.3.5: Windows Update
- Objective 6.3.6: **Windows Server Update Services** (**WSUS**)

## Understanding troubleshooting methodology

This objective may include, but is not limited to, the following:

- Objective 6.4.1: Troubleshooting processes
- Objective 6.4.2: Troubleshooting procedures
- Objective 6.4.3: Best practices

- Objective 6.4.4: Systematic versus specific approach
- Objective 6.4.5: Event viewer
- Objective 6.4.6: **Information Technology Infrastructure Library (ITIL)**
- Objective 6.4.7: Central logging
- Objective 6.4.8: Event filtering
- Objective 6.4.9: Default logs

# What should you expect in the 98-365 exam?

As you already know, exams have questions, and you can expect to see between **30-50 questions** in your 98-365 exam. The exam's duration is 50 minutes, including an additional 30 minutes for an introduction and a survey. The pass score for the 98-365 exam is 700. There is a mark for a review or a flag for a review option, which means that you can check that option if you want to review the question(s) at a later time if the exam time permits it. Other than that, you can move back and forth by clicking the **Previous** and **Next** buttons.

# How should you prepare for the 98-365 exam?

In general, there is no written standard regarding how to prepare for the certification exams, and the 98-365 exam in particular. In fact, that has to do with the use of best practices for the **exam preparation**. In the case of the 98-365 exam, they are as follows:

- Between 6 and 12 months **active work experience** in the ICT industry
- Attending **Windows Server Administration Fundamentals** training at a Microsoft Partner for learning solutions
- Reading **Windows Server 2019** books
- **Practicing** with Windows Server 2019
- It helps a lot if you are certified in **Windows Operating System Fundamentals** or **CompTIA Server+**
- Taking practice tests so that you become familiar with the 98-365 exam format
- Reviewing the objective domain areas carefully so you can identify your weak areas
- Meeting with friends who have passed the 98-365 certification exam and learning from their experiences

Help yourself get prepared for your MTA 98-365 exam by exploring the content at `https://downloads.certiport.com/Marketing/MTA/docs/MTA_SSG_WinServer_individual_without_crop.pdf`.

# How do you register for the 98-365 exam?

In general, MTA exams are delivered by Certiport and PearsonVUE. Thus, there are two types of exams:

- **Proctored exams** delivered at a test center
- **Self-administered** online exams

The 98-365 exam is a proctored exam that is delivered at a test center. A test center is a facility that has been authorized by Certiport or PearsonVUE to deliver certification exams. Knowing that, when you feel that you are ready to take the 98-365 exam, you can schedule your test in two ways:

- **Online** via `www.PearsonVUE.com` (requires a web account)
- By contacting a nearby **test center** (requires you to visit a test center)

To schedule your MTA 98-365 exam with Certiport or PearsonVUE, navigate to the following URL: `https://www.microsoft.com/en-us/learning/exam-98-365.aspx`.

# On the day of the 98-365 exam

Make sure that you have slept well the night before the exam. Do not stress yourself out trying to remind yourself of the things that you learned while preparing for the exam. Make sure to arrive at the test center 30 minutes before the exam is scheduled and that you are carrying the required ID.

On entering the test center, be polite with the test center administrator and carefully read the Pearson VUE Candidate Rules Agreement. When sitting in front of the workstation, simply relax, take a deep breath, build up self-esteem by saying a prayer, read the exam instructions carefully, and begin the exam. Read each question very attentively and do not rush to answer the questions before reading each answer with the same amount of focus. Remember, you can mark questions for review or hit the **Previous** button to go back to questions that you have already answered. So, do not waste time on questions you have doubts about.

At the same time, be rational with the exam time you have because even though there is enough time at your disposal, if you do not manage it properly, then it may not suffice. Do not let panic get in your way; instead, enjoy the exam to its fullness by having fun with the exam questions. Question by question, you will be able to complete your 98-365 exam.

At the end, you will get the score for the exam. Believe me, it is a joyful feeling when you realize that you have passed the exam. However, if the exam result is not the one you expected, then do not let it stress you out. Instead, accept the result as it is, and as of the next day, begin preparing to retake the exam by identifying the points at which you performed insufficiently. Remember that you now have exam experience and that will greatly help you in preparing for the exam again and passing it successfully. Good luck with your exam!

 You can familiarize yourself with the Pearson VUE Candidate Rules Agreement by visiting the following URL: `https://home.pearsonvue.com/candidate-rules-agreement`.

# Post-98-365 exam certification path

Having passed the 98-365 exam successfully, the candidate automatically obtains the MTA certification. On that occasion, congratulations to you on earning the MTA certification! Earning an MTA certification helps prove your knowledge of fundamental technology concepts. Having a validated certification from Microsoft can help you launch a successful career. In addition, if you already have an in-depth understanding of, and hands-on experience with, Microsoft technologies, you might want to start with an MCSA certification or an MCSD certification.

 You can explore Microsoft certifications at `https://www.microsoft.com/en-us/learning/browse-all-certifications.aspx`.

# Useful resources

- *Microsoft Technical Certifications*: `https://www.microsoft.com/en-us/learning/certification-overview.aspx`
- *Start a career in technology*: `https://certiport.pearsonvue.com/Certifications/Microsoft/MTA/Overview`
- *Windows Server Administration Fundamentals training on MVA*: `https://mva.microsoft.com/en-US/training-courses/windows-server-administration-fundamentals-8477?l=LaRRbeXz_5004984382`

# Assessments

As you have noticed, each chapter is accompanied by a considerable number of questions to help you to strengthen and reinforce the concepts and definitions gained from this book. That said, in the following sections, you will find the answers to chapter questions, so you can compare your answers with the ones in this book.

## Chapter 1: Introducing Windows Server

1. True.
2. Clients and servers.
3. All of the above.
4. True.
5. Windows Server.
6. True.
7. **Peer-to-peer** (**P2P**) and client/server.
8. True.
9. Hardware and software.
10. IPv4 and IPv6.

## Chapter 2: Introducing Windows Server 2019

1. True.
2. Docker.
3. Windows Server 2019 Datacenter and Windows Server 2019 Standard.
4. True.
5. System Insights.
6. 1.4 GHz 64-bit processor.
7. False.
8. Storage Migration Service.
9. All of the above.
10. False.

11. Kubernetes.
12. Windows Admin Center.

# Chapter 3: Installing Windows Server 2019

1. **GUID Partition Table** (GPT).
2. False.
3. Nano server.
4. **Windows Assessment and Deployment Kit** (**Windows ADK**) and **Microsoft Deployment Toolkit** (**MDT**).
5. False.
6. A migration.
7. Desktop Experience, Server Core, and Nano Server.
8. Windows Server 2019 installation files are required to be on DVD media and should be bootable. The same as DVD media, USB flash drive is required to contain the Windows Server 2019 installation and be bootable. Network boot requires setting up a WDS server so that Windows Server 2019 is installed over the network.
9. The clean installation overwrites the existing operating system on a hard disk. The WDS server enables installation over the network. An unattended installation has little or no interactivity with the operating system installation. Tools such as the Windows ADK and MDT provide a unique platform to automate desktop and server deployments. An upgrade replaces your existing OS with a new one. Migration takes place when you bring in a new machine (physical or virtual) and you want to move the roles, features, apps, and settings into it.

# Chapter 4: Post-Installation Tasks in Windows Server 2019

1. True.
2. Plug and Play.
3. **Interrupt Request** (**IRQ**), and **Direct Memory Access** (**DMA**).
4. True.
5. Windows registry.
6. Devices and Device Manager.

7. Services Control Manager and Registry Editor.

8. Service account.

9. Any changes made to your server are stored in the registry. That being said, the Windows Registry is a hierarchical database that stores the hardware/software configuration and system security information. After you access the registry, you will notice that its console tree (on the left-hand side) consists of five registry keys known as hives (that is HKEYs): HKEY_CLASSES_ROOT (HKCR), HKEY_CURRENT_USER (HKCU), HKEY_LOCAL_MACHINE (HKLM), HKEY_USERS (HKU), and HKEY_CURRENT_CONFIG (HKCC).

10. Services are background services that keep alive the OS. When accessing services through the Services Control Manager, you will notice that, for each service, there is a description that helps us to understand its purpose. Each service has the following start-up types: **Automatic**, **Automatic (Delayed start)**, **Manual**, and **Disable**.

# Chapter 5: Directory Services in Windows Server 2019

1. True.
2. Group nesting.
3. Roaming Profile and Mandatory Profile.
4. False.
5. Replication topology.
6. Global group and Universal group.
7. True.
8. Domain Controller.
9. Active Directory Administrative Center and Active Directory Users and Computers.
10. True.
11. Primary Zone.
12. Master schema and domain naming master.

13. **Active Directory** (**AD**), a Microsoft technology, is a distributed database that stores objects in a hierarchical, structured, and secure format. AD's objects typically represent users, computers, peripheral devices, and network services. Each object is uniquely identified by its name and attributes. DNS has a tree structure (hierarchical) where each branch represents the root zone and each leaf has zero or more resource records. Each zone represents a root domain or multiple domains and subdomains. A domain name consists of one or more parts, called labels, and these are separated by points (for example, `packtpub.com`). DNS is maintained by a database that uses distributed clients/server architecture where network nodes represent the servers' names.

14. Both **Accounts, Global, Domain Local, Permissions** (**AGDLP**) and **Accounts, Global, Universal, Domain Local, Permissions** (**AGUDLP**) are Microsoft's recommendations for effectively using group nesting when assigning permissions.

# Chapter 6: Adding Roles to Windows Server 2019

1. True.
2. **File Transfer Protocol** (**FTP**).
3. Modify, Write, and Read.
4. False.
5. Software port.
6. **Simple Mail Transfer Protocol** (**SMTP**) and **Post Office Protocol** (**POP**).
7. True.
8. **Secure Sockets Layer** (**SSL**).
9. 3389.
10. False.
11. Share permissions.
12. Change, and Read.
13. Remote Access role in Windows Server 2019 enables remote access to resources inside an organization's network. **Remote Desktop Services** (**RDS**) enables GUI remote access to computers within an organization's network and over the internet.

14. Users can be allowed or denied access to the objects and this can be said to be related to user rights. Each allowance or denial has certain permissions that determine the type of access to the objects. Share permissions have to do with user access to the shared folders and drives on the network.

# Chapter 7: Group Policy in Windows Server 2019

1. True
2. **Group Policy Objects (GPOs)**
3. Enabled and Disabled
4. True
5. Forest pane and GPOs pane
6. `gpupdate /force`
7. True
8. Local Group Policy Editor
9. Turned on

# Chapter 8: Virtualization with Windows Server 2019

1. True.
2. Hyper-V architecture.
3. Fully Virtualized mode, and Paravirtualized mode.
4. True.
5. **Virtualization Service Providers (VSP)** and **Virtualization Service Consumers (VSC)**.
6. Production Checkpoints and Standard Checkpoints.
7. True.
8. Hyper-V Manager.
9. Hypervisor and Root.

10. The nested virtualization refers to a **virtual machine** (**VM**) that runs inside another VM. In other words, the server's hardware can run the Hyper-V inside a VM, which itself runs on a Hyper-V too.

11. Nowadays, when virtualization has become the major network service driver, organizations are migrating their Active Directory Users and Computers (P2V) for reasons such as cost, ease of management, and future expansion. Hence, knowing that VMs are using VHDs, Microsoft engineers have developed the Disk2vhd app to make the **Physical Disk Drive** (**PHD**) conversion to the **Virtual Hard Disk** (**VHD**).

12. Despite the reasons that may stand behind the decision to do **Virtual to Physical** (**V2P**) conversion, it is good to remind ourselves, in the technological era that we live in, that the trend is for **Physical to Virtual** (**P2V**) conversion. Other than that, it can be said that the hypervisor manufacturers, including Microsoft, will not encourage you to conduct V2P conversions.

# Chapter 9: Storing Data in Windows Server 2019

1. True.
2. **Storage area network** (**SAN**).
3. **Direct-Attached Storage** (**DAS**) and **network-attached storage** (**NAS**).
4. False.
5. Disk controller.
6. **Small Computer System Interface** (**SCSI**) and **Fiber Channel** (**FC**).
7. True.
8. **High Availability** (**HA**).
9. RAID 1 and RAID 5.
10. True.
11. **Advanced Technology Attachment** (**ATA**), also known as **Integrated Drive Electronics** (**IDE**).
12. CD-ROM and DVD-RAM.
13. The idea behind the concept of **data deduplication** (**dedup**) is to provide disk space savings.

14. **Storage Spaces Direct** (**S2D**) is an enhanced feature in Windows Server 2019 that enables you to group disks into storage pools, hence creating software-defined storage called **storage spaces**.

15. **Distributed File Systems** (**DFS**) enables the sharing of data from the server in an authorized and controlled way.

# Chapter 10: Tuning and Maintaining Windows Server 2019

1. True.
2. Server baseline.
3. Cache and Cores.
4. True.
5. Processors and HDDs.
6. **Network Load Balancing** (**NLB**) and network separation.
7. False.
8. Word size.
9. Performance Monitor and Resource Monitor.
10. True.
11. Performance monitoring.
12. **Random Access Memory** (**RAM**) and **Read-Only Memory** (**ROM**).
13. Performance Monitor is a Windows MMC that monitors server performance. Resource Monitor is at your disposal to view the real-time usage of both hardware and software resources.
14. Logs are useful for detailed analysis and archiving records. Alerts enable you to be vigilant about the performance and configuration of servers.

# Chapter 11: Updating and Troubleshooting Windows Server 2019

1. False.
2. Event Viewer.
3. Systematic approach and specific approach.
4. False.

5. UPS.

6. Application, and Security.

7. True.

8. POST.

9. NTLDR and BOOTMGR.

10. True.

11. Clustering.

12. Incremental and Differential.

13. The **Basic Input/Output System** (**BIOS**) is a program that controls the functionality of the server hardware components. Bootsector is the sector on the server's disk that contains the information to boot your server. The bootloader is a program that loads the OS kernel into RAM. The bootloader is located in MBR. In Windows OSes, there are two types of bootloaders: NTLDR and BOOTMGR. MBR is created when disk partitions are created too, however, MBR resides outside disk partitions. Multiboot: every time you turn on your computer, you will notice a boot menu that lists multiple OSes. **Boot Configuration Data** (**BCD**) represents a store consisting of a specific file that enables control of what should happen when an OS boots. POST is a diagnostic test that verifies that the server hardware is working correctly. Safe mode is a Windows diagnostic mode that uses a minimal set of drivers and services.

14. Among the dozens of available methodologies, a six-step troubleshooting model known as the **detect method** is used by Microsoft Product Support Services engineers. The steps are: discover the problem, evaluate system configuration, list or track possible solutions, execute a plan, check results, and take a proactive approach.

15. The Event Viewer generates an enormous number of logs; hence, in finding the right information that would help to overcome the issues, event filtering is used. Setting the wrong filtering criteria will result in getting filtered results that will not help to find the right information to overcome the issues. The problem with event logs is that they consume storage space. Hence, changing the default logs' locations helps to overcome the lack of storage space for storing logs. That enables writing event messages to any of the log files due to a lack of storage space.

# Other Books You May Enjoy

If you enjoyed this book, you may be interested in these other books by Packt:

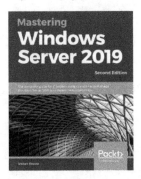

**Mastering Windows Server 2019 - Second Edition**
Jordan Krause

ISBN: 978-1-78980-453-9

- Work with the updated Windows Server 2019 interface, including Server Core and Windows Admin Center
- Secure your network and data with new technologies in Windows Server 2019
- Learn about containers and understand the appropriate situations to use Nano Server
- Discover new ways to integrate your data center with Microsoft Azure
- Harden your Windows Servers to help keep the bad guys out
- Virtualize your data center with Hyper-V

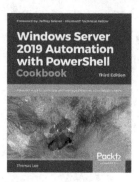

## Windows Server 2019 Automation with PowerShell Cookbook - Third Edition
Thomas Lee

ISBN: 978-1-78980-853-7

- Perform key admin tasks on Windows Server 2019
- Employing best practices for writing PowerShell scripts and configuring Windows Server 2019
- Use the .NET Framework to achieve administrative scripting
- Set up VMs, websites, and shared files on Azure
- Report system performance using built-in cmdlets and WMI to obtain single measurements
- Know the tools you can use to diagnose and resolve issues with Windows Server

# Leave a review - let other readers know what you think

Please share your thoughts on this book with others by leaving a review on the site that you bought it from. If you purchased the book from Amazon, please leave us an honest review on this book's Amazon page. This is vital so that other potential readers can see and use your unbiased opinion to make purchasing decisions, we can understand what our customers think about our products, and our authors can see your feedback on the title that they have worked with Packt to create. It will only take a few minutes of your time, but is valuable to other potential customers, our authors, and Packt. Thank you!

# Index

CPSIA information can be obtained
at www.ICGtesting.com
Printed in the USA
LVHW060538220821
695831LV00011B/1006